REVOLUTION AT THE WALDORF

REVOLUTION AT THE WALDORF

America and the Irish War of Independence

PATRICK O'SULLIVAN GREENE

EASTWOOD BOOKS

First published 2022 by Eastwood Books
Dublin, Ireland
www.eastwoodbooks.com
www.wordwellbooks.com

1

Eastwood Books is an imprint of the Wordwell Group.

The Wordwell Group is a member of Publishing Ireland,
the Irish Publishers' Association.

Eastwood Books
The Wordwell Group
Unit 9, 78 Furze Road
Sandyford
Dublin, Ireland

ISBN: 978-1-913934-39-2 (Trade Paperback)
ISBN: 978-1-913934-40-8 (Ebook)

British Library Cataloguing in Publication Data.
A catalogue record for this book is available from the National Library of
Ireland and the British Library.

Typesetting and design by the Wordwell Group

Printed in Ireland by Sprint Print, Dublin

TABLE OF CONTENTS

DEDICATION

James (Jim) Kavanagh
24 March 1965–26 March 2021

ACKNOWLEDGEMENTS

A special thank you to Ronan McGreevy and Eileen Kelleher for their ongoing encouragement, and to Ronan Colgan and the team at the Wordwell Group for their support.

The archival staff in the Bureau of Military History, the National Archives of Ireland, the National Library of Ireland and Villanova University provide expert digitisation and readily accessible historical records. I owe Eamon Browne and the staff of Kerry Library many thanks.

I was fortunate to source valuable material from Dr. Michael Doorley, Justice Joseph E. Fahey, Eileen McGough and Kelly Anne Reynolds. Megan Kavanagh supported me with early research.

Thanks to family and friends at home and abroad.

This book is dedicated to my late friend James Kavanagh.

QUOTES

Because of our Irish blood, we are handicapped in America and, consequently, have an interest in the freedom of the race.
- Judge Cohalan

The motto of Irish citizens is today, what it has ever been, 'America First', and that motto and the great force behind it will eventually make the whole world free. An America free from entanglements with Old World Despotisms and Oligarchies is the hope of Mankind.
- John Devoy

The incident [rejection of an Irish Republic recognition plank at the Republican Convention] *illustrates in an interesting manner the immense influence Irishmen can exert on American politicians if they proceed wisely; and how ready American politicians are to withdraw themselves from that influence if they can find some colourable pretext for doing so.*
- Sir Auckland Geddes, British Ambassador to the United States of America

There always seems to be something depressing coming from the U.S.A.
- Michael Collins

PROLOGUE

Confession to being a Gael

> '[Amory Blaine] *suspected that being Irish was being somewhat common*'

On 4 September 1919, F. Scott Fitzgerald, still only twenty-three, and recently discharged from the army, began an anxious wait for a reply from Scribners, the New York publishing house. His friend and mentor, Shane Leslie, had delivered the manuscript for his first novel to their offices on Fifth Avenue.

Amory Blaine, the chief protagonist of the novel, represented a new generation of young Americans. Determined to find their place in post-war America, they were 'dedicated more than the last to the fear of poverty and the worship of success; grown up to find all Gods dead, all wars fought, all faiths in man shaken'.[1] But like Fitzgerald, on whom he was modelled, the Ivy League educated Amory Blaine struggled with his 'common' Irish Catholic heritage. It troubled Fitzgerald that his comfortable childhood had depended on a generous, though not substantial, inheritance from his maternal Irish emigrant grandfather, Philip McQuillan, who had built a large grocery wholesale business. Familial pride for Fitzgerald came through his paternal grandmother, Cecilia Ashton Scott, whose southern antebellum roots traced back to the seventeenth century. His father, Edward Fitzgerald, when he lost his job as a salesman, had been 'a failure the rest of his days'.[2]

Fitzgerald had faced little negative Irish or Catholic bias in his young life. St. Paul, where he lived, had been established by French–Canadian Catholic settlers. Being Irish in the city was just common, a little above the Swedes.[3] When Fitzgerald went to Princeton, courtesy of the mercantile labours of his grandfather, he was able to join one of the 'snootiest clubs', helped by his handsome appearance, personality and southern lineage.[4]

In a later letter to a friend, which Fitzgerald called a 'confession to being a Gael', he described himself as 'half black Irish and half old American stock with the usual exaggerated ancestral pretensions'.[5] His Irish heritage, and lack of independent wealth, manifested itself in an inferiority complex. Fitzgerald described feeling like a parvenu. He had a social self-consciousness and a continual need for self-justification.[6]

On 16 September, after two fretful weeks, Scribners informed Fitzgerald that his debut novel, *This Side of Paradise*, had been accepted. The novel was published to instant critical and commercial success. Fitzgerald's future, and maybe even the future direction of America, might have taken a different course if Maxwell Perkins, a brave junior editor, had not made an impassioned plea for publication: 'If we're going to turn down the likes of Fitzgerald, I will lose all interest in publishing books'.[7]

Fitzgerald did not challenge the roots of his own inferiority complex in his writing, but others of the 'Irish Race' devoted their lives to it. They were determined to fight for equal opportunity in an America controlled by an Anglo-American elite.

Fitzgerald's vocation as a writer was not to elevate the Irish Race.

Instead, he launched the Jazz Age.

Saviour

On 10 July 1919 a triumphant President Wilson delivered the Treaty of Versailles by hand to the Senate for ratification. The treaty included the League of Nations covenant; the terms setting out the powers of the new global organisation that formed a core part of his *Fourteen Points* plan for an equitable peace in Europe. President Wilson made a stumbling start to his Senate address, labouring to read his card notes and omitting words as he proceeded; signs of a small stroke. The speech received scattered applause.

The terms of the agreement establishing the League of Nations troubled Democratic and Republican law makers. Many believed Wilson had failed to deliver on his pre-war promises, and had caved to the demands of the leaders of Britain, France and Japan, the three surviving post-war empires, who each had added to their territories under the mandate system.

David Lloyd George, the British prime minister, so pleased with his own performance at the Paris Peace Conference, declared he had done well considering he 'was seated between Jesus Christ and Napoleon.' The reference was to the idealistic Wilson striving to fashion a new world order and the pragmatic Clemenceau, prime minister of France, determined to achieve total victory over Germany in the peace negotiations.

President Wilson's refusal to bring any senior Republicans to Paris had been a strategic mistake. Republicans had taken control of the Senate and a two-thirds majority was required to pass the League of Nations covenant; the terms of which challenged the constitutional core of America, a country barely a century and a half old, and within living memory of its civil war.

Britain had negotiated individual voting rights for each of its dominions, including Australia and Canada, resulting in six votes for the British empire compared to one vote for the United States. A particularly thorny issue was Article 10 of the covenant, which placed an *obligation* on America to deploy its military to preserve the 'territorial integrity' of any member of the League. Under the US Constitution, it was Congress that had the prerogative to declare war and to authorise the deployment of military and naval forces overseas.

Ratifying the agreement meant abandoning the doctrine of avoiding permanent entangling alliances with countries of the Old World. And the treaty terms were seen by some to over-ride the Monroe Doctrine, an anchor of American security considerations since the early 1800s.

American eyes had turned towards the Pacific, in particular to the newly industrialised and militarised Japan. Many predicted a future war with the Imperial Japanese Army. A German-American had left 5,000 marks in his will to the crew of the first American vessel to sink a Japanese warship.[8]

The British and the Japanese empires had entered a treaty of alliance in 1902, which had been renewed in 1905 and 1911. This treaty gave the two empires naval control in the Pacific. Japan had entered the world war on the British side, a Japanese destroyer even serving in the Mediterranean to protect allied shipping. Under the terms of the Versailles treaty, the Japanese empire retained control of the Shandong territories in China, which it had seized from Germany. This was a diplomatic failure for President Wilson who had strongly urged Chinese claims for the return of its territory.

Britain's relationship with her former colony since the end of the Revolutionary War in 1783 had been troublesome. Economic and trade disputes resulted in renewed hostilities during the war of 1812, and British support for the Confederacy – to the point of almost recognising the south – came close to naval conflict. A peaceful but troubled diplomatic relationship had slowly emerged. Rising pan-Germanism, including efforts by Germany to acquire a base in South America, nurtured closer diplomatic relations between the Anglo-Saxon cousins. Some even advocated a reunion with the former colonial power.

Others, however, foresaw war with the British empire, which held considerable naval superiority over the United States, and had used that advantage against trade rivals in the past, as the Dutch, French and Spanish had learned to their cost. They believed that a heavily-indebted Britain had carefully structured the League of Nations agreement to maintain her imperial status using American military power and money. William Randolph Hearst, the media magnate, warned England to 'create her own army and navy at her own expense and not expect us to pay for the creation of these weapons which may at any time be used against us'.[9]

In a February 1918 address to Congress, President Wilson had advocated the principle of 'self-determination' for all nations.[10] It was a speech he had come to regret for the hopes it had raised across the world, including among Irish nationalists. Robert Lansing, his secretary of state, was appalled with the concept, a phrase 'loaded with dynamite.'[11] On board ship to Paris, Wilson thanked George Creel, his propaganda chief, for popularising the theme of self-determination and the rights of small nations, adding, 'But I am wondering if you have not unconsciously spun a net for me from which there is no escape.'[12]

The president had endeavoured to secure a settlement in Ireland when America entered the war. His motivation, however, was not an affinity toward the Irish people; rather, he needed to convince young American men of Irish blood to fight side by side with England as an ally, in a war sold to them as a fight for the freedom of small nations. And the president was concerned by the close ties that had emerged between nationalist Irish–Americans and their German counterparts. Wilson had urged Lloyd George to grant a 'substantial' self-government measure to Ireland, saying, 'Successful action now would absolutely divorce our citizens of Irish birth and sympathy from the German sympathizers here.'[13] The British took no action.

Glass ceiling

Shane Leslie, who had delivered Fitzgerald's manuscript to Scribners, was a thirty-three-year-old Anglo-Irish author, poet, world traveller and part-time diplomat. Born Sir John Leslie in Monaghan, he had adopted an anglicised Irish version of his first name and converted to Catholicism at Cambridge.

When Fitzgerald first met Leslie as a schoolboy he described him as the 'most romantic figure I had ever known'.[14] The Eton-educated Leslie, a first cousin of Winston Churchill, inspired Fitzgerald with tales of meeting Tolstoy in Russia and swimming with Rupert Brooke, the idealistic English poet who died during the war. Fitzgerald took the title for his first novel from the poet, 'Well this side of Paradise! …There's little comfort in the wise'.

Leslie was a passionate advocate for Home Rule; an Irish parliament within the British empire. Home Rule supporters in America, the dominant political opinion before the war, had coalesced around the middle class United Irish League.[15] A small minority of marginalised nationalists, bitterly opposed to Home Rule, advocated for an independent Irish republic. They had opposed America's entry into the war on England's side. Leslie, after being invalided out of the British Ambulance Corps, had embarked on a diplomatic mission to counter nationalist Irish opposition to America entering the conflict. In November 1917, Scribners published his political treatise, *The Irish issue in its American aspect.* But the attraction of Leslie's Home Rule vision for Ireland had already began to wane.

Moderate Irish–American opinion, confounded by British policy towards Ireland, had become disillusioned with Home Rule. Broken promises on the latter, mooted partition, the appointment of Edward Carson to the British war cabinet, conscription and, above all, the execution of the 1916 leaders, shifted American opinion dramatically. The once dominant United Irish League was a spent force, replaced by the pro-independence Friends of Irish Freedom.

William Bourke Cockran, a lawyer and congressman for New York, who was related to Shane Leslie through marriage, described his own conversion in the wake of the executions:

> For thirty years I have been one of those who had believed … that it was
> the part of prudence for Irishmen to forget … the wrongs of the centuries
> in the hope that better days were dawning. … And now, behold the con-
> sequences of this attempt … The noblest Irishmen that have ever lived are
> dead, dead by the bullet of British soldiery, shot like dogs for asserting the
> immortal truths of patriotism![16]

As in America, a new generation had emerged in Ireland, equally determined to establish their place in the new world order. They looked to Paris, New York and the new emerging nation states in Europe. The new leaders in Ireland talked about Irish freedom in a different way.[17] They framed their message around international trade, taxation, monetary policy, development of internal resources and social improvement. They were determined to crack the colonial glass ceiling; the political, economic and social privilege of the establishment, Catholic and Protestant, that would not change under Home Rule.[18]

Sinn Féin won seventy-three out of the 105 seats in Ireland in the 1918 United Kingdom elections. Instead of taking their seats, the newly elected MPs set up a counter-state parliament in open defiance of the Dublin Castle administration. Over seventy Irish and international journalists were present when the national parliament of the self-declared Irish Republic met for the first time on 21 January 1919.

The British government initially ignored the new assembly, dismissing it variously as a ludicrous farce, a stage play and a piece of political window-dressing. By contrast, George Creel, head of the Committee of Public Information, the powerful American wartime propaganda bureau, compared the assembly to the first session of the Continental Congress.

> Some young and reckless, some old and academic, but for the most part a gathering of very intense patriots with sanely constructive ideas about finance, education, economics, industry, merchant marine, foreign trade.[19]

Shane Leslie had tried and failed to convince moderate Irish–Americans to hold faith in President Wilson delivering a Home Rule solution. By 1919, a completely disillusioned Leslie wrote to Joe Tumulty, the president's private secretary:

> For three years I have done my utmost to retain Irish confidence in the President but English policy gives me no choice between Sinn Féin and becoming an American. Could you enable me to enlist in the American forces now engaged in Russia or Siberia?[20]

America First

Within weeks of being presented with the peace treaty, the Senate Foreign Relations Committee held a series of public hearings. On 30 August 1919, it was the turn of the Irish delegation to appear before the committee.

Daniel Cohalan, a lawyer and justice of the New York Supreme Court, chaired the delegation. In his opening statement to the committee, Cohalan called the League of Nations a 'superstate' and an infringement upon the sovereignty of America.[21]

Cohalan had made exhaustive preparations in advance of the hearing. Every night from New York, he discussed, by long-distance phone, the plan for the following day with the head of the Irish National Bureau in Washington, the propaganda office financed by the Friends of Irish Freedom. Every weekend was spent in the capital conferring with senators, rushing from office to office. 'I was exhausted when the time came for him to board the train for New York,' recalled the head of the Bureau, 'after outplaying the British Embassy at their own game of "secret diplomacy".'[22]

Cohalan's grandfather, a widower, had emigrated from Ireland in 1848 with three daughters and one son, Cohalan's twelve-year-old father. The latter became a stone mason and later established a successful glass business.[23] As a boy, the future judge saw his father fight sectarian and race bigotry and support Irish nationalist and cultural causes. Educated at Manhattan College, Cohalan played on the baseball team that defeated Yale, and played against the New York Giants. He also had American revolutionary roots through a great-grandfather, Captain Eugene McCarthy, who had reportedly served as aide-de-camp to the Marquis de Lafayette during the American Revolutionary War, after which he had returned to Ireland.[24]

Admitted to the New York Bar in 1888, Cohalan joined the Democratic party in New York, drafting state party platforms and serving as a delegate to national conventions. A former grand sachem of Tammany Hall, he had been a trusted adviser of Boss Charles F. Murphy.

Cohalan was appointed as a justice of the New York Supreme Court in May 1911 to fill an unexpired term, and he was elected in his own right later that year. In 1916, he was one of the founders of the Friends of Irish Freedom, the public face of the Irish independence movement, while also secretly being a member of the physical force, Clan-na-Gael.

Cohalan loathed the Anglo-American elite and their close relationship with the English ruling class. He believed a stigma attached to the Irish Race[25] as long as the homeland was under British rule. 'Because of our Irish blood,' he wrote, 'we are handicapped in America and, consequently, have an interest in the freedom of the race.'[26]

He believed that recognition of the self-declared Irish Republic by the United States government could only be achieved by showing that an independent Ireland was in America's own geopolitical interest. 'England cannot continue to control the world unless she controls the sea', Cohalan told the members of the Senate committee, '[and] her continued control of the sea is dependent on her continued control of Ireland'.

Cohalan proceeded to outline George Washington's geopolitical reasoning on why England held Ireland; if Ireland was 500 miles further from England there would be no Irish question. 'You cannot approach the southern coast of England without approaching the southern coast of Ireland, and cannot approach the northern coast of England without approaching the northern coast of Ireland,' Cohalan informed the committee. 'Under the circumstances, England is going to insist on control of Ireland'. In his treatise, *The Freedom of the Seas*, Cohalan espoused the view of an inevitable conflict between America and England for control of global sea routes. He repeated this view to the Senate committee; it was in America's commercial and military interest that an independent Ireland, instead of England, controlled the Irish deep water ports.

Cohalan also pressed the cause of Ireland on a standalone basis: over-taxation on Ireland amounted to $1.7 billion over twenty years; England controlled Ireland's imports and exports by forcing all trade through English ports; the population of Ireland had been halved since 1845.

He explained that Article 10 of the League of Nations covenant posed a *new* obstacle to Irish independence; all members of the League would be obliged to protect the territorial integrity of the United Kingdom. '[If] a League of Nations had been in existence at the time of the American Revolution,' Cohalan declared to the committee, 'France could not have come to the assistance of the Thirteen Colonies'. America would be compelled to send her military into Ireland 'not for the purpose of helping them in their struggle but in order to help England to rivet the chains upon her'.

Cohalan was widely praised for his performance in front of the committee. Within weeks of the hearing, however, he was burned out. 'You have overworked yourself as I feared you would do', a close friend wrote to him, 'and you must let up this fall or you will break down'.[27] But there was much work still to be done. Cohalan had presented the case of Ireland to a Senate committee, a prospect unthinkable for a nationalist Irish leader even two years prior. It was not for Cohalan to slow down. He had a voice again.

Two years earlier, on 23 September 1917, just three months after American combat troops had landed in France, and during the Third Battle of Ypres (Passchendaele), the *New York Times* had declared Cohalan a traitor to America: 'Cohalan And Other Irish Leaders Named In *New Expose Of German Plots*' screamed the front-page headline.

In a raid on the office of Wolf von Igel, a German spy, the secret service had seized incriminating papers. The Committee of Public Information, George Creel's formidable government propaganda agency, released the seized documents to the press. The *New York Times* published an image of a translated document implicating Cohalan; a communication dictated to von Bernstorff, German Ambassador to America. The document called on German support for the Easter Rising; aerial attacks on England; a diversion of the fleet; and troop, arms and ammunition landings in Ireland from Zeppelins. 'This would enable the Irish ports to be closed against England and the establishment of stations for submarines on the Irish coast,' urged Cohalan in the communication, 'and the cutting off of food from England.'

The release of the document was part of a deliberate strategy to discredit Cohalan, and others opposed to America's entry into the war. The communication was dated 17 April 1916, seven days before the Easter Rising in Ireland and one year before the United States Congress agreed to join the conflict. Cohalan was not guilty of treason, but he was potentially in breach of the Neutrality Act, according to which an instruction sent within the United States to begin, set in motion or prepare a military or naval expedition or enterprise was subject to a fine of $3,000 or imprisonment for up to three years. George Creel suggested Cohalan continued to have close contacts with German sympathisers even *after* America had entered the war, by disclosing to the press that a German-American paper had put him forward as a senatorial candidate for New York.

Cohalan issued a statement denying everything; it was a British plot similar to the attempt to discredit Parnell with forged letters and Roger Casement with a forged diary. He described one warning given to him in May 1916 'by one who had entry to the British Embassy' that the British authorities were determined if possible to 'destroy' him, and another a year later at a meeting in the embassy attended by Shane Leslie. He declared that he was an American 'who yields to no man in devotion to this country'. Whatever Irish sympathies had been before America's entry to the war they were 'now, as they have always been, for *America, first, last and all the time.*'

The campaign against Cohalan continued through the winter. The *New York Times* published an incriminatory editorial, *The Cohalan Evidence*.[28] The New York Senate requested Secretary of State Lansing, a member of the Committee of Public Information, to supply any additional evidence to establish that Cohalan had violated international law, making him an 'unfit person' to continue to be a justice of the New York Supreme Court.[29]

The attack on Cohalan served another purpose during a divisive New York mayoral election campaign. Cohalan had supported the candidacy of John Hylan, the former railroad worker turned lawyer, against the aloof and Ivy League educated incumbent John Purroy Mitchell. Despite an impressive Irish nationalist heritage through his grandfather, the mayor was a Home Rule supporter.

During a mass meeting in support of Mitchell at Madison Square Garden, Theodore Roosevelt denounced the 'Huns within' as being more dangerous than the 'Huns without'. The former president publicly attacked the loyalty of Cohalan. This was a step too far for the judge, who came out fighting with a statement published in the *New York Times*.[30]

> The man, I care not who he may be, who says that I have ever had a dis-loyal thought … is false and the truth is not in him'.
>
> 'I am thoroughly American … I am with her in this war against Germany … I made it clear and unmistakable from the platform of Carnegie Hall within forty-eight hours after the declaration of war.

Cohalan filed a libel suit against the publisher of the *Evening Mail*, which was settled in his favour in December 1918. The media coverage stopped and impeachment proceedings in the New York Senate came to nothing.[31] But the document released by George Creel was, in fact, authentic. Cohalan *had* requested a telegram to be sent to Berlin on his behalf by von Bernstorff. A copy was kept in the German diplomatic archives in Berlin.[32]

Cohalan had a passion for Ireland; he owned a house in Cork, which he visited frequently before the war. It was only natural that he would support the Irish cause. But he *fought* for Irish independence – risking his reputation, career and even his freedom – as an American. Cohalan had a vocation to elevate the status of the Irish Race; Ireland taking her place among the nation states of Europe was crucial to that objective. He fought against anything that threatened the country of his birth, in particular the imperial ambitions of Britain and Japan. His opposition to the League of Nations was as an American. The fact that the League covenant was a new obstacle to Irish independence was convenient to that fight.

Cohalan was playing a key role in maintaining the unity of a historically factionalised Irish movement in America. He had cross-party political contacts in Washington. Although he could be dogmatic and had mannerisms that hinted of a patronising attitude, he was genuine and sincere in his passion for America and Ireland.[33]

Shane Leslie wrote that Cohalan was 'ready to go to any length and to make any alliance in furtherance of an Irish Republic'.[34] As the recognised leader of the Irish movement, he was willing to take on any opponent, even defending America's right to intervene on behalf of Ireland against Edward Carson's criticism of the Senate hearing.

F. Scott Fitzgerald wrote, 'Between the rancid accusations of Edward Carson and Justice Cohalan, [Amory Blaine] had completely tired of the Irish question.'[35]

Propaganda battle

British government propaganda had played a crucial role in securing America's reluctant entry into the war on the side of the Allies. The propaganda chief on the ground was Sir Gilbert Parker, a Canadian novelist, who had set up a secret propaganda bureau.[36] 'I need hardly say that the scope of my department was very extensive,' he wrote in *Harper's Magazine* on his return to London.[37]

On 4 July 1919, Lord Northcliffe, the owner of *The Times,* whom Lloyd George had sent to America during the war, advocated for a renewed intensive propaganda campaign in America; those trained in the 'arts' of swaying public opinion were 'urgently needed.'[38] England wanted to force Senate ratification of the League of Nations and to counter Irish propaganda, described by Philip Gibbs, a former English war correspondent, as 'elaborate, widespread and brilliantly organized.'[39]

Gibb's statement was a compliment to Diarmuid Lynch, the national secretary of the Friends of Irish Freedom. Within one year of his appointment in May 1918, Lynch had achieved his objective of building an organisation able to mobilise the Irish–American movement 'at the touch of a button.'[40] Without that, wrote Lynch, 'the politicians will sneer at us, and the British propagandists who are working day and night will sneer at us also – and they will be right'. Of the loosely estimated twenty million Americans with Irish blood, 'a mere fraction' had given a thought to Ireland.[41] An education campaign to raise awareness needed to be put in place if Ireland was ever to secure recognition.

Lynch, aged forty and a naturalised American citizen, had arrived back in New York in 1918 after an eventful eleven-year absence; he had played a central role organising the 1916 Rising, served as a captain in the General Post Office, escaped the death penalty and served time in eight English prisons.[42] Secretly marrying his fiancé while he was in prison, so that she could follow him to New York as his wife, he arranged for the marriage to take place on the same date and time as the Easter Rising had commenced.[43] Lynch was shadowed by at least two secret service agents in New York for months after his forced deportation.[44] He was a member of the supreme council of the Irish Republican Brotherhood and was on the executive council of Sinn Féin. He had been elected to the Dáil *in absentia* in the 1918 elections.

Lynch had first come to New York as a young man in 1896. With a natural flair for organisation, attention to detail and endless stamina, he found work as a bookkeeper and shipping clerk with Farquhar & Company, a manufacturer of agricultural machinery shipped throughout America and overseas.[45] His first friends were German-American emigrants with whom he shared accommodation and celebrated his twenty-first birthday in 1899. Within a few years he had become friendly with Cohalan and John Devoy, editor of the *Gaelic American* newspaper. Sensing the changes happening in the country and wanting to be of service, Lynch returned to Ireland in 1907.

On his return to New York, he implemented his ambitious growth plans for the Friends of Irish Freedom. Branch numbers increased from eighteen to 250 and paid-up membership rose from 2,000 to 70,000 in his first eighteen months.[46] Associate branches experienced the same growth rate. In May 1919, he moved the headquarters to larger premises in the Sun Building at 280 Broadway and considerably augmented the staff.

Much work still needed to be done to broaden the membership, of which 40 per cent lived in New York City and 80 per cent in the states of New York, Pennsylvania, Massachusetts, New Jersey, Connecticut and Rhode Island.[47] Lynch appointed a publicity firm to conduct a national press campaign; after they proved incompetent he took the work in-house. Miss Martin from Detroit, a highly qualified Irish–American publicist, was attached to Lynch's staff. News bulletins issued by the publicity department of the revolutionary government in Ireland and special articles prepared by Miss Martin were circulated in large numbers.[48]

A fully staffed national headquarters in New York and nationwide publicity campaigns required funding. The Irish Race Convention in February 1919 had authorised the raising of $1 million through an Irish Victory Fund. The money raised would be used to campaign for the recognition of 'the Republican form of government' established in Ireland; to fight against any League of Nations which did not safeguard American rights; to preserve the American ideals of government; to offset the British propaganda, which was 'falsifying and misrepresenting' American history; and to pay the expenses of an Irish–American delegation sent to the Paris Peace Conference.[49]

Guardian

'Does it ever occur to you that your assumption of infallible judgment is absurd?' John Devoy wrote to Patrick McCartan on the train from New York to San Francisco on 21 April 1919.[50]

Devoy, who was the voice, guardian, theorist and chief organiser of the Irish nationalist movement in America, was endeavouring to maintain unity. He was reacting to McCartan's attack on Cohalan at a meeting of the FOIF National Council and in a letter he planned to send to Ireland. 'You utterly misunderstand the situation here if you think you can overthrow Cohalan on flimsy charges like those contained in your letter. *And who would you put in his place?*'.

'Amiable to meet, vitriolic of pen,' was how Shane Leslie described Devoy, 'the last of the real Fenians.'[51] It was an accurate assessment to a point; Devoy was more than an old Fenian. He spoke French, a legacy from his time in the Foreign Legion, and he had a little Spanish; he was erudite, a voracious reader and a keen geopolitical analyst. A gift for language, peppered with cultural and political references, was paraded in weekly editorials in the *Gaelic American*, the paper he had founded in 1903.

Arrested in 1866, Devoy spent five hungry rock-breaking years in English prisons before being exiled to America, leaving behind a broken promise to marry his fiancé. An innovative and visionary revolutionary, despite being three thousand miles from home, penniless and living in the slums of New York City, he was determined to use his intelligence and organisational skills to continue the republican fight from America.

Four years after his arrival, Devoy organised the rescue of six prisoners from a British penal colony in Australia; a logistics marvel that extended over two years and 12,000 miles, ending in triumph with the arrival of the rescue ship, *Catalpa*, into New York Harbour in August 1876. Shortly after, Devoy arranged funding for the development of the first prototype of a submarine by a young Irish inventor, John Holland, seeing the potential threat to British warships. A later prototype, combining electric motors for submerged travel and gasoline engines, was purchased by the US navy.

News and editorial comment in the *Gaelic American* was partisan; high praise for friends and unsparing invective for opponents. Devoy battled Anglo-American alliances, pro-English interpretations of American history and anti-Irish caricatures. He advocated an 'America First' foreign policy; keeping America out of overseas imperialist entanglements, including the League of Nations, would 'eventually make the whole world free.'[52]

In smoke-filled political back rooms, Devoy abandoned the invective of the revolutionary for the realism of the pragmatist; he strived for what was attainable on the path to the ultimate goal of an Irish republic. He had supported agrarian reform and helped organise an American tour by Michael Davitt, one of the founders of the Land League. Many in Clan-na-Gael had opposed this distraction from revolution, but for Devoy land reform was necessary and attainable.

He moved the cause of Ireland forward in a 'New Departure', a phrase that became synonymous with him, by building a political relationship with Parnell, the Anglo-Irish protestant Home Rule leader. Again, he had faced criticism, but cooperation between the different strands of nationalism would bring the nebulous goal of an Irish republic out of the realm of a small group of conspiracists to mainstream America; agrarian reform had united the Irish–American community for the first time, while participation in political life would ultimately legitimise the goal of an independent Ireland. During this time, Devoy had continued to organise gunrunning funds.

'It is very unpleasant to write as I have done to a man I like and have always trusted as I have you,' Devoy continued in the letter to McCartan.

The forty-year-old McCartan had come to America after leaving school, initially working as a barman in Philadelphia for Joseph McGarrity, a fellow Tyrone native, successful businessman and a senior Clan-na-Gael member. McCartan returned to Ireland in 1905 to study medicine with the financial support of McGarrity. Arrested after the Easter Rising, in which he did not take part owing to receiving a countermanding order, McCartan returned to America in 1917 to deliver a memorandum from the released prisoners to the Wilson administration. McGarrity appointed him editor to his Philadelphia-based *Irish Press* newspaper. He was elected to the Dáil in 1918.

McCartan disagreed with the strategy of the Friends of Irish Freedom for obtaining recognition of the Irish Republic from the US government. At the Irish Race Convention two months earlier, he had demanded that the resolutions make specific reference to the Irish Republic. The FOIF leaders, in line with official policy in Ireland, focused on gaining admission of an Irish delegation to the Paris Peace Conference under the guise of self-determination for small nations. Devoy explained to McCartan that the resolutions had to be 'couched in something as near to diplomatic language as revolutionists can get'.

Declaring a republic was one thing, but securing international recognition required diplomacy and political nuance. 'The writing of our own resolutions was the hardest job I ever had,' Devoy tried to explain to McCartan. 'To demand that Wilson directly recognise the Irish Republic would have brought instant refusal and brought us up against a stone wall.' Diarmuid Lynch, who attended the National Council meeting where McCartan had made a 'bitter personal onslaught' on Cohalan, believed the doctor was 'incapable of grasping the international realities of the situation.' [53]

Devoy resented McCartan's implication that he and Cohalan had 'gone back' on the Irish Republic.

> I am quite satisfied to stake my reputation as a citizen of the Irish Republic, to which I swore allegiance in January, 1861, on the writing of those resolutions, and will continue to defend them as sound in principle and the best service to Ireland that could be rendered in the circumstances.[54]

McCartan had even criticised the leaders in Ireland, including the president of the new assembly, whom Devoy defended in the letter.

> And now you appear to be ready to turn your batteries on De Valera. Your statement that he was influenced in making what you hint is a change of front by our action here is very foolish and wholly inconsistent with the descriptions you have given me of him.
>
> I judge him by his public acts and speeches and am convinced that he is the best leader that Ireland has had for a century. After your bad failure with Cohalan you would be well advised to let De Valera alone. The men at home are as fully competent to take care of their own business as we are here to take care of ours.

Devoy also disagreed with McCartan on Irish strategy regarding the proposed League of Nations, criticising him for initially wanting the fight against the League dropped.[55] The editorial stance in the *Irish Press* would flip-flop on the League. On one occasion, it declared that 'Defeat of Article 10 Will Not Free Ireland',[56] before, in an editorial somersault, proclaiming that the League of Nations was 'a perpetual declaration of war on Irish liberty, and the sooner the friends of Ireland realize this the better.'[57]

On his return to America in 1917, McCartan had become close to the leaders of the Irish Progressive League, a politically left-leaning group, centred in New York, with a core membership of 150 labour, socialist, suffragist and liberal activists, many of whom had been born in Ireland. Initially established to support a socialist mayoral candidate in opposition to Hylan and Mitchell, the organisation continued to advocate support for Irish independence during the war and was publicly critical of Britain, America's wartime ally, as well as Wilson, the wartime president.[58] Such a stance was not possible, or even considered wise, for the FOIF; the latter had pledged loyalty to America once she entered the war on the Allies' side, reduced its criticism of Britain and dropped overt German–American connections, focusing instead on building an organisation powerful enough to have influence in post-war Washington. Devoy was 'simply adjusting … tactics to the new situations'.[59]

The Irish Progressive League was founded close to the time of the release of the von Igol documents. Devoy accused McCartan of the 'constant coddling' of them in their efforts to 'supplant our organisation.'[60] A weary Devoy saw McCartan as another in a long line of revolutionaries coming from Ireland who 'not alone misunderstands America, but is filled with preconceived notions that are wholly without foundation, as well as a belief that he knows America better than those who have spent most of their lives in the country or were born in it.'[61] At least McCartan would be gone soon; he was arranging to go to Moscow to secure recognition of the Irish Republic from the Soviet government.

But a new threat to the unity of the Irish movement had emerged.

Neurologist

When Cohalan had defended himself against the accusations in the von Igol papers by publicly disclosing a British Embassy meeting at which

Shane Leslie was present, he also named two other attendees: William J. Maloney, a neurologist and former captain in the British army, and Lord Eustace Percy, a valued friend of Maloney who worked with the British Foreign Office.[62]

Doctor William Maloney, born in Edinburgh, had moved to New York in 1911 at the age of twenty-nine as professor of nervous diseases at Fordham University. A talented practitioner, he had completed fellowships in Paris, London and Munich under leading specialists in the fields of psychology, psychiatry and nervous diseases.[63] Though of Irish heritage, he had exhibited no material interest in Irish nationalism.

Maloney left his practice and enlisted as a lieutenant in the Royal Army Medical Corps when England declared war on Germany. He was wounded at the Marne, and again at Gallipoli when going to the aid of an officer, which earned him a military cross, promotion to captain and partial paralysis in one leg. His younger brother was killed at the Somme.

In August 1916, Maloney resigned his commission, on excuse of his wounds, disillusioned by the imperialist war aims and 'disgusted' by the brutality of the English towards the 1916 leaders, in particular the execution of Roger Casement. He returned his military cross. After spending months recuperating in Jamaica, Maloney returned to New York in April 1917, immediate on America's entry to the war.

Maloney had married Margaret McKim, daughter of a renowned American architect, and in New York he moved in high society, in particular among the reforming elite. The McKims were close to Oswald Garrison Villard, a pacifist and liberal, and owner of the *New York Evening Post* (until 1918) and *The Nation* weekly journal. Villard had written to Maloney in May 1919 with his view on the Irish cause: 'A government which has to be upheld by 80,000 troops is a government to be done away with—of course I mean, being a pacifist by pacifist means only.'[64] He was introduced to Revd Norman Thomas, another pacifist, and a Presbyterian minister, socialist and editor of *The World Tomorrow*, a Christian social magazine.

Maloney used his ready access to liberal New York newspapers to criticise British policy in Ireland, bringing the Irish case to the attention of a new progressive audience that was interested in political activism, civil liberties and nationalist movements. He was a talented writer and proved to be a brilliant propagandist. After becoming involved in the Irish Progressive League, he was introduced to McCartan, thereby becoming the most prolific contributor to the *Irish Press*, of which McCartan was nominally editor, writing articles and editorials, and setting policy.[65]

John Devoy had deep suspicions of Maloney, a new convert to the Irish cause and a former British army captain who was close with Leslie and Percy. Those factors would have been enough to arouse his suspicion, but they were compounded by the fact that Devoy had once fallen victim to a talented British spy. Henri Le Caron, another physician, a French-Canadian with an Irish mother, who had fought in the Fenian invasion of Canada in 1870, had joined the senior ranks of Clan-na-Gael. But it turned out that Le Caron was in fact Thomas Beech who, in addition to feeding information to the British, appeared as a government witness at the Parnell Commission linking the Irish leader with Devoy, and had provided to the commission dozens of documents, including secret Clan-na-Gael memos.[66]

Spy or not, Devoy saw Maloney as another threat to the unity of the Irish movement in America, at a point when unity was required more than ever in the fight against the League of Nations and for recognition of the Irish Republic. With the zeal of a convert and the passion of a crusader, and the support of McCartan and McGarrity, Maloney had aggressively pushed the Irish Race Convention to demand immediate recognition of the Irish Republic from the Wilson administration. He had also tried to remove condemnation of the League of Nations from the convention resolutions.[67]

Devoy described Maloney as 'one of the keenest, shrewdest, and most versatile men I ever met.'[68] He was convinced that Maloney was pushing for his and Cohalan's removal. 'He tells his friends the Clan is in control of the Friends [of Irish Freedom],' he wrote in his letter to McCartan, 'and that it must be ousted.'[69] Devoy added, 'He would be powerless to do any mischief but for you.'[70] His dislike of Maloney was visceral: 'the expression of his face and his furtive eyes, and his thin velvety voice.' [71] In a letter to Oswald Garrison Villard, Maloney had accused Cohalan of 'capitalizing the Irish cause for big money Republican purposes.'[72]

But Maloney presented little challenge to the leadership of Cohalan and Devoy. They commanded the support of the majority of the FOIF and Clan members in New York.

Unless, of course, something unexpected happened.

Irreconcilables

'Several of the Senators, Republicans and Democrats, with whom I talked admit that they do not regard a separate Irish Republic as either feasible or desirable,' Sir William Wiseman, a British intelligence officer in New York, reported to London in June 1919, 'and all they meant by the resolution was to register their conviction that something ought to be done.'[73]

The Senate had just passed the Borah Resolution. Sponsored by Republican Senator William Borah, the first part was an official request from the Senate to the American Peace Commission in Paris to secure a hearing for an Irish delegation at the peace conference, while the second part, which had been significantly diluted in committee, expressed the Senate's *sympathy* with the aspirations of the Irish people for a government of its own choice.[74] The resolution passed by a majority of sixty to one.

Cohalan had developed a close relationship with Senator Borah, arousing in him a special interest in the Irish situation.[75] In 1916, Borah had called for the end to the execution of the Irish leaders and criticised the 'midnight judgements' of the courts martial sitting at Dublin. Borah, along with Senator Hiram Johnson of California, was the leader of a small but powerful group of Republican senators, known as the *Irreconcilables*, opposed to the League of Nations.

Borah and Cohalan were political realists. Borah's original resolution had specifically referred to 'international recognition of the government, republican in form, established by the people of Ireland.'[76] Both knew that text would never make it out of committee; pro-English support in both parties was too strong to support a straight recognition resolution. The revised text was worded deliberately to garner bipartisan support. Passage of the resolution, albeit diluted, was another step, and an important one, on the recognition path.

Senator John Sharp Williams, a Democrat from Mississippi and supporter of the League of Nations, voted against the resolution, describing it as 'ill-advised, and really none of our business'.[77] While most politicians had sympathy for Ireland, Sharp William's view was shared by the majority in both parties when it came to recognition of an Irish republic. It was not in America's interest to upset England, a recent war ally and partner in the unstable global order that had emerged after the destruction of four empires, by recognising the alternative government established in Ireland. For many, Ireland was a 'domestic' matter for England; Irish independence was equivalent to the secession of the Confederacy. Some sympathised with the loyal and industrious Ulster protestants falling under the yoke of a Catholic majority; some even feared religious persecution. Others believed that an independent Ireland would result in 'an orgy of legislation, in jobbery, and in financial ruin … an Irish Tammany Hall.'[78] None of this stopped Republicans or Democrats, however, playing politics with the Irish question during the League of Nations debate.

In that debate, clear battle lines had been drawn: on one side, President Wilson, principle architect of the League of Nations, determined to deliver the exact terms agreed in Paris, on the other, Senator Henry Cabot Lodge, Republican majority leader, who believed that the president's 'internationalism' was a step too far. For Lodge, the Paris Peace Conference had passed far beyond its primary business of making peace with Germany; though he was not an isolationist, he opposed any treaty that usurped congressional powers.

Lodge proposed five 'American' reservations to the Treaty of Versailles (which he later increased to fourteen) relating to: the Monroe Doctrine, congressional consent, domestic issues (immigration, tariffs, 'racial matters'), withdrawal terms and Article 10. On the latter, he declared that Congress retain 'definitely the right to say when and where American soldiers are to fight.'[79] But for President Wilson, Article 10 represented the heart of the League, without which it would be a mere 'debating society.'[80]

Republican *reservationists* had no objection to the 'territorial integrity' provision of Article 10, which threatened to permanently prevent recognition of the Irish Republic by the United States government and, as most Democrats supported the treaty including Article 10, it became evident that the status of Ireland was not critical to either party in the debate. Sean T. O'Kelly, the unofficial Irish envoy in Paris, had reported to Dublin that there was 'no doubt now that Wilson looked upon the Irish Question as a "domestic" one for the British Empire'.[81] Republicans raised the question of Ireland in the Senate mainly to place Irish-supporting Democrats in an awkward position and to highlight failings in the treaty. With outright rejection of the treaty being the only way to block Article 10, Senators Borah and Johnson, the *Irreconcilables*, became natural allies of Cohalan and Devoy.

President Wilson, burdened with failing health, was forced to embark on a nationwide tour to shore up wavering support for the treaty; the war had ended in victory, but peace was proving problematic. He also faced multiple domestic and international challenges. While the public health threat had waned, further influenza cases were expected in winter. He faced anarchist bombings and police, steel and coal strikes. The revolution in Russia fuelled a *Red Scare*. The Ku Klux Klan had become a political force and interracial violence was rife in what newspapers were calling the *Red Summer*. America was struggling to define itself and its role in the global order.

The outcome of the battle for Senate ratification of the League of Nations would determine America's relationship with the outside world for a generation. The stakes were high, passions rose and opponents were willing to use any weapon to crush it, including the Irish question. Into this maelstrom arrived an unexpected visitor from Ireland.

PART 1

1

RETURN OF THE NATIVE

Meet the press

If he was expecting the reporters to take it easy on him, he was mistaken.

'Are you an American citizen?'[1]

'I am an Irish citizen.'

'Did you foreswear allegiance to the United States?'

'I ceased to be an American when I became a soldier of the Irish Republic.'

'How about the Irish bond Issue?'

'I can't talk about that now; not now.'

On 23 June 1919, Éamon de Valera was taking questions from reporters gathered in the reception room of his suite in the Waldorf Astoria Hotel. In his first official statement since his arrival in America, he had deliberately avoided mention of the proposal to float a bond on behalf of the self-declared Irish Republic, yet this topic attracted most of the questions. 'The "President" of Ireland,' commented the *New York Times*, 'proved an adept in the art of talking and saying nothing.'

Facing reporters again the following day, de Valera announced that the Irish Republic would be issuing its first bond of £500,000 ($2.5 million), of which half would be floated in Ireland and half in America.[2] He downplayed the importance of the bond issue, however. It was secondary to his objective of compelling the United States government, through the force of public opinion, to officially recognise the Irish Republic. 'The loan is only a minor issue with me,' he replied to persistent questioning. 'Some time in the future I will announce the plans whereby it will be floated'.[3] But the reporters would not let go. Asked to explain the use to which the money would be put, he answered, 'for purely national purposes'.

De Valera was cautioned by the reporters that money raised in the United States for the prosecution of Irish national aspirations would be in 'violation of American laws and might lead to serious complications between this country and Great Britain'. De Valera attempted to deflect to a higher authority. 'The law of humanity is more fundamental, and I would appeal to that. When municipal and international laws conflict with humanity I regard them as no law.' But the seasoned reporters refused to accept such a vapid answer; one that might have worked on a town hall platform in Ireland, but not in the cauldron of a New York press conference.

'Will American money, obtained through bond sales, be used to buy guns for the Irish Volunteers?'
'It will be used for the Irish Republic.'
'…including the maintenance of a military establishment?'
'It will be used for the full administration of the Government of Ireland.'

Before ending the conference, de Valera was forced to deny 'most emphatically' that Russian or German money had ever been used to fund the Sinn Féin movement.

Man of mystery

The American newspapers knew almost nothing about de Valera, other than that he was the revolutionary Sinn Féin leader. He had been sentenced to be shot in 1916, saved only by 'his American citizenship'.[4] He had been imprisoned as part of a *German Plot* while America was still at war, elected to the British parliament while in prison, and had escaped story-book style from Lincoln Jail just four months previously. The mysterious ease at which de Valera eluded the British since his escape added to his popular interest.

Tipped off about his presence in America prior to his first public appearance, the *New York Times* had dispatched a reporter to the Rochester home of his mother, Mrs. Charles Wheelwright. She had sent her son to Ireland when he was two years old following the death of his father. Mrs. Wheelwright was 'amused' when told that her son had been in the city.[5] She had not heard from him since he was imprisoned, 'if he has really got away, it would be more probable that her son was in Paris.'[6] The *Irish Press* carried a dispatch from the French capital that well-informed circles reported that he had arrived in Switzerland.[7]

In fact, de Valera had landed in New York on 11 June as a stowaway on a steamship, cramped, seasick and with mainly rats for company. His mother, in whose home he had stayed on his first night, and Joe McGarrity, the owner of the *Irish Press*, whom he had also visited, were part of the subterfuge to disguise his presence in the country. Since his arrival, he had visited the influential Cardinal Gibbons in Baltimore, called on several senators in Washington and met Irish–American leaders in Boston.

Two days before de Valera's official appearance, Harry Boland, another absentee member of Westminster Parliament, had gathered reporters at the Waldorf Astoria to announce that de Valera would hold a press conference at the hotel on 23 June.[8] Boland had come to New York five weeks earlier working as a ship stoker; the still chafed and blistered hands of the former tailor testament to days feeding the ship's furnace.[9]

Boland was not registered at the hotel and disappeared immediately after the brief conference. Reporters went to the offices of the Friends of Irish Freedom, where it was confirmed that de Valera had really reached America. 'Right there the plot thickened, the mystery – the hallmark of the Sinn Féin Movement – deepened,' commented the *New York Times*. 'Somewhere in America was de Valera; somewhere in New York was Boland but nobody, not even their friends, knew where.'[10]

Newspapers dug up details on de Valera's life, learning that he had been born in New York thirty-six years earlier.

His father was a Spanish-American, his mother an Irish woman. When de Valera was two years old his father died and the family re-moved to Ireland [*sic*], where the boy was educated. He held the Professorship of Mathematics at several colleges in Dublin at different times, then became active in the free Ireland movement.[11]

Official appearance

At 5.45pm on the day of the press conference, a large touring car carrying de Valera had swung into Thirty-third Street from Fifth Avenue amid cheers and tumult. On leaving the car, de Valera was kissed heartily by an elderly lady pushing past two policemen. Entering the Waldorf Astoria, smiling but hurriedly, he was met by the cautious gaze and discreet applause of tea sippers.[12] Accompanying him were Patrick McCartan, Diarmuid Lynch and Liam Mellows, another exiled revolutionary, and with them Judge Cohalan and John Devoy.[13]

After checking in to his suite, de Valera held an informal reception for 100 prominent supporters in the hotel's Gold Room. Returning to his rooms for a pre-arranged press conference, he welcomed the fifty journalists who had gathered in his private reception. One of them noted that de Valera wore glasses and a collar almost of collegian highness, and that he had a scholarly stoop that detracted from his height, a high forehead, deep set brown-black eyes, a rather prominent nose, and a general expression of eagerness.[14]

'I have been traveling incognito and now my private life here is ended and I am now in an official capacity', de Valera informed the reporters.[15] His first public appearance had solved the mystery of his location, but now the reporters wanted to know how he had come into the country. He mischievously suggested that he might have come by air. Nine days earlier, Alcock and Brown had taken off from Newfoundland and sixteen hours later had landed safely in Clifden, completing the first non-stop transatlantic flight.

Miss Martin hurried into the room with her arms full of copies of a type-written statement.[16] De Valera told the reporters that he wished the statement printed word for word, so that 'British propagandists' could not misrepresent what he said. 'From today I am in America as the official head of the republic established by the will of the Irish people in accordance with the principles of *self-determination*.' Establishing a connection between the Irish fight for freedom and the American revolution, he said that the degree of unanimity in Ireland was 'higher than that claimed by the American colonies when they declared their Independence ... You had your Tories and your Loyalists, too'.[17]

He reminded the American people that their revolutionary leaders were called traitors and murderers, noting, 'so are we.' While they had sought the support of France, 'We seek the aid of America.' The American nation had come to the aid of the people of Poland, Greece, Hungary and the Latin republics of this continent. 'Ireland, the one remaining white nation in the slavery of alien rule, will similarly be free unless Americans make scraps of paper of their principles and prove false to the traditions their fathers have handed down to them.' He ended by decrying Britain's economic control of Ireland and the population collapse. 'Had Ireland been under Kaiser, Emperor or Czar its population would have been doubled or trebled, as the population of the three divisions of Poland, of Bohemia, of Alsace-Lorraine have been.'

After a photoshoot on the roof of the hotel, de Valera received a rousing welcome at a reception organised by the Friends of Irish Freedom in support of the Irish Victory Fund, at which he was introduced by Judge Cohalan. 'For the first time in Irish history we have the President of the Irish Republic on American soil.'[18] The celebrations continued until 4 a.m., when de Valera retired in the presidential suite. He could sleep soundly that night without fear of arrest. 'The President has been in Washington, as you know,' one of his entourage had informed reporters earlier in the day, 'and while there he saw many influential men, men more powerful than some of President Wilson's appointees. We have no fear of an arrest. His safety is assured here.'[19]

Reporters had ascertained from official sources that de Valera would not be interfered with unless he violated American law, with officials at the State Department intimating that if the object of the money was to create or equip a military force he would make himself liable under the Neutrality Act.[20] When questioned by reporters, Senator Lusk, chairman of the committee investigating Bolshevism and other seditious activities, said he was 'quite sure that De Valera's activities do not come within the purview of the committee's work.'

De Valera's public appearance in New York was front-page news the following morning. Meeting reporters again, he declared that Ireland desired the closest possible commercial and political relationship with the United States.[21] The elected government of the Irish Republic, he said, would send accredited representatives to the Paris Peace Conference, and ambassadors and consuls to other countries. 'It is obvious that the work of our Government cannot be carried on without funds,' he proclaimed. The money would be raised in such amounts 'as to meet the needs of the small subscriber.' When interrupted by a reporter inquiring about the rate of interest on the Irish Republic bonds, and also when they would be payable, he responded, 'As to the rate of interest, I can't say just now, but the interest will start six months *after* the British troops evacuate Ireland.'[22] This was not what had been agreed by the cabinet in Dublin, however. Interest *payments* would commence on British withdrawal, but the interest *liability* started from the time of subscription, consistent with standard government bonds.[23]

His means of arrival in the States continued to attract interest. One story doing the rounds was that he had stepped onto a seaplane in front of British officers, which took him to a waiting yacht, and that another seaplane had met him off the coast of New York.

De Valera changed to a new suite on the eleventh floor that one reporter said outranked the former apartments 'by many pounds of gilt, a heap more fancy clocks, no end of French vases, and the like.' [24]

The following day, just the third of his official visit, reporters noticed de Valera's irritability at questions on the bond. 'It appeared as if the stress which had been placed on the Irish loan annoyed Dr. de Valera because he made it evident that his main mission here was to get official recognition for Ireland.'[25] The *New York Times* had published an editorial attacking the stance of the Irish Republic during the war, the bond funding and alleged links to radicals, and interpreted de Valera's comments as being pro-German.

> Many thousands of Irishmen – men like Tom Kettle and William Redmond – were dying for the freedom of the world; and for the sake of the memory of those men, if for no other reason, justice is due to Ireland. But where was the Irish Republic?'[26]
>
> … it was a little tactless of Professor De Valera to tell us how much better off Ireland would have been under the rule of 'Kaiser, Emperor, or Czar'. It is six months since fighting ceased, but the Kaiser is not yet a popular hero in this country. Our distinguished visitor has hitched his wagon to a fallen star.'

According to the paper, Soviet Russia, acting through its 'intensively investigated' envoy Ludwig Martens, had recognised the Irish Republic.

The same morning as that editorial appeared, Sir Charles Carrick Allom, a well-known English sportsman and aeroplane manufacturer, was thrown out of the St. Regis Hotel on Fifth Avenue. While walking through the lobby, two eighteen-year-old girls, standing by a table on which the American and Irish flags were displayed, had asked him if he wished to subscribe to the Irish Victory Fund. Sir Charles protested the display of the Irish flag to the hotel manager and, when the discussion turned animated, he was ejected through the main door onto Fifty-Fifth Street by porters of Irish heritage. 'There is no reason why we should discriminate against the Irish in their campaign,' said Mr. Haan, the Austrian-born hotel manager, when interviewed about the incident. 'The Serbians, the Armenians, and all the other nationalities that conducted drives for funds were allowed to solicit funds in this building, as well as in all other hotels, and the Irish can solicit here, too.'[27]

Shipping up to Boston

On Sunday 29 June, de Valera basked in the adulation of the vast crowd of at least 50,000 people packed into Fenway Park, home of the Boston Red Sox.[28] Newsreel footage shows de Valera waving his panama hat, his face alight, smiling and nodding, mouthing acknowledgements of his welcome. A sea of hats filled the playing field, along with American flags, tricolours and banners in support of Irish freedom.[29] Sharing the platform with de Valera were a senator, two mayors, three majors, one colonel, a district attorney, an ex-congressman and an ex-mayor.[30]

It was an engagement that de Valera had initially turned down. At his first press conference, he told reporters that he did not plan to go on a speaking tour of the country, 'since the American people understand the Irish situation.'[31] He rejected an invitation to address the meeting in Boston, which had been organised by the Bench and Bar Committee of the Irish Victory Fund,[32] and mapping out his programme at a meeting with Irish leaders, de Valera said he would address state legislatures, chambers of commerce and representative groups, but would not speak at large public gatherings. Cohalan, however, believed a series of mass meetings would be of value, as did Harry Boland, who was 'enthusiastic for it.'[33] It seems de Valera came to see their point of view; as Devoy wrote to Cohalan, 'It looks as if they had changed their minds a bit and come round to our way of thinking about a series of big meetings.'[34] In the *Gaelic American*, Devoy called the Irish president 'a very modest man who underrates his ability to sway great public gatherings.'[35]

In his short speech to the Boston audience, de Valera called for a *new* League of Nations agreement to be created in Washington.

A League of Nations and a covenant for a League of Nations can be framed in Washington as well as in Paris. Now is the time to frame it – it is not enough to destroy, you must build.

He delivered an abstract critique of the entire Treaty of Versailles: 'Peace was nominally signed between the two great combating sides … Peace that gives us twenty new wars instead of the one that it nominally ends … Does it not already seem a mockery … A new "holy alliance" cannot save democracy.' An incredible contribution to the treaty debate by a foreign representative, one that positioned him publicly at odds with both President Wilson and the irreconcilables who were opposed to any League, even one framed in Washington. The pro-League *New York Times* responded bitterly in another editorial comment. 'The establishment of a new nationality requires some practical qualities in the statesman who is at the head of that nationality.'[36] Acknowledging de Valera's right to oppose the League when it provided no place for Ireland, the paper said he should 'get down to practical details, as other representatives of oppressed nationalities have done and tell us just what he wants.' If de Valera thought it was a mockery, he 'might at least be kind enough to tell us why.'

The Fenway Park meeting, however, was a monster propaganda success. According to the *Gaelic American*, the New York papers gave de Valera 'more space than they have given to anything Irish for many years and were much fairer than is their habit'.[37] Devoy praised the Hearst newspaper group as being the fairest. The *Boston Post* commented that it was impossible to see and hear de Valera 'without feeling the most profound conviction that the cultured leader of the new Ireland is supremely in earnest and full of the fire of faith'.[38] The *Gaelic American* noted that de Valera received the 'greatest reception ever accorded to any man visiting the city.'[39]

On an automobile tour of Boston and Cambridge, de Valera placed wreaths at the elm tree under which Washington reputedly took command of the American revolutionary army, at the Minute Man statue in Lexington, and at Bunker Hill in tribute to the men of Irish blood who fought there.[40] Later that day, he addressed the Massachusetts House of Representatives. He had not received an invitation to speak to the Senate, however; the president of that chamber, although favourable to receiving de Valera, had not wanted to commit an impropriety by recognising the Irish government.[41] Amid some confusion, a solution was found by which the Senate accepted an invitation to hear de Valera in the House, where the whole assembly rose to its feet and cheered loudly when he entered.

On the same day in Indianapolis, Cohalan criticised the 'English-made' League of Nations.

> The day of equality and freedom is coming in. A *real* League of Nations in the end *may* be formed that will include all peoples, great or small, that will not be as this proposed League of Nations is, a cover for a special alliance between England and America, but will be a step in the direction of the brotherhood of man.[42]

Unlike de Valera, however, Cohalan knew the prospect of a *real* League of Nations was aspirational. President Wilson was committed to the agreement he had signed in Paris and, while Republicans would fight for their reservations, they had no appetite for negotiating a new League in Washington.

On 10 July, de Valera spoke at a reception held for him in front of 17,000 people in Madison Square Garden.[43] A 'struggling mass of humans' in the streets outside tried to gain access. Cohalan, who received 'quite a reception himself', outlined the purpose of the FOIF organised event. They were here to welcome to the metropolis of the world the president of the Republic of Ireland, to welcome home the delegates sent by the FOIF to Paris, and to protest against the League of Nations. 'We say that if there be anything in the doctrine of Self-Determination,' asserted Cohalan, '… President de Valera must be acknowledged as the leader of the Irish people.'

In his speech, de Valera denied absolutely that Ireland was a domestic question of Britain, criticising the hypocrisy of English propaganda for championing liberty as if Ireland, Egypt and India did not exist, and for making it appear as though the situation in Ireland was due to 'some inherent defect in the character of Irishmen'. At the first mention of President Wilson's name, the crowd burst into 'a medley of disapproving noise.'[44] De Valera, noticeably, did not mention the League of Nations in his address.

Two days later, arriving in Chicago at 9.45 on a Saturday morning, de Valera went to the Congress Hotel, where, in the humming lobby, he smiled as he greeted waiting reporters asking them to make it as easy as possible for him. In the barrage of questions that followed, one reporter asked whether he disapproved of the hissing of President Wilson's name in Madison Square Garden. De Valera stopped smiling. The question 'disturbed' him.[45] He gave a rambling reply, avoiding open condemnation of the jeerers, and suggested blame be put on the enemies of the Irish cause. He would later blame press exaggeration of the incident.[46] After that, de Valera avoided direct mention of President Wilson's name at public meetings.

The following afternoon, on his arrival at the Chicago Cubs baseball park, de Valera was cheered for over thirty minutes by a crowd of between 25,000 and 60,000 people, depending on the source.[47] In a dangerous repetition of events at Fenway Park, the crowd surged past the police cordon and through the barriers, almost toppling the speaker's stand.

The chairman of the meeting declared that American citizens were 'unalterably opposed' to the League of Nations, which would impair their sovereignty, imperil the Constitution, destroy the Monroe Doctrine, and guarantee world supremacy 'of the two remaining despotic empires of the world, Great Britain and Japan.'[48] In his speech, de Valera acknowledged these 'American grounds' for opposing the League. Recognising that he had meddled in American domestic politics, he restricted his own opposition to the negative impact of Article 10 on Ireland.[49] De Valera no longer publicly called for a new League of Nations.

A five-day stay in San Francisco began on 18 July, during which de Valera received the freedom of the city and addressed a crowd of 12,000 people at the Civic Auditorium. On his way back to New York, he stopped in Salt Lake City, where he was greeted by the Utah governor, and in Butte, where he received the freedom of the state of Montana, spoke before the state legislature and visited Anaconda, the copper mining centre.[50]

Arriving back in New York on 3 August, de Valera told reporters, who had been gathered at the Waldorf Astoria by his new press agent, Charles Sweeney, that he had found a 'very definite' opposition to the League of Nations 'in the minds of the working classes.'[51] The bond drive remained a secondary objective for him. 'If we gain recognition by the United States, we shall not lack for money.' He announced an upcoming extensive ten-week tour of the country, after which, he said, he may return to Ireland.[52] The FOIF would provide a $10,000 loan out of the proceeds of the Irish Victory Fund to pay for the tour.[53]

In another comment to the press, de Valera channelled Cohalan's concerns on trade and the freedom of the seas. 'It has seemed obvious to me,' he said, 'that if there is another war it would be England and Japan against the United States. The history of England shows that it always has been her policy to combine against her nearest rival in alliance with the next nearest. Just now the United States is England's greatest commercial rival.'[54]

What happens in Paris should stay in Paris

On 8 July, President Wilson, the first sitting president to travel to Europe, had arrived back in New York on board the *George Washington*, after an absence of 147 days.[55] He was greeted by a naval escort and received a salute from a squadron of sea planes, one of which developed engine problems and was forced to land in the open sea; an augur of difficult days ahead for the president as he anticipated a fractious treaty ratification battle in the Senate.

Hundreds of thousands of people waved as the presidential motorcade moved slowly up Fifth Avenue. Seated at a window in the Waldorf, de Valera watched the standing president doff his silk hat to the crowd.[56] With him were Frank Walsh, chairman of the American Commission on Irish Independence, and Edward Dunne, former governor of Illinois and mayor of Chicago, a member of the commission. They had also returned to New York that day having failed to obtain a hearing at the peace conference for a delegation from Ireland.

The waiting party that met Walsh and Dunne at the West Fourteenth Street pier included Joseph Shannon, a senior Democrat and future member of Congress.[57] The triumvirate of Frank Walsh, Joe Shannon and George Creel, the former head of the wartime propaganda bureau, had cut their political teeth together in Kansas City, where elections were contested 'with a vigor that stopped short only at mayhem.'[58] Within the Democratic party, Shannon led the Rabbits against the Goats faction of a rotund saloonkeeper. 'At Joe Shannon's right hand, and the brains of the faction, stood Frank P. Walsh,' wrote Creel, 'a man who had won my love and admiration at our initial meeting. A great lawyer, a persuasive speaker, and the most authentic liberal I have ever known.'[59]

Walsh was now a well-known labour attorney and a former pacifist who President Wilson had appointed joint chairman of the National War Labour Board and chairman of the Industrial Relations Commission. Walsh's experience in Paris, however, turned him against Wilson and the League of Nations; he described the plenary session of the peace conference as akin to 'mob primaries out in Missouri'.[60]

The commission to Paris had almost no chance of success, but it did generate significant publicity. Walsh's lack of political diplomacy, however, ensured the mission ended in controversy. A meeting with President Wilson, arranged just three weeks before his return to America, turned into a tetchy and provocative encounter with threats made by both sides, where Walsh succeeded, not for the first time, in getting under the skin of the man for whom he had once campaigned. At it, he informed Wilson that unless some relief was given to Ireland, 'workers there would have, in self defence, to set up Soviet governments or do something else to relieve the situation.'[61] Wilson explained that no small nation could appear before the peace conference unless there was unanimous consent from the committee of four, which would not be forthcoming as the conference only considered nations actually concerned in the war. As one American plenipotentiary put it, Irish affairs had 'nothing to do with making peace with Germany and Austria.'[62] Walsh proceeded to quote Wilson's own self-determination statements back to him, angering the president who, forgetting himself, shouted that he 'didn't give a damn.'[63]

The encounter might have remained private had the full transcript of the meeting – much of it politically sensitive to the president – not been released to the press after a slip-up by Walsh in front of the Republican-controlled Senate Foreign Relations Committee. Walsh told the committee that he would submit his Paris interviews in private 'because they might prove embarrassing to some gentlemen.' Republican senators, seeing an opportunity to embarrass the president, voted to receive the interviews only as part of the public record.[64]

While in Europe, the commissioners made a high-profile visit to Ireland and addressed the third session of Dáil Éireann, the counter-state parliament. This led to the British prime minister, Lloyd George, complaining to Colonel House, Wilson's chief adviser: 'I now find these gentlemen, so far from investigating the Irish problem in a spirit of impartiality, announced on arrival in Dublin that they had come there to forward the disruption of the United Kingdom, and the establishment of Ireland as an independent Republic.'[65] Walsh's outbursts in Ireland lost him the support of Colonel House and the official American delegation in Paris whose help he had been receiving.

The cooling of the relationship between Walsh and Wilson had begun earlier in the year. On a brief return to America in March, the president had reluctantly agreed to meet a delegation from the Irish Race Convention, his only stipulation being that Cohalan could not be part of the delegation, which resulted in it being led by Walsh. After the meeting the president complained to colleagues, 'They were so insistent ... I had hard work keeping my temper.'[66] His first impulse was to tell them to 'go to hell'.[67]

The Irish mission in Paris was funded by the Friends of Irish Freedom through $10,000 cabled to Walsh in May and another $10,000 sent to Sean T. O'Kelly, the envoy from Dublin.[68] O'Kelly wrote to thank Cohalan for his work in organising the commission.[69] When Devoy complained to O'Kelly about McCartan's criticism of the self-determi-nation strategy, the envoy replied with a message of support: 'I hope the president will be able to settle that now that he is with you. If he cannot succeed in bringing those people to their senses, nobody will.'[70]

Independence day

A sweltering Fourth of July weekend saw huge crowds escape Manhattan by train and ferry, with hundreds of thousands taking the subway to Coney Island and the other beaches. The authorities were on high alert for threatened Bolshevik, anarchist and other 'red flag' violence.[71] Two days earlier, the *New York Times* had published a cable from Switzerland suggesting collusion and cooperation between de Valera and Russian Bolshevists and German propagandists,[72] while the *Chicago Tribune* carried a report on an Irish–American Independence Day celebration in Berlin held by Americans who had remained in Germany during the war, the most prominent attendant being Kuno Meyer, a German national who held the Celtic chair at the University of Berlin.[73]

The left-leaning Irish Progressive League, headed by Peter Golden, an Irish-born actor, poet and journalist, celebrated with a meeting in support of the Irish Republic at the Lexington Theatre. The speaker list included leading New York liberals and socialists, alongside an Indian nationalist, who were joined by McCartan and Mellows.[74]

Independence Day celebrations at Tammany Hall were marked by resolutions supporting both the League of Nations *and* Ireland, and condemning radicals.[75] Boss Charles F. Murphy introduced a resolution advocating Irish freedom, while Senator Ashurst of Arizona commented that he didn't wholly like the League of Nations, 'if I had my way I would have written it in that Ireland is a free state.' Senator Harrison, who praised President Wilson's support for Irish self-determination, pointed at the Stars and Stripes while addressing the Bolshevik threat, 'Every man who doesn't love that flag and wants to tear up the Constitution should be sent from the shores of the United States. That flag and the red flag of anarchy have no place side by side in America.'

17

Jack Dempsey's defeat of Jess Willard in the world heavyweight title fight in Toledo united all Irish supporters. The Pottawatomie Giant, who hit the canvass six times in the first round, lost the belt when his team tossed his towel into the ring at the end of round three. The Knights of Columbus had installed a ticker service direct from ringside to give round by round updates to soldiers in the New York area.

2

FLOATING THE BOND

Millionaire group

William Bourke Cockran invited John Ryan, Nick Brady and Joe Grace to dine with him.[1] He wanted their opinion on de Valera's proposal to raise the Irish loan in the form of a government bond. Ryan and Brady were part of what Harry Boland called the 'millionaire group'.[2]

Ryan, aged fifty-four, was a copper mining magnate and one of America's leading industrialists and financiers.[3] He was president of Anaconda Copper Mining and an investor in many banks and utilities throughout the country, as well as being a pioneer in the electrification of the railroads.

Brady, aged forty, was chairman of the board of New York Edison.[4] He controlled vast family interests known on Wall Street as the 'Bradys'. He was close to Ryan, who invited him on the board of Anaconda Copper. They were both directors of National City Bank of New York and trustees of the Emigrant Industrial Savings Bank. Other members of the millionaire group included Edward L. Doheny, a self-made oil magnate and inspiration for the character of Daniel Plainview in the 2007 film *There Will Be Blood*, and Judge Morgan J. O'Brien, a director of Metropolitan Life Insurance.

The consensus among the New York diners was that the proposal to raise funds in the form of a government bond was not feasible. Bourke Cockran wrote to Cohalan on 14 July that 'the idea that a loan could be floated on *normal* financial grounds they scouted as preposterous.'[5] The money could never be raised as a 'cold financial investment.' The only alternative might be raising it 'as a matter of sentiment'.

The first instructions for raising an Irish loan in the form of a government bond had been brought to America by Harry Boland in May.[6] The plan was undeveloped, offered no detail on organisational structure and took no account of the legal and regulatory framework. Devoy considered the scheme 'very crude and wholly unworkable' and in 'utter ignorance' of conditions in America.[7] According to the instructions from Ireland, the bond drive was to be managed by a board of American trustees.[8] The prospectus was to be signed by the three Dáil members in America – Lynch, McCartan and Mellows – and two Irish people resident in the country; Devoy was suggested as one of the latter, while the second Irish resident was not to have been previously prominent in the Irish movement. Devoy, however, insisted that his name should not be used in that capacity.[9] Boland was 'very much disappointed' with the reaction to the scheme, but 'kept his temper.'[10]

A second set of instructions was sent from Ireland following the visit of the American Commission on Irish Independence (ACII) to the country.[11] On the advice of the visiting commissioners, new instructions on arrangements for the bond issue recommended that a bank be secured to act as trustee for the loan, or, failing that, an Irishman of high financial standing. De Valera and Michael Collins, the recently appointed minister for finance, sent a cablegram to New York requesting the withholding of the original prospectus until the commissioners returned.

On the evening after de Valera's first public appearance in America, he discussed the second set of instructions with Cohalan and the other Irish leaders. He proposed to find a bank to underwrite *and* sell the bonds, to conduct the campaign on the same lines as the war bond drives, and to complete the funding within *one week* simultaneously across all forty-eight states.[12] He increased the funding target to $5 million.

The four lawyers in the meeting – Judge Cohalan, Judge Goff, Richard Dalton and Michael Ryan (also a banker and a member of the American Commission) – pointed out critical flaws in the scheme. There were two legal impediments and several operational obstacles.[13] On the legal side, they advised that bonds issued on behalf of a self-declared government would be prohibited under federal law and would breach Blue Sky state regulations devised to protect the investing public from fraudulent overseas investments. On the operational side, even if the legal impediments were overcome, banks would neither underwrite a bond issue of an unrecognised government or sell them across the counter as they had done with the war drives. Furthermore, Irish–American financiers would not cooperate in the sale of such bonds. John Ryan later told Bourke Cockran that even 'love of country would not suffice to make men of high standing in business sponsor such a loan'.[14]

Diarmuid Lynch, who was also at the meeting, explained to de Valera that the organisation and cooperation that ensured the success of the war drives could not be replicated within a reasonable timeframe, and to think of completing the bond drive 'in a week or even a month was ridiculous.'[15] Nevertheless, de Valera insisted on implementing the plan regardless of the legal and operational advice received. He was influenced by Joe McGarrity, a hotelier and alcohol distributer, the only person at the meeting to support his proposals, who said that 'several times' $5 million could be subscribed within one week.[16]

Two weeks later, Boland read a letter from de Valera explaining the bond campaign plan to a meeting of the FOIF National Council.[17] De Valera, who was on his way to Chicago and San Francisco at the time, had left behind the inexperienced Boland to prepare the bond issue. The National Council perceived the proposals put to them as 'impossible propositions' presented as an ultimatum.[18] Believing the sale of bonds to be legally out of the question, a special committee of bankers, businessmen and lawyers was formed to find some alternative medium of raising the funds.[19] The committee members were: Thomas Hughes Kelly, a New York banker and treasurer of the FOIF; Richard Dalton, an attorney and president of the New York Architectural Terra Cotta Company; John D. Moore, former National Secretary of the FOIF; William Bourke Cockhran; and Judge Daniel Cohalan.

Immediately after the meeting of this committee, Boland had a 'nasty breakdown'.[20] Confined to his Waldorf apartment until ordered out of New York by his doctor, William Maloney, to recuperate in Orange County, he was taken out of the picture at a critical time.[21] Boland had come to admire his physician. 'If Maloney is as brilliant a spy as he is a doctor, then England has a very able man working for them.'[22]

Before falling ill, Boland had delegated the responsibility for setting up the bond campaign to Joseph Walsh, the former co-editor, with Shane Leslie, of the *Home Rule Ireland* paper. Walsh made arrangements with a man called Hill who apparently had managed the Knights of Columbus war drive.[23] This arrangement collapsed even before it got off the ground.

Cohalan and Devoy had reason to be concerned about Walsh's involvement in the funding campaign. Not only was he close to Leslie, but according to Devoy, Walsh, as special correspondent at the peace conference for *America,* a Catholic publication, had promoted Maloney as the 'coming leader' of the Irish Race.[24] Moreover, Maloney publicly credited Walsh with converting him to the Irish cause, while Walsh declared a series of five articles written by Maloney in 1917 as the 'real beginning' of the Irish republican movement in America.[25] 'He may be a genuine convert,' Devoy said of Walsh, 'but he was Captain Maloney's man.'[26]

A recovered Boland returned to New York at the end of July.[27] By then, progress on the bond drive had come to a halt. 'I cannot go further with this,' he wrote to McGarrity, 'until I hear from DeV the result of his interview with Bankers'.[28] The Irish president had arranged to meet financiers in Chicago to discuss the sale of bonds, but the meeting had been cancelled at the last moment.[29] During his time away, and on his return, Boland did not consult with the FOIF special committee, as had been arranged.[30]

Irish Victory Fund

The workaholic Diarmuid Lynch also fell ill during July. 'It's hard lines to be on the sick list now,' he wrote to his sister, 'with so much on hand that needs attention.'[31] He continued to work from home, however, including engaging with Cohalan on a *New York Times* report regarding a $5,000 contribution to the Irish Victory Fund made by Samuel Untermyer, a German–Jewish lawyer and Zionist, as well as a friend of Cohalan.[32]

Lynch had been busy transferring many of the activities of the FOIF headquarters in New York to an expanded presence in Washington. On 9 August, a press release announced the official opening of the new Irish National Bureau offices in the Munsey Building.[33] 'This period was a critical one in Ireland's fight for independence, and in America's fight for the preservation of her own,' recalled Lynch. 'America was deluged with cabled material from British sources; it was overrun with British propagandists seeking to prejudice American opinion against Ireland, and to secure the adoption of the League Covenant by the United States.'[34] By this point, the FOIF had taken over running of the bureau from the Irish Progressive League.

Daniel T. O'Connell, a Harvard-educated Boston lawyer, and former journalist and congressional secretary, was chosen as director of the bureau and as the person to shape its policy.[35] He had been discharged from the army with the rank of captain after serving in the JAG Corps. According to Lynch, 'No better selection could have been made.'[36] Katherine Hughes, who had been running the bureau for several months, continued as secretary, as well as writer and lecturer for the FOIF.[37] A Canadian who had relocated to New York, she was an author, journalist, activist and skilled orator. While working in London before the Easter Rising, she had met members of the cultural revival and republican movement.[38]

The FOIF immediately launched an ambitious publicity campaign in opposition to the League of Nations. Full and half-page advertisements were placed in Washington's main daily newspapers, including the *Washington Post*.[39] The advertisements changed daily over a five-day period, addressing the themes of self-determination, Shantung, American sovereignty and Article 10: 'Are You Willing to Delegate to

Foreigners the Power to Send Your Boys to War?' It was a deliberate strategy to fight the League of Nations on both American and Irish grounds.

The costs of the Irish National Bureau and the publicity campaign were met from the Irish Victory Fund, which after a slow start had accumulated rapidly from early June.[40] Unexpectedly, and to Lynch's dismay, de Valera demanded that the FOIF shut down the Victory Fund to provide a clear run for the bond campaign. Devoy suspected an alternative motive. Under the influence of McGarrity and McCartan, de Valera was depriving the FOIF of its primary funding source. Wrangling over the *use* of the Victory Fund proceeds had commenced months earlier. At a meeting of the national executive in May, before de Valera's arrival, McGarrity had proposed that $50,000 be made available for the Dáil envoys in Paris.[41] Cohalan informed the meeting that only $5,000 of the Victory Fund had been received at that time and that only $12,000 cash was on hand. Instead, it was unanimously agreed that $10,000 be cabled to the envoys.

The following month, on the eve of de Valera's arrival in New York, Devoy proposed that 25 per cent of the fund be sent to Ireland, and that this be followed by a larger proportion as soon as it was available.[42] An initial instalment of $50,000 (in addition to previously-made transfers) would be sent immediately. Two members of the National Council had proposed that 75 per cent of the fund be sent to Ireland, but received no support. Lynch believed Maloney had pushed for the *entire* proceeds to be sent to Ireland, in order to deprive the battle against the League of Nations from funding.[43] Frustrated, Lynch issued a circular announcing the closure of the Victory Fund and requesting the FOIF branches to forward all monies collected to the national treasurer before 31 August.[44]

Bond shock

Meanwhile, the FOIF special committee had continued to work on an alternative to raising the Irish government loan as a bond. After preparing a set of points on which legal advice was required, the committee wanted to confirm the principal details with de Valera.[45] Like Boland, however, de Valera had ignored the committee since returning from San Francisco.[46]

When Cohalan then suggested a meeting at his chambers on 21 August, de Valera wrote to Frank Walsh that it would give an opportunity 'to straighten out matters *finally*.' [47] At the meeting, he dropped a bombshell, telling the FOIF leaders that he was placing management of the bond campaign under the direction of Walsh and the American Commission for Irish Independence, a nameplate organisation without staff or structure that had been set up solely to give authority to the work of the commissioners when in Paris.

Walsh had developed a loyalty to de Valera since their first meeting in Dublin, declaring to an acquaintance that he 'must decide *every* question'.[48] Prior to going to Paris, Walsh had not played a leading role in Irish affairs. Like other new adherents to the cause, he brought the zeal of a convert with him. He saw his role, however, as more honorary than practical. He wanted no responsibility for the day-to-day operations of the bond drive. Fearing the work would fall 'very heavily' on him, he intended to appoint someone on a 'proper salary' to represent him at headquarters.[49]

De Valera had a special reason to appoint Walsh to direct the bond drive. On his unexpected arrival in New York, he had arranged for two seamen to get a note to a surprised Boland.

'Rather unexpected this! ... I learnt a number of things since you left *dealing with the matter you came to investigate...*' [50]

One of Boland's reasons for coming to New York, in addition to gun-running and as an Irish Republican Brotherhood liaison to Clan-na-Gael, had been to settle the dispute that had arisen between Devoy and McCartan.[51] Prior to de Valera's arrival, his conciliation mission had been meeting with 'good success'.[52] McCartan was arranging to go to Russia and his criticism of Cohalan had waned. On de Valera's arrival in New York, however, McCartan postponed his travel plans. De Valera could swing the balance of power in his favour.[53] The appointment of Walsh was a deliberate decision to isolate the FOIF leadership, in particular Cohalan and Devoy.

Optimism was high within the new bond management team on the size funds that could be raised. 'The impression I have gained from the several chats I have had on the subject with a variety of persons,' de Valera informed Walsh, 'is that it should be *ten millions of dollars.*' [54] Encouraged by McGarrity and McCartan, de Valera requested approval from Ireland for discretionary power to raise up to $25 million.

When de Valera decided to hold at $10 million, the *Irish Press* declared that it was a 'pity'; had not the Poles and the Czechs raised larger sums in this country; $10 million could be raised in a 'very short period of time'.[55] On 23 August a press release announced the opening of bond drive head-quarters at 280 Broadway in an office provided by the FOIF. Boland was placed 'in charge of the offices.'[56]

A week earlier, de Valera wrote to Diarmuid Lynch on the logistics around his planned tour. 'As you are aware, the success of this tour depends mainly on your organization.' Lynch was instructed to rush circulars 'at once' to FOIF branches to procure invitations and to set up welcoming committees. De Valera made an awkward attempt at moti-vating Lynch, still upset at the forced closure of the Victory Fund. 'It is a case of full steam up.' An ambitious start date of 10 September was set for the tour.

First doubts

An outline plan for the bond drive, most likely prepared by McCartan and Maloney, both medical doctors with little administration experi-ence, envisaged 'possible' completion within weeks.[57] Frank Walsh was charged with opening offices, recruiting staff and field workers, arrang-ing a system of accounting, setting up a speakers' bureau, organising campaign literature and preparing the funding documents. He was to engage a principal depository bank to act as a financial agent for the bond issue. The plan required obtaining an 'advance of $100,000' to fund the set-up costs. The only body which could fund such an amount was the spurned FOIF.

Frank Walsh faced an immediate and serious impediment to his plans. The two commissioners who had travelled to Paris with him, Edward Dunne and Michael Ryan, refused to become involved with the bond drive. Walsh sent a letter to Dunne pleading with him to reconsider his decision:

> The President was greatly distressed about your refusal … it should be the whole Commission or none … we ought to make this *sacrifice* … it would be almost a disaster for us to refuse.[58]

The sixty-six-year-old Dunne wanted the afternoon of his life to be peaceful. His reason for refusing Walsh also exposed a contradiction at the core of the bond drive. 'It is one thing to ask [for] contributions for a good and holy cause, where the contributor understands what he gives is a *gift*, and another thing to sell a *bond* for money.'[59] Dunne feared being assailed by people who would be induced to buy bonds on the false statements of salesmen, and by subscribers who, subsequently becoming hard-up, would demand a refund. As a practicing attorney and judge, he had seen many such cases, where 'hard feeling, bitterness, and even homicidal assaults had occurred.' When Walsh put considerable, even unfair, pressure on him to reconsider his decision, he held firm.[60]

Faced with the realities of organising a nationwide funding campaign, de Valera wrote to Arthur Griffith in Dublin admitting 'considerable difficulty' in getting the bond drive started. He put the blame on the unfortunate Boland, whose attempt at launching the drive in July had been stalled by inexperience, illness and delay as he waited for de Valera to update him on his cancelled meeting with the Chicago bankers. 'The bond question is backward. Harry did not come to California. He was to make the preliminary arrangements re bonds but unfortunately got ill.'[61] Americans were also apportioned blame. 'People take plenty of time to do things here and we have no time to spare like that.' In de Valera's opinion, he did not have the advantages of those organising the loan in Ireland. 'There is no close knit organisation here as at home. One must be created for the purpose.' He expressed the wish to devote himself entirely to the task.

De Valera did not mention the FOIF's administration structure, branch network or the work of the special committee. Neither did he refer to his decision to force the shutdown of the Victory Fund prematurely, which would still have been taking in funds. He did acknowledge that the FOIF was picking up his tab. 'Living expenses here enormous but borne by Friends of I. Freedom'. He anticipated significant expenses to run the bond campaign. 'Cost of collecting the bonds subscriptions will I fear be very high.' A personality flaw became a badge of honour for him. 'I have got a bad reputation here as being "a very stubborn man."' De Valera also had to justify news cables published in America 'well calculated' to give rise to false impressions. 'What I say in America is what I say in Ireland. Apply that test for truth always etc.' It was a phrase he would use regularly in letters home.

Michael Collins, who was preparing his written finance report in advance of the Dáil meeting on 19 August, struggled to piece together the sporadic information reaching him on the status of the bond drive. 'Up to the time of writing this note, there is *no definite report* from America on the issue of the Loan.' He was limited to giving a vague positive outlook, 'We are given to understand that the prospects are bright.'[62] But there was doubt in his verbal statement to the Dáil. 'As to the Loan, the *actual* issue had not *yet* been made, and the prospectuses had not *yet* been issued to the public in America.'[63] He appeared hesitant when explaining the reason for the delay, 'It *appeared* that the Friends of Irish Freedom were engaged in a campaign to raise funds for propaganda purposes for themselves, and it was not considered advisable at the time that the Loan Issue should be made simultaneously.'

By contrast, preparation for his own bond issue in Ireland was in an advanced state. The sixteen-member finance committee set up by Collins had finalised the organisational machinery for the issue of the loan. A broad marketing campaign included full-page newspaper advertisements and a seven-minute promotional film. Collins printed 250,000 copies of the prospectus under the watchful eye of Dublin Castle; weeks earlier he had to authorise the shooting of Detective Patrick Smith.

The possibility of further delays to the funds from America made it imperative that the domestic loan succeed.[64] The credibility of the Dáil government as a viable alternative to the Dublin Castle administration was at stake. Without money, the Dáil Éireann experiment could end in failure — maybe even with the Sinn Féin elected representatives crawling back to Westminster, as many in London predicted.[65] While Collins anticipated a 'considerable' response to the launch of the loan at home,[66] he underestimated the nature, depth and level of violence involved.

Get the Big Fella

Four days before Collins presented his finance report to the Dáil, Harry Boland was returning to New York from Chicago on the overnight *20th Century Limited*, a modern train offering barber and secretarial services to travellers on the twenty-hour journey. Boland was enjoying his star status in America and was returning from the United Irish Societies annual picnic in the Windy City. In a fiery address to the crowd, he had declared that Ireland refused to be 'the only white nation in the world in chains.'[67] Two weeks earlier, race riots had ripped apart the south side of Chicago; the most severe civil disturbances in the country during the *Red Summer*.

Boland was troubled about the lack of progress in the bond drive. Desperate times required desperate measures. Writing to Collins on 26 August, he informed him that the organising of the bond issue was a 'tremendous undertaking' and that it was his judgement 'that you are now wanted here.'[68] The suggestion appealed to Collins, who had planned to go to America before the 1916 Rising. While working as a business clerk in London, his skills underutilised and his titanic ambition unsated, he had received an offer of a position in America. 'It was in 1914, just before the declaration of war, that the chance came to take passage to New

York. I could have gone under the most advantageous conditions, and with the one thing I had been looking for—*a fair chance to get ahead.*'[69] Tom Clarke, however, had convinced him to remain in London. 'He said there was going to be something doing in Ireland within a year. That was good enough for me. I changed my mind about going to America, and plodded along in my uncongenial job.'

And now, despite the appeal of the offer, he found himself yet again unable to go. Collins replied to Boland that 'at present, and for the purpose you outline – no – it is quite impossible'.[70] Intriguingly, he added, 'there is still only one thing that would take me away, and when the time comes for that, *I'm off without delay*'.

Two cabinet members, Cathal Brugha and Austin Stack, pressurised Collins to leave Ireland. Other members were also in favour of Boland's suggestion.[71] When, on 12 September, Collins narrowly escaped arrest during a raid, the close shave almost convinced him to go. But things were heating up in Dublin; two days earlier, Dáil Éireann had been prohibited, and a ten-week circle of suppression against the civilian arm of the counter-state, triggered by the launch of the loan campaign, had begun. The now underground government went on a war footing. Collins made it clear to Boland he had to remain in Ireland because of his work with 'communications, Volunteers, etc'.[72]

'Harry's hair is falling out with worry,' Sean Nunan joked to Collins in a letter on 3 September. 'Your remarks to him at Vaughans on the night of his American wake, he often repeats. "I am a poor lonesome whore".'[73] Nunan, a 1916 GPO veteran, had been sent to America the previous June to aid de Valera, and had since then spent a considerable amount of time with him. Unaware of Boland's request to Collins to come to New York, he expressed a similar sentiment: 'I wish to God that yourself and a few of your satellites were here to make things hop.'

Like de Valera, Nunan placed blame for the bond delay on others. 'Everyone seems to be out for some game of his own. But [de Valera] is beating them, and in spite of a lot of *trouble and jealousy* will come out on top.' He declared that the 'smart Yankee business man is a cod.'

Two weeks later, on 17 September, Nunan again wrote to Collins saying progress on the bond was 'very slow.' They were not getting the cooperation expected. 'From the *very beginning* they have been apathetic but now things are getting a move on.'[74] Collins advised pragmatism. 'The best not the worst must be made of them, and there is little doubt that eventually things will be all right.'[75] Collins wished him the best of luck, noting that 'so do all the cailini [*sic*].'

The misleading information flowing to Ireland frustrated Devoy. 'They stuffed the people at home with such glowing misinformation as to prospects here,' he explained to a friend, 'that the Dáil voted the other day to increase the American loan to $25,000,000. They also misrepresented us, but I have sent our side of it over.'[76] He continued to publicly support de Valera in the *Gaelic American*.[77]

Quarrel

A frustrating dispute erupted between de Valera and Collins. The latter had read an American newspaper cutting announcing that de Valera had agreed to repay the $500,000 worth of Fenian bonds issued in America in the 1860s.[78] 'That, of course, is quite right,' Collins wrote on 12 July. 'It was worth going to America to be converted to that idea. I am serious. It is the right thing to do.'[79] An annoyed de Valera replied in early August, 'What did you mean by saying it was worth going to America to be "converted" to the idea of paying up the Fenian Bonds? Surely I never opposed acknowledging that as a national debt. You must mean something else. *What is it?*[80] A tired and overworked Collins responded on 29 August, 'For God's sake, Dev, don't start an argument about its being from the prospectus only, etc. Don't, please. It's quite all right.'[81]

De Valera had told reporters that the redemption of the Fenian bonds would be on the basis that the interest *liability* would start six months after the British troops evacuated Ireland.[82] This was incorrect; interest liability commenced immediate on subscription; *payment* would be made on British evacuation. Writing again on the same subject in October, Collins remarked:

> By the way, you will probably have seen some of the Fenian Certificates since you arrived in America. If you have, you will notice that we are responsible for an *accumulated interest*, at the rate of six per cent, per annum, from varying dates during the period 1864-1867. This was in my mind when we were going over the original draft prospectus. You remember I talked a good deal of "continuity of responsibility."
>
> I am sorry to be always fighting with you on these matters.[83]

De Valera opened a similar spat on the current bond drive. On 6 September he wrote to Collins informing him that the interest liability should only begin '*of course*' after recognition and evacuation.[84] 'I hope you have not made that *mistake* in your proposed issue in Ireland.' De Valera was concerned that the accumulated interest 'might be a very serious handicap later.' The cabinet, however, had agreed that the liability for the interest rate on the bonds would commence from the date of subscription (as for the Fenian bonds). The terms had been presented to the Dáil on 19 June.

A flabbergasted Collins replied to de Valera, 'Your remark … astonishes me. So far as I am concerned, I was fully aware at the time of the liability we were incurring, and deliberately drafted the particular paragraph accordingly.'[85] He added, 'there certainly can be no question of alteration now.' On 16 September, days after Collins had escaped arrest, de Valera wrote that the liability on the American loan would not start from the date of subscription, 'It *must* not be so in any foreign subscription.'[86] After a secret cabinet meeting at which the matter was discussed, Collins reported to de Valera that '*all present* were agreed that the statement on the Prospectus accepting liability for interest from the time full payment is made, was what was meant.'[87]

The Irish prospectus had already been distributed in Ireland and Great Britain, copies had also been sent to Australia, and an advertisement had been submitted to the Paris edition of the *Chicago Daily Tribune*. On the basis of these developments and the cabinet decision, Collins informed de Valera, 'You will, I am sure, agree that, having in mind all this, it is not possible to alter the conditions of the Loan anywhere.' Collins advised that the terms of the bond in America should match those in other jurisdictions, 'it would be very damaging if the issue in America were made on much more unfavourable terms than the issue in Ireland.'

During the correspondence, Collins took the opportunity to apprise de Valera on family, colleagues and the situation on the ground in Ireland. 'All friends are well, most of them working very hard.' He had called to see Mrs. de Valera in Greystones. 'All well there too, and cheerful in spite of everything.' He also mentioned that British pressure on the loan campaign in Ireland had intensified. 'You will be interested to hear that the enemy's *chief offensive* here at the moment is directed against the Loan. Men are now being arrested for making public reference to the subject.'

3

TROUBLE BREWING

Invasion of New York

'Until I came the attack on the L.[eague] of Nations was conducted by our people as if they were American Republicans,' de Valera wrote to Griffith.[1] He intended to adopt an alternative strategy, one that placed them in line 'with liberal thought everywhere':

> I am trying to give Wilson to know that if he goes for his 14 points as they were and a true League of Nations men and women of I.[rish] blood will be behind him. So Democrats and Republicans are bidding for our support – Democrats by amending covenant, Republicans by destroying it.

Just as Collins lacked clarity on the bond situation in America, Griffith must have been confused as to de Valera's exact strategy regarding the League of Nations. Publicly against the League, he was privately advocating in favour of a *true* League of Nations being ratified in the Senate. But President Wilson could not deliver on a true League of Nations, even if he wanted to. Committed to the terms signed in Paris after months of hard negotiation with Lloyd George and Clemenceau, he was not going to change those terms for de Valera's offer of Irish support, which he could not guarantee anyway; working class Irish–Americans would oppose any League that would satisfy President Wilson's objectives. Democrats were not amending the covenant in a bid for Irish support, and if Republican reservationists sought to destroy the League (as some suspected) it was on American grounds of sovereignty and protection of congressional powers.

In a postscript to his letter to Griffith, de Valera made an interesting revelation. He had met Shane Leslie at the Cedars, the Long Island estate of Bourke Cockran. Leslie, who was related through marriage to Cockran, had brought F. Scott Fitzgerald to the same estate earlier in the year; the Cedars inspired the fictional home of Jay Gatsby. De Valera raised the meeting because he was concerned that a picture taken of him playing with one of the Leslie children might be used to make it appear he was on 'very intimate terms' with the Home Rule advocate. He was worried that Leslie, who was 'in the Northcliffe and British service', would use the photo in a clandestine way. De Valera suggested that the meeting had been accidental, but it is unlikely that Cochran would not have informed him that Leslie would be a guest in his home at the same time.

During the final two weeks of August, the FOIF was preparing for the Senate committee hearing on the League of Nations, at which Cohalan had presented the case for Ireland. The logistics had been organised by Lynch in New York and by O'Connell at the Irish National Bureau in Washington. De Valera was 'very anxious' to lead the Irish delegation.[2] He was supported by Frank Walsh and Boland; four days prior to the hearing, Boland wrote to McGarrity, 'Some of our friends think that it is unwise for him to appear, though I cannot see this point of view at all.'[3] But the spokesperson for the other national delegations, including the Estonian, Indian, Latvian, Lithuanian and Ukrainian representatives, were American citizens.

Devoy was frustrated with de Valera's increasing reliance on the advice of McGarrity and McCartan and, by extension, Maloney, especially as the FOIF was doing most of the day-to-day work on his tour and on the bond drive. He wrote to Boland on 6 September complaining that the FOIF leadership was 'treated as if they were unfriendly' and that de Valera's actions were dictated by 'a very insignificant minority *who can deliver nothing*'.[4] He believed the situation was 'becoming dangerous'.

A clear-the-air meeting was organised. Updating Cohalan on the outcome, Devoy noted, 'D.V. was straight and he *evidently* meant every word he said. Of course he defended Joe [McGarrity] and the DR [McCartan], but I think the air will be cleared and that it will be plainer sailing in future.'[5]

But one week later, on Sunday 14 September, the Philadelphia-based McGarrity and McCartan, with the support of Maloney, organised a meeting at the Lexington Theatre in New York to protest the prohibition of Dáil Éireann. They did not inform Devoy about the planned meeting, who only learned of it from a notice in the evening papers. After reluctantly attending, Devoy informed Cohalan that he watched 'Joe, Dr. McC, and Maloney … on the platform together with an *unmistakable air of ownership*.' For Devoy, it represented the 'latest development in the effort to sidetrack us'. He added, 'For the first time we have proof that they worked with Maloney.'[6] Lynch described the event as an 'invasion'.

The *Evening World* reported that the meeting was held under the auspices of a 'group of liberals.'[7] The *Irish Press* said it had been called by 'representative American citizens.'[8] Frank Walsh delivered the opening speech, and all the speakers who followed were prominent New York liberals, progressives, pacifists and socialists, all of whom were close to Maloney.

J. W. McConaghy was the former director of the news department of George Creel's Committee on Public Information. Three weeks later, the pro-Wilson McConaghy would pen a front-page article in the *Irish Press*.[9]

R. H. Massey worked for *The Nation*, the weekly journal owned by Oswald Garrison Villard, the pacifist and leading liberal champion, to whom Maloney was related through marriage.

Alfred W. McCann of the *New York Globe* had previously worked with Maloney, and had started taking a more active interest in the Irish movement.

Allen McCurdy was secretary of the national executive of the Committee of 48, a liberal political association established with a view to setting up a new political party.[10]

Other speakers included Revd Norman Thomas and Lincoln Colcord, an author and journalist, and a contributor to Villard's *The Nation*.[11] Colcord would later write to Santeri Nuorteva, a Soviet representative in New York, urging the advisability of the recognition of Ireland by Russia.[12] 'With the Irish in America on the side of the Russian Soviet Republic,' he wrote, 'I believe that it would be impossible for the present anti-Bolshevik madness here to get out of hand.' Colcord impressed on Nuorteva his Irish connections. 'It happens that I have personal relations with men in America who are empowered to determine the foreign policies of the Republic of Ireland.'

De Valera was not in New York on the day of the meeting, though Frank Walsh had consulted him and received his approval to hold the event.[13] An upset Devoy cancelled an appointment to accompany de Valera on a trip to Newark. 'The point is that a man on D.V.'s staff [McCartan] was one of the prime movers in the work of shoving us out of the way and parading Maloney as the man to be trusted.'[14] Lynch criticised the involvement of Maloney, which was 'certain to strain still further the personal relationships between those old colleagues [Cohalan, Devoy and McGarrity] in the Irish–American movement.'

Devoy refrained from publicly criticising the Lexington meeting to which he gave front-page coverage in the *Gaelic American*, and continued to support de Valera in the paper.[15,16] However, all the distractions had started to take a toll. 'This continual recurrence of sudden crises precipitated upon me,' he wrote to Cohalan, 'is a bad blow to my efficiency. It unfits me for serious work ... I am very, very tired of it all.'[17] It must have also frustrated him that de Valera happened to have met James Wilson, the sole remaining survivor of the Catalpa rescue, during the weekend.[18]

But he continued to defend the Irish Race against attacks from all quarters, including from an increasingly embattled President Wilson, who, on his nationwide tour promoting the peace treaty, issued a warning to his Irish opponents from Cheyenne, Wyoming:

I am going to keep my face toward the enemies. The only organized forces outside the halls of Congress who opposed the treaty are the hyphenated forces: the pro-German forces and the other forces who showed their hyphens during the war.[19]

Devoy's retort was to defend the war record of the Irish Race in an editorial.[20] Under the heading 'Wilson and the Hyphenated Americans', he declared that the sons, brothers and relatives of the men who opposed the League of Nations had fought 'magnificently under the Stars and Stripes in France in the war with Germany.' Devoy valued logical argument and he saw none in Wilson's racial undertones. 'If you have no case, abuse the Plaintiff's attorney'.

Battle of 3 October

Six days after the Lexington Theatre event, de Valera sent a letter to the FOIF asking that it fund the initial costs of the bond campaign. 'To meet these expenses I would *suggest* that the Friends of Irish Freedom give in *advance* their subscription for the amount of certificates which the organization proposes to take.' In a passive threat, De Valera added that he intended to publish the larger amounts subscribed to the drive; he trusted that the FOIF 'will find it possible to head the list with an encouraging figure'.[21]

An advance of funds required the approval of the National Council. Ahead of its meeting, Diarmuid Lynch issued another cheque for $10,000 to cover de Valera's tour expenses.[22] On 3 October, the National Council approved a *loan* of $100,000 to the American Commission on Irish Independence, rather than give an advance subscription to the bond drive.

At the same meeting, McGarrity proposed that the FOIF pay the full expenses of the bond campaign, a motion that, if approved, would have bankrupted the organisation; de Valera had informed the FOIF that he expected the costs for the bond campaign to be between $600,000 and $1 million.[23] Unsurprisingly, the motion was voted down. McGarrity's proposal particularly annoyed Lynch because the FOIF in Philadelphia had retained $25,000 of the Victory Fund proceeds, which it refused to forward to headquarters.

The National Council meeting turned tempestuous when McGarrity then provocatively proposed that the cost of the Lexington Theatre event of $1,515 be paid by the FOIF.[24] Devoy moved an amendment that the money be paid under protest; his objection was not to the holding of the meeting but to the manner in which it was organised. He called Maloney a 'British agent', citing several instances in which his advice would have 'wrecked the movement by making impossible the several important steps taken by the FOIF during the past ten months.' McGarrity took issue with Devoy as to Maloney's conduct and refused to accept one cent of the money. Devoy described the events of the meeting to a friend, 'We had a hot time for about an hour, but finding practically everyone against him, including most of the Philadelphia men, he refused to accept the money under protest and withdrew the bill. He defended Maloney hotly and said that it was "cowardly" to attack him, etc. He is completely committed to support him. The case is hopeless.'[25]

Devoy also related his concerns to Cohalan. 'We have preserved the appearance of unity on the surface for the sake of the big things at stake and through fear of giving comfort to the enemy, but it is only on the surface. It can't remain for long'.[26]

4

ELEGANT SOLUTION

Boy Mayor

One minute it's 'the brutality and inhumanity of these Prussians' –
the next it's 'we ought to exterminate the whole German people'.
Amory Blaine.

On 10 September, Boland wrote to James K. McGuire that while the
'details of the Bond Issue are not yet worked out satisfactorily', they were
'hastening slowly and I hope by the end of the week to have final details
completed.'[1] McGuire, fifty-two, was a successful businessman, political
lobbyist and local newspaper publisher. Elected mayor of Syracuse at the
age of twenty-seven, he had attracted the sobriquet 'Boy Mayor'. A fluent
German speaker – his first education was in a Lutheran school – McGuire
was close to the German-American community with whom he had aligned
in opposition to America's entry to the war on the side of the Allies.[2] He
published *The King, the Kaiser and Irish Freedom* in 1915 and *What Germany
Could Do for Ireland* the following year.[3] The first book was endorsed by
the editor of a German language newspaper in Syracuse:

> During the thirty years he lived in our midst, no man occupied a warmer
> place in hearts and affections of the German people ... It is perfectly nat-
> ural for him to defend German ideals and causes, for he is a student and

writer in German history, philosophy and poetry, as well as a firm friend and son of Ireland with an international reputation.[4]

McGuire's opposition to America's entry to the war extended beyond publishing; he also worked with the German Information Service, the propaganda department of the Imperial German government.[5] Like Cohalan, however, to whom he was close, he abandoned pro-German activities once America entered the war, a sound tactical move as anti-German sentiment steadily rose. In October 1916, six months before America joined the conflict, it had been acceptable for German submarine U53 to surface at Newport, Rhode Island to put ashore a letter for transmission to von Bernstorff, the German ambassador. An Irish activist even presented the tricolour to an officer, who promised to hoist the flag in honour of Ireland when they sunk their first British ship. Less than two years later, John Meintes, a farmer in Minnesota, was tarred and feathered for allegedly not supporting war bond drives.

On 18 September, de Valera summoned McGuire, with whom he had stayed in his home in New Rochelle,[6] to see him 'as soon as possible.'[7] He wanted McGuire to take over the speakers bureau for the troubled tour, which had been due to commence eight days earlier. As McGuire explained to Cohalan, de Valera thought he might be able to make good connections in the south and west.[8] Earlier in the month, Boland had sent a draft tour itinerary to Cohalan for his approval to which he cordially replied 'on the whole it is very well done', though he urged more attention on the southern states.[9]

McGuire told de Valera that he could not accept the role because his business kept him out of New York most of the time. Under persistent pressure, however, he allowed his name to be used, but only on condition that he would not do any clerical work and that Charles Wheeler, the recently appointed tour manager, would be responsible for the day-to-day activity.[10] Despite his reluctance, McGuire could not help but get involved in the detail of the tour and the bond drive.[11]

Charles Wheeler, the new tour manager, had prior experience organising presidential campaigns. A Presbyterian without Irish heritage, he had been a correspondent for the *Chicago Tribune* in Europe during the war. In 1919, he published a well-researched book on Ireland based on his experiences in the country, in which he exhorted England to free Ireland: 'Take her into the family of nations. She will be your friend in a fortnight, as Cuba became ours.'[12]

Wheeler was close to Frank Walsh, who he had met in Paris, and to Joe McGarrity, who he referred to as his boss. 'Whatever you want me to do,' the new convert told McGarrity, '... I shall be glad to do even to the shining of shoes ... I shall not be hurt, piqued or humiliated at anything you may determine upon.'[13] John Devoy believed Wheeler had done 'great service' for Ireland and was a 'very good fellow', but he was 'utterly uninformed' on Irish organisations in America.[14]

De Valera made an even more important appointment when he recruited Colonel Patrick Callahan as director of organisation for the bond drive. Tall, distinguished and always impeccably dressed, Callahan had a quick mind and a powerful speaking voice.[15] He had received the honorary title of colonel from a Kentucky governor and had been chairman of the Knights of Columbus Committee on War Activities, until he left, before the end of the war, due to personality and leadership conflicts.[16] After a short professional baseball career with the Chicago White Stockings, he had become president of the Louisville Varnish Company. A labour advocate as well as a businessman, he introduced an innovative profit-sharing scheme that had received national attention. An ardent Catholic, prohibitionist and polemicist on social, economic and moral issues, he was also close to Frank Walsh.

McGuire, however, was not overly impressed with Callahan when de Valera introduced him, informing Cohalan that he was 'probably as good a man as can be obtained under the circumstances.'[17] McGuire elaborated that Callahan 'has been a successful business man at Louisville, does not know much about Ireland, but like many other converts is quite enthusiastic now.' In the face of the 'great difficulties' confronting the bond drive, McGuire concluded that 'we are fortunate to have him.' Devoy considered Callahan to be 'honest enough', but working on the Knights of Columbus war drive was 'a very different proposition from our own.' He would later say that Callahan was 'wholly unfit for the work.' [18]

A third senior appointment, albeit a part-time one, was completed when Thomas Maloney, president of Lorillard Tobacco, became director of finance.[19] Lorillard, which was quoted on the New York Stock Exchange, reported over $9 million profit in its previous financial year.[20] Maloney was also chairman of the Hudson County Bank and a director of the Emigrant Industrial Savings Bank of New York, where John Ryan and Nick Brady, two of the millionaire group, were trustees.

De Valera, taking full advantage of McGuire's presence in New York, included him in a meeting on the appointment of state chairmen for the bond drive. 'Whether the men selected for the task will accept is another question,' McGuire apprised Cohalan with scepticism. 'I await their replies with some interest.' [21]

On the recommendation of Cohalan, McGuire met with Martin Gillen, a lawyer, businessman and public servant. After a two-hour meeting at the Waldorf, McGuire was impressed. 'He looks like a down town broker or banker, a very alert, cool and decisive man.' Gillen had organised a special war bond train on which he was the sole speaker that stopped at 131 cities in 30 days, leading his native Wisconsin to first place in subscriptions in the first war drive.

Gillen's Irish mother had come to America as an orphaned two year old and had died when he was fourteen. His father, who was three-quarters Irish, was one of the advance guards that entered Atlanta with Sherman, before later building a successful marine contracting business in which Gillen was put to work during high school and college holidays, building wharves, piers, bridges and breakwaters, and living and working with men 'one meets in the roughest place in America'.[22] After practicing law for fourteen years, he took over the loss-making Mitchell wagon and motor business, returning a profit to shareholders within three years. His summer vacation work served him well; he was appointed executive assistant to the chairman of the US Shipping Board in 1919, later refusing the commissioner role owing to other interests. As an adviser and consultant, Gillen was in demand, particularly by steamship lines and banks. McGuire persuaded him to draft a 'memo' for Callahan on the bond issue.

Much of the bond drive work was landing on the desk of Lynch. Following a visit to the FOIF headquarters in early October, McGuire recommended to Cohalan that all work unrelated to the FOIF be lifted from Lynch's shoulders, which would relieve him of a 'great deal of pressure.'[23] McGuire was a believer in the FOIF mission seeing the potential for 5,000 branches across the country 'if operated intelligently.'[24] Hinting at the tensions with de Valera, he expressed the view to Cohalan that the work of the FOIF would have to be carried on 'long after the other *diversions* have passed', because Ireland was 'not to be free this year or next year'.[25]

McGuire was impressed with de Valera's 'most extraordinary' meetings, though with the caveat 'in spite of more or less *poor management.*'[26] He believed that advantage should be made of them to organise new FOIF branches and that 'special attention should be paid to women, who I notice form the greatest percentage of the visitors to our Washington headquarters.'[27] But de Valera did not use the big audiences he attracted to recruit new members to the FOIF. Neither did he promote the bond drive at his meetings. On 18 September, the FOIF organised a mass meeting in Brooklyn at which de Valera, Frank Walsh and Bourke Cochran addressed a crowd of between 12,000 and 20,000, the largest ever gathered under one roof in the borough. Mayor Hylan and the police commissioner were seated on the platform. 'Nothing was said by any of the speakers about the Bond Drive,' an incredulous McGuire later informed Cohalan, 'which was a mistake because it was a great audience to whom it would have been explained.'[28]

In contrast, a little over a week after the Brooklyn meeting, Alex McCabe was arrested for speaking and soliciting subscriptions at a small loan meeting in Ireland. The Dáil deputy for South Sligo had encouraged people to subscribe to the loan because the 'American people had subscribed two and a half million in pounds.'[29] McCabe had read the massively exaggerated press reports of *pledges* being made to the bond drive in America, which had not even been launched, and had been convinced of its imminent success by de Valera's request the previous month for the Dáil to increase his discretionary target to $25 million. He was sentenced to three months' imprisonment with hard labour. His fellow TD, James Dolan, was arrested on 5 October for unlawful assembly and soliciting loan fund subscriptions.

Legal opinion

Two months after being informed of the legal obstacles to raising the Irish government loan as a bond, de Valera finally sought independent legal opinion from Martin Conboy, an experienced New York attorney. The forty-one year old was the son of an Irish emigrant father who was a veteran of the civil war and recipient of the Medal of Honour.[30] Softly spoken, polite and often smiling, Conboy would later be appointed attorney for the southern district of New York at the urging of President Roosevelt. A devout Catholic, he appealed a court ruling that Joyce's *Ulysses* was not obscene. Later again, in returning to private practice, he would represent mafia boss Charles (Lucky Luciano) Luciana.

'We have had legal opinion on the Bond Issue,' Boland wrote to McGuire on 10 September, 'and find that while it does not offend Federal law in its original form it might be stopped under the Blue Sky law of the Western States.'[31] Boland relayed the same message to Cohalan.[32] Permission would have to be obtained from over thirty separate state regulators to float the bond, an option not available to the time-and-resource-constrained campaign team.

A member of the dissolved FOIF special committee was 'primarily responsible' for coming up with an innovative solution.[33] On 17 September, Nunan informed Collins that the issue was to be floated 'as a <u>bond certificate</u> which will be <u>exchangeable</u> for a bond on the Republic when same is established.'[34] This was an elegant workaround, but it fundamentally changed the nature of the funding. Instead of issuing bonds to subscribers, they would receive *'certificates of money advanced'*. There was to be no obligations attached to the 'bond certificate' – no commitment to repay, no interest rate. What gave the funding quasi-government bond status, elevating the bond certificate above a mere receipt (which it had amounted to), was that it could be exchanged into bonds of the Irish Republic one month after international recognition and withdrawal of British forces. Six months after issue of those bonds, the funds would be redeemable and pay interest at 5 per cent. The bonds would be a first charge on the revenues of the Republic.[35]

De Valera secured a second legal opinion from Franklin D. Roosevelt, fourteen years before he became the 32nd President of the United States.[36] 'The form of the subscription is harmless,' McGuire concluded to Cohalan, 'it is practically a voluntary subscription.'[37]

De Valera admitted to Frank Walsh what the millionaire group and the FOIF leaders had known from the beginning. 'Our Bond Certificates cannot be issued on a purely financial basis.'[38] Nevertheless, three months after his arrival in New York, there was room for cautious optimism. 'Colonel' Callahan was in charge of the bond drive and the legal obstacles had been overcome. Nunan wrote to Collins that 'the thing should go along pretty well now.'[39] The launch was fixed for the first week in December, giving the campaign team two months to complete the necessary organisation.[40] The start of de Valera's tour was pushed out to a more realistic 1 October. Wheeler was on board to organise the tour and Liam Mellows was to travel ahead of the party to arrange the logistics.

5

GRAND TOUR

Lovely women, fast horses, strong whiskey

Harry Boland started his new diary on 1 October under the heading 'Grand Tour of America'. By then, he had settled into the American way of life and was excited by the prospect of visiting every state in the union. 'There is something very breezy about the people here that is a delight to me,' he wrote.[1] But the initial excitement of welcoming committees and cheering crowds at train stations, motor cavalcades and mounted escorts, receptions and banquets, as well as all the newspaper attention, would quickly wear off. The speeches became monotonous; it was difficult to select a novel theme at every meeting. Late nights, early starts and constant travel took a toll. Most of all, poor organisation of the tour irked him.

On the morning of 1 October the touring party left New York by train.[2] The first day of the tour in Philadelphia went well, despite the pouring rain. The case containing the Liberty Bell was opened so that de Valera could touch it.[3] He was then escorted to the statues of George Washington and Commodore Barry, and he placed a wreath at the tomb of Benjamin Franklin, where, recalling the latter's visit to Ireland in 1771, he declared, 'The Patriots of Ireland are one in spirit with Franklin. I hope my mission in America will be as successful as was his.'[4] That evening a banquet for 613 guests at the Bellevue-Stratford Hotel, costing $7,000, was held in his honour.[5]

On the second day in Philadelphia, a visit to historic sights around the city had to be cancelled due to inclement weather.[6] That evening, at a full-to-capacity Metropolitan Opera House with an overflow of 30,000, de Valera quoted the speech made by George Washington in support of Irish freedom. 'Patriots of Ireland! Champions of liberty in all lands! Be strong in hope. Your cause is identical with mine.'[7]

On the following morning the touring party headed west on a ten-hour train journey to Pittsburgh, arriving one and a half hours late at 8.30 p.m. A crowd of 10,000 people greeted them at the train station, accompanied by a band and a military escort. 'If cheers and parades mean anything we have won,' Boland cynically noted in his diary. 'Wish we could translate cheers etc. etc. into deeds. Bed.'[8]

The next day got off to an inauspicious start. A logistics failure caused de Valera to miss a planned conferring of a doctor of laws degree on him at De Quesne University. Boland described it as an 'unfortunate misunderstanding.'[9] The rest of the day passed well, though a 'strong Orange element' in Pittsburgh dissuaded the mayor from offering de Valera an official reception.[10] The American Legion of Pennsylvania passed a resolution declaring de Valera to be an American who 'should have served in the army or navy and that he should not be accepted or recognized by any city of the United States.' The resolution was passed with 'considerable cheering', but only after attempts to speak against it.'[11]

The next phase of the tour was through Ohio; heading north west towards Cleveland situated on the shores of Lake Erie before heading south west to Cincinnati. Their first stop was at Youngstown where Boland was not satisfied with the organisation. 'Youngstown could have been much better,' he wrote to McGarrity. In his diary he noted, 'Boys at home more capable to organise than any I have met here so far.'[12]

At Akron they arrived to another crowded train station and received a mayoral reception. A packed meeting did not go well, however. 'Bad form stale, so is deV.'[13] The excitement was wearing off. 'Fed up. Banquet.'[14] Akron was followed by the short journey to Cleveland by car. An escort of two aeroplanes as they arrived in the city failed to enliven Boland, who was 'not well'.[15] He did not speak at the meeting that evening.

On 8 October they were met by another 'Band & Committee' at the train station in Columbus.[16] Boland continued on to Cincinnati which he found 'very backward. No good men to stir up gizz.'[17] The reception committee was 'very slow'.[18] Baseball was the talk of the town. The Cincinnati Reds had lost game seven of the nine-game World Series to the Chicago White Sox at Redland Field. The home team was still four–three up, with outright victory possible in Chicago the following evening. The next day Boland met de Valera off the train and they attended a meeting that was only 'fair'.[19] He noted in his diary, 'Cincinnati won ball championship.' The Reds had clinched the series in a 'slugfest' at Comisky Park. Rumours were rife, however, that the White Sox had thrown the championship. Hugh Fullerton in the New York *Evening Post* would run a story, *'Is Big League Baseball Being Run for Gamblers, with Players in the Deal?'* Eight White Sox players were banned from the game for life, including the great 'Shoeless Joe' Jackson whose innocence is still debated today.

Boland was dissatisfied with the Ohio leg of the tour. 'I must say that I am a little disappointed,' he complained to McGarrity. 'Phila[delphia] Pittsburg and Cleveland were very good … Akron fine. Columbus and Cincinnati were very poor.'[20] Boland's frustration was evident. 'I feel that we are not getting at our people as we could do if proper attention were given to organisation.'

But the 'dark and bloody' soil of Kentucky appealed to him, as did the 'lovely women, fast horses, strong whiskey.'[21] Arriving in Louisville by train at 3 p.m., they stayed at the elegant Seelbach Hotel, a favourite of F. Scott Fitzgerald that appears in *The Great Gatsby*; the fictional Jay Gatsby fell in love with 'flapper' Daisy Fay while stationed in Louisville, but she married a rich socialite in the grand ballroom of the Seelbach. Maybe Boland sympathised with Gatsby, 'rich girls don't marry poor boys'.[22] In any case, the mood of the touring party rose in Louisville, despite the reception committee being a 'likely lot' and having to attend another 'inevitable' banquet. One meeting went well and de Valera was 'extra good.' Boland informed McGarrity that the president was now in 'great form', though a 'little impatient' at the slowness of some of the committees.[23]

Getting to Indianapolis required the touring party veering northwest on a 'good fast' train.[24] There, de Valera was presented to the governor and mayor, but a big meeting at Tomlinson Hall was 'not good' and the committee were a 'poor lot'. A second day in the state capital was not much better, 'Glad to leave here. Could have been 20 times better in proper hands.'[25] The Indiana synod of the Presbyterian Church branded de Valera an opportunist and traitor, and adopted a resolution recommending that 'no official act should encourage this person.'[26] While in Indianapolis, the *New York Times* published a letter criticising the planned bond sale for threatening to absorb the hard-earned savings of 'thousands of innocent maid servants.'[27]

The tour rolled northward through Indiana, stopping at Muncie for three hours ('meeting fair'). In Fort Wayne, home to many Irish and German emigrants, they were met at the station by the mayor. A good meeting attended by several thousand people was marred by problems with the local committee; 'resolution not put, *double crossed. DeV in hell of a way.*'[28] Problems had not been unexpected, however; Mellows had alerted Boland to a 'bad mess' in the city owing to 'very poor' organisation.[29] Following a successful visit to Valparaiso University, de Valera celebrated his thirty-seventh birthday in South Bend, enjoying a 'great welcome' and a 'good' meeting. Boland was 'fond' of Indiana and was looking forward to going to Notre Dame University, where they received a 'Wonderful greeting.'[30]

Next stop was Detroit, where the booming automotive sector had turned 'motor city' into the fourth largest in the country. Labour unions were strong there, though so was the Ku Klux Klan. It was a successful visit, the highlight for Boland being the 'wonderful' interview with the 'extraordinary' Henry Ford.[31] The stubborn de Valera met his match in the innovative entrepreneur: 'DeV & Ford hot and heavy on League of Nations. Ford fanatic. Bad league better than no league. Holds de Valera wrong… argued 3 hours.'[32]

Chief Dressing Feather

De Valera and Boland enjoyed their 'best day so far' as guests of the Chippewa tribe in a remote region of northern Wisconsin. They had set out from Detroit by rail on their long journey to the reservation; travelling westward across the state, changing trains in Chicago, heading north along Lake Michigan into Wisconsin to their first destination, Milwaukee. The city had a strong Germanic influence and a vibrant brewing sector; there, de Valera received a good welcome and was introduced to the governor. At midnight they continued their journey, travelling all night by rail to Spooner followed by a two-hour trip to the reservation in a fleet of automobiles.[33]

At a mass in the village, de Valera spoke in honour of the Chippewa war dead. Then, squatting on the ground in a chilly clearing of Wisconsin forest, he was made Chief 'Nay Nay Ong Gabe' (Dressing Feather) and adopted into the tribe. The honour was conferred after three hours of speeches and dancing in a natural amphitheatre with 3,000 members of the tribe attending. De Valera took an active part in the ceremony and smoked the pipe of peace. The most iconic images of the tour were taken that day, including de Valera in full head dress. In a poignant report on the meeting between the leaders of the Chippewa and the Irish, the *Chicago Tribune* commented, 'Each represented peoples downtrodden, robbed of liberties and lands ... but neither was resigned to the fate offered them.'

6

RIVAL ORGANISATION

Coup exposed

News of the stormy National Council meeting on 3 October reached Boland on tour. 'I heard you and D[evoy] had it hot at the Council,' he wrote to McGarrity.[1] 'I am very sorry I was not there to hear myself.' Boland advocated patience. 'I fear we may have to hit out but *not yet*.'

The most surprising news to reach him was a wire from McCartan that he intended to return to Ireland.[2] Boland did not know his reason, but he suggested to McGarrity, 'if I were him I would stick it out & not have his <u>friends</u> [Boland's underline] who are anxious for him to quit crowing at his departure.'

The timing of McCartan's decision was surprising as a plan had been put in motion giving the American Commission on Irish Independence (ACII) a much broader role in the Irish movement beyond management of the bond drive. The first hint of the plan was revealed by an exuberant Callahan in front of an energetic audience at the Metropolitan Opera House on the second day of the tour in Philadelphia. Callahan declared that he was confident of raising $10 million 'in about sixty days', and expected to have 'an organisation in every hamlet, in every community, in large and small cities, with State organisation from one end of this great country to the other.'[3]

Days after the Philadelphia meeting, Callahan sent a letter signed by Frank Walsh to Devoy. The circular – to Devoy's astonishment – revealed plans for the ACII to take on propaganda and other activities that were in the remit of the FOIF.

> It has been suggested that the organisation be extended into a *national association* on *very broad lines*, so as to include everyone with any Irish sympathies, and while primarily it will conduct President De Valera's tour … and the Bond Certificate issue … it will have many other duties such as that of *counteracting anti-Irish propaganda* … and centralising and crystallizing *all* of the Irish sentiment.[4]

Devoy immediately informed Cohalan, 'This will mean a rival organisation and taking the work out of the national council.'[5] And it put de Valera's request for funding from the FOIF in a new light for him. 'Evidently, that is what they want the $100,000 for, to use the money collected by the Friends to start an organisation to supplant it.'

Devoy found himself in an awkward position. The circular had been sent across the country. He would have to address the situation in the *Gaelic American*, but without suggesting even a hint of a dispute with de Valera because of the negative consequences for the bond, recognition and the League of Nations campaigns. He made a subtle appeal for unity to de Valera in an editorial without mentioning his name or the reason for the entreaty. Declaring that the Irish people were 'more united, better organised and more able led than at any time in their history', and that it was the 'high tide of Irish sentiment and enthusiasm', he pleaded:

> All that is needed to win the final victory is the preservation of the *unity* we now have, the full development of *existing* organisation and the gathering in of the resources that are at the call of Ireland's leaders, if that call is properly directed.[6]

Frank Walsh told Devoy that he did not write the letter, but signed it when it was sent to him in de Valera's absence by Callahan.[7] Sending the letter to Devoy looked like an act of stupidity on Callahan's part, but he had no prior experience of Irish affairs and was not privy to the dispute between McCartan and Devoy. Furthermore, de Valera and Boland had upped and left New York shortly after his appointment, giving him no strategic direction and leaving him under the influence of McCartan and Maloney, who most likely arranged for the circular to be sent. Devoy published the letter the following week, together with a succinct analysis of its contents.[8] Deliberately understated, the report was positioned on page six.

> It must not be supposed that Mr Frank Walsh's statement ... means the starting of a rival organisation to the Friends of Irish Freedom intended to supplant it.[9]

Writing in the third person, Devoy commented that the editor 'understood' from President de Valera prior to his going on tour that the new organisation was to consist of '*committees*' in various cities to sell bond certificates and would have no other duties.[10] He added that the president had 'too much good sense to listen to any suggestion ... to set up a rival organisation of an undemocratic kind and led by men not chosen by the people themselves.' Devoy concluded that the work of the bond drive was a task 'so great that it will absorb all the time and energy of those in charge of it.'

Lynch, who had built the FOIF into an influential organisation over the previous eighteen months, was incensed on hearing the plan to turn the ACII into a rival organisation, describing it as 'distracting and unpropitious'.[11] Charles Wheeler, the tour manager, informed McGarrity that Lynch was 'not disposed' to cooperate with the ACII, until he was satisfied that it was not intended to 'supersede and injure' the FOIF.[12] Sympathetic to Lynch, Wheeler referred to the 'big organization he has built up after so much hard work', on which the ACII relied almost entirely to function. It had failed to build its own infrastructure after becoming accustomed to using the 'well organized mailing force' of Lynch. 'It will be necessary to *hurry up* the bond drive organization,'

Wheeler warned McGarrity, 'so that we can get out the literature and publicity stuff on our own hook.'

Wheeler was uncomfortable with the notion of there being 'any ulterior motive' behind the ACII's movements. 'I know nothing of it, and I am sorry such suggestions should be entertained.' He suggested to McGarrity that the leaders should all get together to ensure a 'harmonious' drive; the differences may be easily adjustable 'if everybody will give and take a little.' He remained diplomatic in the face of what he saw as an ill-considered move. 'I am not writing this to you, my boss, in any spirit of anger or resentment.' He understood the importance of Lynch and his resources to a successful bond campaign, 'you will have the fight more than half won if the F.O.I.F. organization will swing into line and put the punch into the bond drive.' If unity could be maintained, 'you would get not $10,000,000, but nearer $50,000,000.'

7

BOGGED DOWN

No bank

Frank Walsh began to have personal doubts about becoming bond drive chairman. When de Valera sent a formal request to him to take up the position, Walsh delayed his reply. 'In view of its grave importance I have taken the privilege of considering the matter for a few days.'[1] It was a privilege Walsh had not granted to Dunne. A reluctant acceptance was finally given to de Valera, 'notwithstanding the pressure of other duties and obligations.' Walsh made it clear that he would be relying upon the 'ungrudging support and assistance' of those around him.[2]

De Valera appointed McGarrity as his 'personal representative' for the bond campaign while on tour. Before departing, de Valera wrote to McGarrity with a few of his 'thoughts' that needed to be carried out 'at once.'[3] The thoughts were a diluted version of the original outline plan, and showed that little progress had been made since the first organisation meeting.

McGarrity had much on his plate at the time; his wholesale liquor business was in crisis following the passage of the eighteenth amendment and the business would be liquidated within a year, having generated sales of $125,000 in 1918, while the *Irish Press* was running at a loss.[4] His appointment was sure to antagonise Devoy, as it signalled that de Valera's actions would continue to be dictated by him, and influenced by McCartan and Maloney. Devoy's relationship with McGarrity had become strained after he launched the *Irish Press* in March 1918, just two months after the *Gaelic American* had been banned from the US mail under the Espionage Act. McGarrity had also fallen out with Cohalan, most likely over the organisation of competing events in New York and Philadelphia in December 1918.[5] Lynch blamed the breakdown in their relationship on the machinations of William Maloney.[6]

De Valera asked McGarrity to prepare instructions for the state organisers to select a bank, 'if possible a correspondent of a central bank chosen in New York.'[7] But securing a depositary bank in New York for the bonds of an unrecognised government, as had been highlighted in June, would be a challenge, even with the bond certificate solution in place. When on 16 September Martin Conboy wrote to the Chatham Phenix National Bank asking if it would agree to become the 'depositary of funds' for the first loan subscriptions of the elected government of the Republic of Ireland, the reply he received the following week from a partner of the bank's attorneys was not heartening.[8] 'I do not see how I could properly pass any documents issued by a foreign government,' the letter read, 'until, at least, that government had been duly accredited by the United States of America'. The partner added, worryingly, 'I am quite certain you would find other banks taking the same view'.

With little prospect of securing a depositary bank in New York, McGarrity switched focus to Philadelphia. On 16 October, well-known lawyer Michael Francis Doyle sent a request to the Land Title and Trust Company, a business that insured real estate purchasers against losses from defective title.[9] The forty-three-year-old Doyle, whose offices were in the same building, was the first American lawyer to practice in English courts when defending Roger Casement. He was chairman of the American Committee at the League of Nations and would later become the first permanent president of the electoral college and be appointed to the Hague International Court.

Doyle's letter stated that he desired to open an account to receive subscriptions and deliver as acknowledgements the bond certificates. He received a response the same day to his 'valued communication'.[10] The Land Title and Trust Company only confirmed that it would be 'very

glad' to act as depositary for the funds, but it would not deliver the certificates to subscribers and it would not act on a nationwide basis.

Meet me in St. Louis

De Valera and Boland endured four hectic, tiring and sometimes frustrating days following the visit to the Chippewa reservation, with stops at
St. Paul, Minneapolis, Des Moines and Bloomington, the latter reached
after a tiresome twelve-hour overnight rail journey. Moreoover, reports
from New York on the bond drive were 'disquieting'.[11] De Valera was 'not
pleased' with the situation in New York and Washington.[12]

Summoned by wire to go to St. Louis to meet Joe Shannon, the
friend of Frank Walsh and George Creel, who was organising the tour in
Missouri, Boland noted in his diary 'fear that Bond has not been properly
organised.' McGarrity and Wheeler were 'impatient'. The bond organisation had 'bogged down'. On 23 October Boland came off another
overnight train in St. Louis to learn that 'No arrangement yet made for
Banks.' Shannon had brought 'Cert. for meeting', most likely temporary
bond certificates.[13] Still hoping to secure a depository bank, no attempt
had been made to engage a specialist security printer. A temporary certificate fix would lead to an administrative nightmare. But the pressure to
start the campaign and get money into the ACII was overwhelming. 'All
anxious to start on drive,' wrote a concerned Boland. 'I fear start as no
proper organisation to handle sale.'

The following morning, de Valera arrived in the city to a presidential
twenty-one gun salute followed by a parade of the city.[14] Frank Walsh
arrived later in the day.[15] De Valera had also wired Edward McSweeney
in Boston to come to St. Louis to attend a critical meeting on the
status of the bond drive. McSweeney, aged fifty-five, had been active in
Democratic politics from a young age. His abilities as a fundraiser and a
publicist came to the fore in the 1892 election of Grover Cleveland.[16] He
was chairman of the Port of Boston, as well as one of the city's leading
journalists. A member of the FOIF national executive and Clan-na-Gael,
he was close to Cohalan and shared his opposition to closer cultural and

diplomatic alliances with England, and to a revisionist interpretation of history designed to lure America into reunion.[17] The FOIF distributed 100,000 copies of his 'America First' pamphlet, an exposé of English propaganda and agents.[18] He battled the Ku Klux Klan and other nativist groups during the 'Tribal Twenties'.

McSweeney travelled almost 1,000 miles by rail to attend the meeting. While on the train, he drafted a scheme to rectify the absence of bond campaign literature, a banker and 'any organization'.[19] McSweeney understood that significant changes needed to be made if the bond campaign was to succeed; he had previously met with de Valera and Boland at the Waldorf, after which he had concluded that there was 'no adequate systematization of the work, and no clear or definite idea of the handling of the mass of detail necessary for such a campaign.' Presenting his plan at the meeting in St. Louis, he recommended nationwide preparations, a postponement of the start date to March, a substantial marketing budget and an increased funding target to $20,000,000. But de Valera was 'decidedly unfavorable' to his recommendations. The experienced fundraiser was incredulous at the rejection of his plan by de Valera, who wanted rapid results without any 'elaborate organization'.[20] McSweeney found de Valera to be 'dissatisfied with everybody and everything.'[21] He noted that Frank Walsh 'had little to say', while Boland moaned the failure of the FOIF to hand over more of the Victory Fund proceeds.[22]

De Valera's reaction to the crisis in the bond campaign had a sense of *déjà vu* about it. 'I am ordered back to New York,' noted Boland despondently, 'to see to organisation of Bonds.'[23] Boland's exploration of America was over. At least he had made it halfway across the continent. In July, he had been left behind in New York to take care of the bond drive. The disappointed soldier accepted his orders without complaint. 'I had looked forward to seeing the Rockies & California. "Tis but in vain etc."'[24]

Incredibly, a new plan was drafted, entitled 'Scheme to sell bonds *without an organised machine*'. Probably prepared by McCartan and Maloney,[25] it never went any further. In Ireland, by contrast, things were moving.

Following the prohibition of the Dáil assembly and the suppression of newspapers, Collins had expanded his nationwide organisation. He increased the print run of the prospectus to 400,000, distributed three million promotional leaflets and sent 50,000 customised letters to prominent Sinn Féin supporters. Four provincial organisers and forty-three sub-organisers were transferred from the payroll of Sinn Féin to the funding campaign.[26] On the same day as the meeting in St. Louis, Collins wrote to de Valera.

> I said in my last letter to you that the enemy's *chief offensive* was directed against the Loan. This continues to be true, but its vigour has been increased, and the arrests of people who have been active in Loan work have now reached quite a respectable figure.[27]

Three days later Arthur Griffith told a meeting of the underground Dáil that de Valera was 'thoroughly sanguine' on the success of the bond drive in America.[28] Funds were desperately required in Ireland for setting up a new national bank, using a dummy corporation to disguise its ownership by the counter-state government, to provide loans to small farmers and landless workers to stem growing agrarian agitation. An urgent solution was required to prevent political and financial capital being lost to a new land conflict. In reply to a motion to make £200,000 ($1 million) available to Robert Barton, director of agriculture and promoter of the new bank, Griffith said that the proposal was an 'impossible proposition'. In the end, the Dáil voted just £1,000 for initial set-up expenses for the bank.

On the same day as the Dáil meeting, Devoy issued a circular to all Clan-na-Gael members calling on them to set up committees to cooperate with the ACII.[29]

> It is only by *systematic, energetic and persistent work* that such an enterprise can be made a success and our organization must play the leading part ...

... an exact record of the number of Bond Certificates sold ... and a copy of this record should be forwarded when complete ... so that the work done by our organization may be recorded...

This is the *most important task ever* assigned to our organization.

Down, up, and down again

Boland managed a few days recuperation in Chicago before taking an overnight train to New York after almost a month's absence. News on the bond organisation in the Windy City had not been good, 'Fear Chicago will not come up to expectation in Bond drive.'[30]

On his arrival in New York he found the bond arrangement 'incomplete.'[31] This was an understatement – Colonel Callahan had resigned as director of organisation. Devoy later explained the circumstances. '[Callahan] attempted to base the bond drive on the Knights of Columbus, which was folly to start with, and bungled it by sending out his circulars on a six year old directory of the Knights. Of course, hundreds of circulars came back undelivered, the attempt was a failure, and Colonel Callahan resigned.'[32] So Boland found himself meeting with the newly appointed director of organisation – Benedict Elder – at the Waldorf.[33] Aged thirty-seven, Elder had come to New York with Callahan to work on the bond drive. He was a lawyer, editor of the *Catholic Record* in Louisville and president of the Catholic Press Association of America. He had turned around the fortunes of the *Catholic Record*, which had been in 'hopeless debt'.[34]

If Boland was to get the bond drive back on track, he had to mend the relationship with the FOIF leaders. He decided to go to Philadelphia to get the advice of McGarrity and McCartan, who concluded that it was necessary to get Cohalan to aid the drive.[35] On his return to New York, Boland met Lynch for 'chat & lunch.'[36] This was followed by a meeting with Cohalan and Devoy, where Cohalan 'promised all aid possible', though he was not satisfied with the bond drive arrangement. This made Boland 'fear more trouble.'

Devoy was satisfied with the outcome of that meeting. 'We'll have lots of small troubles in the future,' he wrote to a friend, 'but it looks as if the big one was over.'[37] The attempt by de Valera and Boland to start a separate organisation had 'fallen flat' and they had to 'fall back on us.' He interpreted the meeting as the 'surrender' of de Valera to their side.

Boland was in a buoyant mood on the Saturday morning after the meeting. He went into the details of the bond drive and was satisfied that 'things will go well.'[38] After a long talk with McGarrity by phone, he wrote in his diary 'love him more and more.'[39] His good form extended into the following day, with him sleeping late that Sunday morning.[40] At a meeting with John O'Dea, the national secretary of the Ancient Order of Hibernians, at bond headquarters, O'Dea agreed to put the resources of his organisation at the disposal of the bond campaign, including the valuable membership list. Elder and Wheeler were also present and, after lunch, Boland enjoyed a walk and tea with Wheeler before spending a 'pleasant evening' at the home of Frank Walsh where he played with Walsh's children. The following morning, after another meeting with Lynch, he wrote, 'I square with Lynch & talk over Bond'.[41]

His optimism rose further with the unexpected arrival of James O'Mara in New York to help with the bond campaign.[42] Without telling Boland, de Valera had requested the cabinet to send O'Mara to be his 'representative' while he was on the tour.[43] O'Mara was a highly respected, successful and innovative businessman, who had joined Sinn Féin in 1907, when the organisation was in its infancy, after resigning as a Home Rule MP, and had been re-elected in 1918. The university-educated O'Mara was well-travelled, and had been to America on many occasions, including accompanying his son who was accepted at Georgetown University in 1915.[44] He had spent most of his working life in London in the family bacon business, until he returned to Ireland in 1914. He did not take part in the Easter Week Rising, 'too suicidal'.[45]

Enticing O'Mara to America had advantages beyond his experience and expertise. He was one of the three trustees of the Dáil loan, along with de Valera and Dr. Michael Fogarty, bishop of Killaloe. Boland

and Nunan had worked under him during the 1918 election campaign. Boland, unaware of his pending arrival, had written a warm letter to O'Mara reminiscing on their days working together. 'I suppose you are easier in mind now than when I was around giving that big heart of yours palpitations.'

O'Mara had no desire to leave his family and business in an increasingly unsettled Ireland. But de Valera issued the call of a president. 'The cause needs you and I know you will respond. I shall await you *anxiously*.' De Valera placed immense faith in him. 'Your coming I will personally regard as an absolute guarantee of success'.[46] O'Mara responded to the call. 'For him there was only one decision', recalled his daughter. 'He knew that he would go.'[47] He did so as a stowaway.

Boland's optimism was not to last long. O'Mara was anxious to see de Valera who was still on tour,[48] while Boland, desperate for support, wanted him to remain in New York. A wire from de Valera in Salt Lake City settled the matter to Boland's dismay, 'O'Mara goes'. He travelled 3,000 miles by train to meet de Valera in Portland. On 4 November, just four weeks before the planned launch of the bond drive, Boland noted in his diary 'very uneasy'.[49] The management team was not working out. 'No idea of detail shown by Wheeler, Elder.' The bond was getting inside his head. '"Where do I get off", Bond Bond Bond,' he screamed into his diary. Stressed, tired and out of his depth, his plan to hit out at Devoy was postponed. 'Must try to secure unity on Bond issue.'

There was no let up for Boland during the week. 'Office not yet ready. I am *very much upset* at present position of Bond. No system, cannot take up affairs.' Then Elder resigned. Devoy later explained the background to his resignation.[50]

Elder was sent from town to town in the Eastern states to 'prepare the way for the bond drive', and he did it by abusing Judge Cohalan and 'the New York Gang' for 'attacking President Wilson' and opposing the League of

Nations … He was only recalled after complaint had been made of his folly by men active in the Irish movement …

With no director of organisation, no administration infrastructure, no underwriting bank, no security printer, Boland could only see one option: 'I fancy we will have to scrap present plan.'[51]

8

PROPAGANDA OF DISSENSION

Surprise attack

Boland attended the National Council meeting on 7 November 'to have all out … so that we may all get together.'[1] But McCartan and Maloney had exploded a bomb under his unity plan. On the morning after he had met Cohalan and Devoy, the *Irish Press* published a thinly disguised editorial attack on Cohalan.[2]

> There may be some *so called Irish leaders* in the United States who have capitalised the Irish support and sympathy for their greedy and selfish ends … [for] social, political and business entanglements …
>
> Éamon de Valera has the right to expect the support of every Irish organisation in the United States … It is not for any *self-appointed leader* to question either his appeal or the method he has laid down …

The attack piece built up de Valera as a 'splendid and almost tragic figure', a man of 'unimpeachable honour and fine integrity', while the bond drive would give him the financial independence to act promptly without being 'humiliated, obstructed and degraded.' Cohalan, by contrast, had 'sold his priceless birthright for a mess of mephitic pottage'. A second editorial criticised the fight against the League of Nations for side-tracking the recognition campaign.

Devoy privately attributed the 'vicious' editorial to Maloney, seeing it as part of a 'remorseless' public and private 'propaganda of dissension' against the New York leadership.[3] His public response came in his own editorial, 'On His Majesty's Service.' The unnamed McCartan and McGarrity were the 'honest, but infatuated' dupes of the unnamed Maloney, who was 'the cleverest and most subtle agent of the British Government'.[4] He saw the editorial as a continuance of Maloney's support for the League of Nations as, on the eve of victory, he 'makes a last desperate effort to split the opposition to it on the pretence of helping the Irish Republic.' He described Maloney's action as consistent with his record on Irish affairs; his 'absurd' call for the resolutions at the Race Convention to demand immediate recognition of the Irish Republic and his 'desperate' effort to remove the condemnation of the League of Nations. From that time onwards, Devoy wrote, Maloney began 'discrediting' and 'undermining' the men who defeated him.

The public attack in the *Irish Press* was accompanied by a word-of-mouth smear campaign, forcing the exasperated Devoy to condemn the 'malicious lie' being circulated that he and others were hostile to the loan and were endeavouring to frustrate de Valera's mission.[5] Another lie circulating claimed the proceeds of the Irish Victory Fund had been 'improperly applied'. The *Gaelic American* continued to support de Valera, calling the recent leg of his tour a 'veritable series of triumphs'.[6] But Devoy despaired that the new attacks had come just as the 'whole trouble appears to be on the eve of settlement by the surrender of DV to our sides.'[7]

While the bond organisation was crumbling around Boland, the *Irish Press* declared that $10 million was a '*paltry sum*' to ask of the men and women of the United States 'in these days when everybody is talking in billions.' Such confidence might explain the absence of concern that an open rupture in the Irish movement would damage the bond drive. 'If recognition could be secured – and it could be –,' proclaimed the paper, 'the bankers would tumble over each other to aid in floating a loan a hundred times greater than the *modest* one proposed.'[8]

Boland told the members of the National Council that he could *'guarantee'* on behalf of de Valera that the ACII was for 'one object and one object alone' and that they had 'no intention of interfering with the work of the Friends of Irish Freedom.'[9]

The problem with that statement is that it was not true.[10]

At the same meeting, an infuriated Lynch 'went off like a soda water bottle.'[11] He produced letters from Vermont and Chicago which 'clearly showed' that people got the impression from the Callahan circular that the ACII intended to build up a rival organisation. Even more damning was a letter Lynch had received from the FOIF in Kansas City where Joe Shannon had discouraged the setting up of a new branch because the FOIF 'would be discontinued about November to be superseded by another.'[12] Shannon went onto describe the FOIF as 'a small organisation which had outlived its usefulness.' The chairman of the meeting suggested that it would be 'advisable' for de Valera to 'state definitely' that there was no intention of building up another permanent organisation.[13]

Devoy proposed resolutions that put on record the FOIF's 'most earnest and hearty support' for the bond drive, and respectfully recommending that the ACII devote its 'whole attention' to the bond campaign.[14] But he faced opposition. Michael Francis Doyle, the Philadelphia lawyer, moved an amendment, though later withdrew it, that the ACII should not be instructed to confine itself exclusively to bond work.[15] Others present suggested that consideration of the resolutions should be postponed until de Valera returned to New York.

In a gesture of goodwill, Devoy seconded a motion of Hugh Montague, a building contractor close to McGarrity, to pay the expenses of the Lexington Theatre meeting, though McGarrity proposed that the total expenses of the bond campaign be paid by the FOIF. The motion was ruled out on a point of order.[16] Lynch said McGarrity's proposal would have 'crippled the FOIF financially.'[17]

The next edition of the *Gaelic American* carried a message of unity on the front page, while the *Irish Press* commented that the FOIF would give 'whole-hearted support' to the bond campaign. But the latter could not resist a pop at Cohalan. 'Those who do not help Ireland now should never again be heard speaking for or against the Irish nation or people.' Boland noted in his diary, 'Attend F.O.I.F. … Have a free for all row, find everything ends well … Old man and I square things up. *Some hope.*'[18]

The day after the meeting, Lynch handed another $10,000 to James O'Mara for transmission to the Irish envoys in Paris.

Organisation collapse

Boland's sole diary entry on 8 November reflected the dire state of the bond organisation and his stressed state of mind.

> Bonds by day and night.
> Bonds will be all right?
> Bonds not yet in sight.
> Talk Bonds all day, talk Bonds all night.
> I had better stop.[19]

The following day saw no let up. 'More Bonds, no office yet. More Bonds, *fed up*.'[20] The situation was becoming untenable. 'Every day some of Callahan's appointees resign.'[21] A chairman had not yet been appointed in New York and New Jersey and there was faction fighting in Boston. On 11 November, despite the recent attacks on them, Cohalan and Devoy met with Boland to 'get down to Bonds again.'[22] Meanwhile, the *Irish Press* appeared to operate in a parallel world. Announcing the appointment of Judge Bonniwell, a forty-seven-year-old Philadelphia native, as state chairman in Pennsylvania, it expected that the $10 million would be 'subscribed twice over.'[23]

The search for a depositary bank continued without success. On 13 November McGarrity wrote to the Harriman National Bank in New York,[24] only to receive a negative reply from an assistant cashier, stating, 'we regret to advise you that we cannot so act, nor receive funds on deposit for said proposed account.'[25] McGarrity then contacted the New Netherland Bank of New York, but its president declined the request, being 'unable to meet the conditions called for in the matter of the account.'[26]

Maloney ordered Boland out of New York for a few days, the second time he instructed him to recuperate away from the city at a critical time.[27] En route to Atlantic City, Boland stopped in Philadelphia for two nights, where he addressed a meeting and had 'good fun' with the McGarrity family.[28] The optimism in Philadelphia almost infected him. 'All may yet be well for the Bond Drive. Hope so, have me doubts.' [29]

Earlier that month, when optimism still reigned, Boland had written to Collins that they had 'definitely decided on a *general* plan of action' with the 'invaluable' support of O'Mara.[30] Collins wrote his reply when Boland was in Philadelphia. He was relieved to learn that Boland did not require 'any more assistance from Ireland on the Bond Issue'.[31] Collins had troubles of his own. On 11 November, the headquarters of the department of finance had been raided; Collins escaped through a skylight, but most of the head office staff had been arrested.

Red Peril

The League of Oppressed Peoples was publicly launched in New York on 4 November. The liberal organisation was set up to enhance the cause of Ireland by linking it with the fight for freedom and justice in China, Egypt, India, Korea, Persia and Russia, and by protesting against the failure to protect the Jewish population in eastern Europe.[32] The founders included Frank Walsh, Revd Norman Thomas, Allen McCurdy and Oswald Garrison Villard. Maloney was a member. At a private meeting on 29 September, Boland had spoken on behalf of Ireland. Lala Lajpat Rai, representing India, also spoke at it. 'The Irish are being sent to kill the Indians, and the Indians are being sent to kill the Irish, but really their cause is the one, the cause of freedom.'[33] Dudley Field Malone, the chairman, stated that the time for the hyphenated American had passed.[34]

Four days after the public launch of the group, seventy-three offices connected with the Communist Party were raided in New York.[35] The simultaneous raids were carried out on behalf of the Lusk Committee investigating seditious activity.[36] Two weeks later, Ludwig Martens, the Russian envoy, refused to answer questions in front of the committee, pleading diplomatic privilege. The attorney general produced a check stub showing a payment from Martens to Dudley Field Malone for legal services in connection with the purchase of $9.5 million worth of goods. It was claimed the money was paid to Malone to speak in favour of the recognition of Soviet Russia. The *Irish Press* came to the defence of Martens, attributing the attention on him to the 'hand of British intrigue'.[37]

One of the first picked up in the raids was Jim Larkin, 'one of the most dangerous of the agitators' according to the *New York Times*.[38] Larkin had organised the 1913 Dublin Lockout, the most significant labour dispute in Irish history. He had met Cohalan, Devoy and McGarrity and, prior to the Easter Rising, had engaged with German agents.[39] Accused of criminal anarchy, Larkin was held at police headquarters on bail of $15,000.[40] Devoy helped bail him out by putting up $5,000 on his behalf, but Larkin was eventually convicted and incarcerated in Sing Sing prison until 1923 when he was pardoned and deported.[41]

Isolated

Meanwhile, de Valera continued on his tour. After leaving St. Louis he spoke in Kansas City, where the mayor refused to officially meet him owing to his opposition to the League of Nations. This was followed by stops in Nebraska, first at Omaha and then at Lincoln, before moving west into Colorado for meetings in Denver and Pueblo, then on to Salt Lake City, followed by a brief incursion into Idaho to Pocatello. He continued northward to Butte, Montana, and westward to Spokane, Tacoma, and Seattle in Washington State.

On 12 November he cancelled the southern leg of the tour. Instead, Katherine Hughes, secretary of the Irish National Bureau, undertook a three-week tour of Tennessee and Georgia to gauge opinion on Ireland. Hughes, a 'star for facts and figures' who created a 'profound impression', according to McGuire,[42] found that a considerable proportion of the people in every community she visited in the south could be classified as 'Protestant Irish.'[43] Following her tour, the FOIF published an address given by Irvin Cobb, a noted war correspondent who publicised the celebrated Harlem Hellfighters regiment, entitled 'The Lost Irish Tribes in the South'.[44]

De Valera was joined in Portland by James O'Mara, after which they headed south by train to San Francisco and on to Los Angeles, where they received negative coverage from the *Los Angeles Times*, which the *Irish Press* accused of engaging in the 'bitterest and most malignant campaign of misrepresentation and hatred that has been witnessed in this country in years.'[45] After the owners of an indoor venue cancelled the reservation for de Valera's meeting, Joseph Scott, an attorney, secured a baseball park as an alternative. In his speech, which lasted one and three quarter hours, de Valera rejected Lloyd George's Home Rule proposals. 'We will not sell or barter our birthright for a mess of pottage after an agony of seven hundred fifty years.'[46]

De Valera was anxious to head back to the East Coast. Although the tour continued to have propaganda value, there were no bonds to sell and he faced mounting opposition. But most of all, almost 3,000 miles from events in New York and Washington, de Valera felt isolated. On the day he arrived in Los Angeles, the Senate was voting on the Treaty of Versailles.

9

SENATE VOTE

Americanism

On 19 November the Senate rejected the Treaty of Versailles after four months of bitter campaigning. The treaty was not dead, but it had received a near fatal blow. On a vote to ratify the treaty *including* the Lodge reservations, Democrats voted against ratification. On another vote to ratify the treaty as signed in Paris, with no reservations, Republicans voted against ratification. The Borah Irreconcilables happily sided with the opposition on each vote.

The rejection of the treaty was a triumph for Cohalan. In addition to his successful appearance in front of the Senate Foreign Relations Committee, and his marshalling of resources in Washington, he had spoken at meetings in the east and mid-west on twenty consecutive Sundays.[1]

Under the front-page headline 'Senate's Action a Splendid Vindication of Americanism', the *Gaelic American* declared that the upper chamber had won the 'greatest victory' for American ideals of government since the overthrow of the Confederacy.[2] Borah and Johnson, alongside Senator Reed of Missouri, would go down in history 'with the three Romans who held the Tiber bridge.' Irish citizens had 'stood in a solid phalanx behind them.' The resolutions at the Irish Race Convention had been a 'bugle blast' to the American people, and the Victory Fund the 'sinews of war'. Devoy provided a forceful insight into his 'Americanism'.

The Irish in America are the most loyal Americans that live. America is their home. Their children and descendants will remain here for all time. … With or without Irish freedom they are against an Alliance with England because they know it would be bad for America.

Devoy's editorial criticised the stance taken by the *Irish Press* on the League of Nations. Rather than side-tracking the recognition campaign, it was necessary to get Article 10 'out of the way before we could do any effective work.'[3] He succinctly addressed the specious argument put forward by Maloney that defeat of Article 10 would not free Ireland. 'Nobody ever said it would.' Irish people with a 'sound view' saw Article 10 as a '*new* and most formidable obstacle' to achieving Ireland's independence.

In an about turn, as signs increased that the treaty might be defeated, the *Irish Press* recognised the part played by Irish–Americans in warning the nation of its 'impending danger.'[4]

Boland was upbeat following the Senate vote. 'Treaty dead. Great news for Ireland. England has now to reckon with a United Race. We can now go ahead with direct Irish appeal for recognition.'[5]

Hearts and Minds

'The Sinn Féin crusade has its tentacles everywhere,' wrote Frederic Wile, a correspondent for the *London Daily Mail*. 'Their propaganda is at the present moment the most sinister thing on the Anglo-American horizon.'[6] Noting that the Irish had a 'valiant ally' in pro-Germanism, he reported that sentiment in the United States toward Britain had 'apparently begun to veer around to something of its ancient rancor.'

During the fight against the League of Nations, Captain O'Connell, head of the Irish National Bureau, was at the coalface of the propaganda campaign. The bureau reacted aggressively to political developments in Washington that risked ratification of the treaty.[7] When Republican Senator Frelinghuysen of New Jersey weakened in his support for the

Lodge reservations, the FOIF mailed 50,000 cards addressed to the senator's office to 5,000 of its members for distribution to his constituents.

At one point in the campaign, Senator John Sharp Williams interrupted a debate on the Shantung amendment, declaring he was 'sick and tired' of the Irish propaganda being carried on in this country.[8] The Democratic senator was particularly incensed by claims that the Irish had won the revolutionary war. He was equally animated on claims that the Irish were responsible for the defeat of the south in the civil war. 'As a matter of fact, of course, the Irish never whipped the South at all,' the senator from Mississippi declared. 'They could not whip the South at any time. It is a part of the braggart nature of the Irish.' Captain O'Connell sent to Williams a letter authored by a historiographer of the American Irish Historical Society.[9] The letter stated that at least 38 per cent of the American revolutionary army was of Irish birth or of Irish descent.

A month before the Senate vote, Senator Walsh of Montana, a Democrat and League supporter, threw a curveball into the debate when he introduced a resolution which would enable the US government to *present* to the League of Nations the 'state of affairs in Ireland and the right of its people to self-government.'[10] Walsh admitted that his amendment only granted the Irish an opportunity to present their cause; that recognition would not be considered and the assembly of the League of Nations could not take any definite action. Nonetheless, an administration source described the resolution as a significant move to meet the objections of Irish–Americans to the League.[11]

Three hours of lively debate saw Republican senators, concerned that the amendment could win some Irish support, argue against the resolution. Poindexter described it as a futile attempt to impress Irish voters; Lenroot pointed out that Britain could prevent presentation of the Irish case by claiming 'external aggression', or that the Irish question was a domestic one; Penrose remarked that the resolution was 'the crowning and most insolent effort to bunco the Irish.'[12]

When Captain O'Connell sent a letter protesting the resolution to Senator Lodge, who put it into the record, de Valera sent McCartan to criticise O'Connell for this action.[13] 'I was then visited at the Bureau in Washington by Dr. McCartan,' he recalled, 'who, with some agitation, gave me a message from de Valera *ordering* me not to speak further against the League.'[14] The army captain resented being instructed as such. Later in the day, McCartan returned with a written message.

> The President asked me to tell you to be careful with your statements on such things as Senator Walsh's (Montana) resolution, as he might be forced to repudiate you, and that would do harm to the whole movement.

O'Connell told McCartan '*politely* to mind his own business.' Later, de Valera was to deny that he had given the message to McCartan. 'When confronted with the document,' O'Connell recalled, 'he first said it was false, and then repudiated McCartan, saying that he had no authority to write such a message'. The Walsh amendment never went to a vote.

10

BOND UPDATE

Confidence

Boland arrived in Atlantic City on 24 November for a two-night recuperative stay. He spent his first day at the salt water baths, playing skee ball and rifle shooting.[1] He might have preferred to stroll the boardwalk with Kitty Kiernan, then dine and attend the theatre with her. The latter he did alone, after which he wrote home and went to bed.[2] He did meet three old Fenians, 'All gold and a yard wide. Never lost the faith.' Enjoying their company, he extended his stay by a day.[3] He was still in holiday mode when he arrived back in New York on Thanksgiving; after meeting McCartan, who was still determined to return to Ireland, he caught an American football game, the Buffalo Prospects against Rochester Jeffersons, neither team scoring.

The following morning, when he went to his office to face into the bond crisis, he found the situation had not improved. 'Wheeler and I snarl,' he wrote. After a check-up with Maloney, he was ordered 'off smokes'. The next day he saw Navy beat Army in a 'great' game at the polo grounds. That evening, Boland joined a large crowd to welcome de Valera off the train at Pennsylvania Station, after a near two-month absence.

De Valera had appointed O'Mara to head the bond organisation on the return journey to New York, the fourth appointment to that role. Frank Walsh gave him authority to sign his name as chairman of the ACII.[4] Boland was ecstatic, writing, 'I am free of Bond.'[5] He gladly took up his old job as secretary to the chief, a new appointment that lasted a single day, 'Have orders as free lance which suits my disposition.' His confidence was high, 'O'Mara in command guarantees success.'[6] He was not alone; enthusiasm filled the Irish camp. De Valera was in 'great form', 'bursting with energy' and determined to carry out the loan 'cum weal or woe.'[7] Writing in his diary, Boland noted, 'This month should see the end of indecision. I have hopes that Bond drive shall be accomplished in time.'[8] He ended the entry with a roar, 'Up de Valera.' But a sensible decision was taken the following day to postpone the launch to the New Year.

A press release issued on 2 December confirmed that the drive would commence 'about' 15 January.'[9] De Valera and O'Mara were 'well pleased with themselves.' Boland, however, had come down from his euphoric high, 'hope it will work out'.[10] O'Mara was doing 'great work' getting the offices in order, but Boland feared 'Bond may be harder work than we realise.'[11] Then he received bad news from Maloney, 'I must quit tobacco. Heart trouble.'[12]

The ACII issued a statement from 411 Fifth Avenue announcing the launch of 'Irish Loan Week', which was to take place between 17 and 26 January.[13]

Certificates

James O'Mara quickly realised the organisational disarray into which he had steamed. He hurriedly penned a letter to McGarrity in Philadelphia. 'I was wrong about Bond Certificates. Please push on the preparation of these as quickly as possible.'[14] Without a bank to act as a financial agent, headquarters would have to issue bond certificates direct to subscribers.

The culture within the bond organisation and the poor state of preparation for the launch prior to O'Mara's appointment were illustrated in the *Irish Press* on the day he arrived back in New York. 'What we all need to remember, when that time comes,' the paper declared, 'is that it is a *relatively simple affair*.'[15] No marketing campaign was required; 'Publicity is not a thing to worry about, for every reader of a newspaper has had the Irish issue brought to his notice day after day for months past.' Administration and record keeping would be at a minimum; 'It all comes down to a *simple* matter of numbers ... securing of lists, easily obtainable and men and women ... making five or six calls a day'.

O'Mara injected energy into the campaign, which was evident in the tone of his letter to McGarrity, who immediately contacted the Philadelphia branch of the American Bank Note Company. The reply he received on 12 December was not encouraging: 'it is *absolutely* contrary to the custom of our company to execute orders for Governments which have not been recognized by, or have not duly accredited representatives to the Government of United States of America.'[16] With five weeks to the launch date, the ACII did not have bond certificates to give to subscribers.

11

EQUIVOCATION

Evidence

On his return to New York de Valera spoke to reporters at the Waldorf Astoria. He challenged the floating of a $250 million bond by J. P. Morgan on behalf of 'the United Kingdom of Great Britain *and Ireland*', which had been promoted in the press.[1] At the same time, he admitted to the reporters that he did not promote the Irish bond on tour. Raising the funds was one of his objectives in coming to the country, 'but he did not touch on it in his public speeches on tour as the loan is to be the subject of a separate "campaign of education and instruction to the American people on Ireland's right of self-determination."'[2] De Valera stressed that the loan was a sentimental appeal, rather than an appeal to investors, and that it must be 'distinctly understood by each subscriber to the Loan that he is making a free gift of his money.'[3]

The attempt to turn the ACII into a rival organisation to the FOIF came back to haunt de Valera on 9 December, when Lynch handed him letters received from Massachusetts containing new evidence of the plan, despite Boland's 'guarantee' on his behalf that no such intention existed.[4] In addition, Charles Wheeler had inadvertently sent a circular giving 'explicit instructions' on how to start the new organisation to a number of FOIF officers in New York and Brooklyn.[5] Almost a repeat of Callahan's error, it cost Wheeler his job.

Devoy explained exactly what had happened to Luke Dillon, an old friend and fellow Clan-na-Gael member.[6] The circular, which had been prepared in early November, had been set aside following Devoy's exposure of the plan. It was then sent out due to a 'clerical error', providing new evidence that plans to start a rival organisation 'had been definitely made.' Devoy was disparaging of the bond drive head office. 'This is the way a lot of things are done.' They had been 'groping blindly' for people to take care of the bond drive and had made a 'mess of it'. They wanted 'anybody at all except our men and the Friends.'[7]

Luke Dillon, aged seventy, had been released from a Canadian jail in 1914 after serving fourteen years for attempting to blow up Welland Canal. Imprisoned under an assumed name, his family had mourned him as dead.[8] Devoy told Dillon of his frustration, both over this confirmation of the plan and with the 'falsehoods' being spread under Maloney's direction. The chief purpose of the Lexington Theatre meeting had been to put Maloney 'to the front' of the Irish movement, he said. Devoy was struggling to land a punch. 'Personally I would do anything in my power to stop it amiably, but I am met only by defence of Maloney and denials that anything is wrong.'

Devoy admitted that he had no proof that Maloney was a British agent, 'but his whole conduct justifies the belief.' He believed Maloney to be the 'most dangerous man I have ever met and also the most skilful disruptionist. His great zeal for the Irish Republic is only a mask but it is also the lever he uses to make trouble.' Striving to be reasonable, he added, 'I want to have no fight with old friends, or with men who are doing right, If I can help it,' before noting that the leadership of Clan-na-Gael and the National Council were in 'perfect agreement' with him. He ended the letter on a note of hope. 'I believe most of it is over now and that we shall be able to deal with any new trouble that may arise'. He had not anticipated Lynch receiving the letters from Massachusetts.

A showdown came on 10 December, the day after Lynch handed the letters to de Valera, at a well-attended National Council meeting at the Waldorf Astoria.[9] Most of those present were travelling on to Washington to attend an important hearing on recognition of the Irish Republic and when de Valera arrived he was given a rapturous reception. 'He looked hale and hearty,' wrote Devoy in the *Gaelic American*, 'and not a bit fatigued after his long and strenuous tour of the country.'

De Valera spoke for over an hour before addressing the two elephants in the room.

The 'rumours' that Cohalan and Devoy had failed to properly support him he characterised as gossip, saying he 'personally paid no attention to such statements as there was no foundation for them.'[10] De Valera complimented Devoy, remarking 'more people in every part of the country had spoken kindly of him than of any other man.'[11] But Devoy did not appreciate de Valera's equivocation. 'While he was naturally pleased [with the compliment], because it was such a contrast to his experience during most of his life, there was a much more serious thing at stake than compliments to an individual.'[12] He demanded that de Valera settle the matter by making a 'clear and definite statement in regard to the clear and definite *charges*' that were 'steadily spreading and threatened the success of the Bond Drive.'[13] To this, de Valera replied with a firm statement.

Judge Cohalan and John Devoy had given him *every assistance* in their power; that he had several conferences with them and always found them ready with advice and help; that nobody had tried to 'trip him up', and he hoped there would be an end to all such mischievous statements.[14]

De Valera then made an appeal for union and harmony, which evoked strong applause.[15]

On the more substantive issue of turning the ACII into a rival organisation, de Valera equivocated again; knowing that 'no such intention existed', he had paid 'very little attention to the remarks' until he received copies of letters on the subject from Lynch.[16] After investigating the matter, he agreed that the Callahan circular 'undoubtedly gave ground for the doubts which had arisen.' He had arranged for another circular to be sent immediately to remove all misconceptions.

Secure Lynch

Earlier in the day, de Valera had sent a private letter to Lynch. 'Undoubtedly,' he wrote, 'that leaflet should never have been sent, for even a casual reading would show that it was bound to give rise to all sorts of troubles. It represented neither the nature nor the general intention of the organisation for the Bond Drive desired by the President, and gave legitimate ground for complaint by the existing Organisation.'[17] Pressure was then exerted on Lynch to resign from the FOIF and join the staff at bond headquarters.[18] Lynch declined on the grounds that organising the FOIF and extending its membership was 'vital to the success of every phase of the movement, including the sale of Bond-Certificates.'[19] The loss of Lynch would have been catastrophic for the FOIF, possibly even fatal.

Around this time Lynch received a letter from his good friend Terence MacSwiney, TD for Mid-Cork. 'I envy you all the exciting times & doings you can enjoy uninterrupted in America. In Ireland, the IR [Irish Republic] is proclaimed, in America you seem to have it pretty well established. Of course we shall reach that point in time.'[20] Like Lynch, MacSwiney had a flair for organisation, successfully building a robust loan structure in his constituency, despite intense police pressure.[21] Lynch must have longed to work with colleagues of the stature of MacSwiney. Instead, he was clearing up a mess created by Wheeler connected to de Valera's cancellation of his southern tour.[22] And while organising the sending of 70,000 sets of bond literature to FOIF members, an increasing number of branches refused to return the Victory Fund proceeds to the head office.[23]

12

MASON BILL

House hearing

Lynch was also preparing for the House Foreign Affairs Committee hearing on the Mason Bill on 12 December. Representative Mason had introduced the bill that provided for a $14,000 appropriation for salaries for a minister and consuls to the Republic of Ireland. Mason, a 69-year-old former Republican senator, was one of fifty representatives who had opposed declaring war on Germany, and Lynch regarded him as a 'great friend' of Ireland.[1] The FOIF issued a press release calling on all Irish organisations to send delegations to the hearing.[2] In addition, Lynch sent a copy of the bill and speeches made by Mason to the FOIF branches.[3]

When de Valera and Boland arrived in Washington they made their headquarters at the iconic New Willard Hotel, two blocks east of the White House and a favourite of US presidents. McGarrity and McCartan stayed at the equally luxurious, though less iconic, Raleigh Hotel where the general headquarters was established.[4] De Valera wanted to appear before the hearing, just as he had wanted to appear in front of the Senate hearing on the League of Nations. He was forced to issue a statement to the press denying this, however, in which he acknowledged that recognition was a purely American question in which only Americans should participate.[5]

Hundreds of delegates travelled to Washington from across the country for the hearing. 'Large crowds filled the committee rooms and interrupted the speakers with applause and hisses as their utterances excited approval or denunciation,' reported the *New York Times*.[6] The Stars and Stripes and the tricolour were both 'conspicuous'. Opponents of the Irish cause saw an absence of etiquette.[7] Devoy saw 'keen enthusiasm.'

The hearing was another triumph for Cohalan. 'You and I are old friends', he remarked to Congressman Flood as they exchanged preliminary pleasantries. As chair of the delegation, Cohalan handled most of the difficult questioning. His detailed preparation and breadth of knowledge were clearly evident; he debated with Flood on congressional recognition powers; he outlined the conditions in Ireland, the 1918 election, the formation of the Dáil and the campaign of repression against the civil government; and he demonstrated the importance of Irish independence to America. Only once did he find himself cornered, when under intensive questioning from Congressman Tom Connally, a staunch Wilson supporter, on the concept of 'recognition without intervention'. Cohalan said that he favoured passage of the bill even if it meant going to war with Great Britain, though he did not believe it would be necessary to resort to arms. Coming to the aid of Cohalan, Flood asked whether England was in the financial condition required to engage in war with the United States. 'Absolutely not,' came the reply. 'You would have to loan England the money to fight you with.'

Boland wrote in his diary, 'Cohalan, good.' McCartan would later describe Cohalan's performance as 'Quick, decisive, with his facts and figures on his fingertips, he excelled himself.'[8] But in 1919, with Cohalan in his sights, McCartan in the *Irish Press* downgraded his role to 'counsel to those in favour of the Bill'.[9] John McGarry, an Irish leader in Chicago, wrote to Cohalan to congratulate him on his 'magnificent presentation' of the case of Ireland and America at the hearing.[10] He informed Cohalan that Congressman Rainey of Chicago had said to him, 'I was prejudiced against Judge Cohalan, I suppose I got it from the newspapers.'

The hearing took a surprise turn when Congressman Flood asked whether it might be wiser to substitute a *resolution*, which was not legally binding, for the Mason Bill. Flood reasoned that a resolution would be free of the objection that the legislature was trying to usurp executive functions.[11] He suggested a resolution similar to the one made by Henry Clay in 1821 dealing with the South American republics:[12]

> Resolved, that the House of Representatives … will give its constitutional support to the President of the United States whenever he deems it expedient to recognize the Sovereignty and Independence of any of these Powers.

When the Hearing closed, it was unclear whether the original Mason Bill or the Flood resolution would be reported out of committee. The *New York Times* expected inaction by the committee as it believed the hearing was held only because it would be unwise to offend Irish voters in a presidential year.[13] De Valera was frustrated by the introduction of the Flood resolution; as Boland noted, 'Chief mad not consulted again.'[14] De Valera needed a victory to bring back to Ireland. While the consensus of those in Washington, however, was that the Flood resolution would have to be accepted in the face of political reality,[15] de Valera was 'prepared to fight it out.'[16] He was 'getting madder', Boland noted. As his sojourn in America lengthened far beyond his expectations, and the winter days became colder and darker, de Valera experienced frequent mood swings.

13

SHOCK WAVE

Fake News

'Mr. O'Mara and myself are here working on the loan issue,' Sean Nunan wrote to Collins on 11 December when almost everyone else had left for Washington. 'It's a hell of a big job, but be certain that the ten million will be got.'[1] Nunan had heard about the raid on the department of finance. 'Very sorry to hear that the Parson [Diarmuid O'Hegarty] and the other lads were lifted some time ago.' Boland, as usual, was the butt of Nunan's banter. 'I'm doing me best to steer a straight course for Harry, but his fatal beauty and melliferous voice make it difficult.'

Diarmuid Lynch received a letter from Liam Ó'Briain, a good friend and 1916 veteran, who was serving three months in a prison for organising a loan meeting. The witty professor of romance languages wrote from the '*Royal Arms* Hotel, Belfast.'[2]

I am taking a rest from my work in Galway University in this salubrious seaside resort. I am thinking of stopping here just about *three months* when I think a change will do me no harm. It was after some heavy exertions of mine at a meeting dealing with certain *complicated financial schemes* in which both we and you over there are interested, that some friends of mine (and yours) invited and even pressed me to stay a while here for my health. *I really couldn't refuse them.*

> Mick [Collins]…does 10 mens work. There are certain people & those who recommended you to the States – who for a very long time back would like to have him as their guest but it's marvellous how he manages to dodge their enthusiasm.
>
> We wish we had you here to give us a lecture on the precise differences between an Anti-Wilson Democrat and an anti-League of Nations Republican … Anyway, this country is I believe, none that satisfied with the efforts that our friend, the lanky Dago [de Valera] is leading.

Ó'Briain sent his 'warmest greetings' to everyone, including Harry Boland, 'another hustler!'

Shortly after both letters were written, an event in Ireland sent a shock wave across Britain and America. On 19 December, a convoy of cars carrying Lord French was attacked near the Viceregal Lodge in the Phoenix Park. The Lord Lieutenant survived the attack but Martin Savage, a young Volunteer, was shot and killed. French was the highest British official in Ireland and regarded as a hero of the Second Boer War and of Ypres. The attack on French made the front pages across America, with many newspapers carrying his picture. A strong, informed, albeit biased, editorial appeared in the *New York Times* three days after the attack.[3]

> This senseless effort at assassination ought to be disavowed and denounced in the strongest terms by the Sinn Féin leaders. Policy as well as humanity requires that they dissociate themselves from an act which may be presumed to have been planned by weak if not criminal heads. … [H]ow much forbearance or goodwill toward and even sympathy with many of the aspirations of Southern and Western Ireland must this revival of assassination chill or destroy!

A reporter from the *Evening World* pushed a copy of the first news despatch from Ireland in front of de Valera. Taken by surprise, he had 'no comment to make.'[4] Soon, however, the Irish mission was preparing a press strategy that sought to cast doubt on the veracity of the reported shooting. 'I'm thinking it may be a tire exploded on the Viscount's automobile,' de Valera told reporters later. 'So panicky are the British that I'm half wagering that the Lord's guards began shooting wildly at nothing.'[5] Frank Walsh told members of the Washington Heights Catholic Club that the 'real news' of the attack would not leave Ireland for ten days.[6] 'The dispatches regarding the *alleged* attack were so contradictory,' commented the *Irish Press*, 'that it is impossible at present to say whether the whole thing was an organized fake, an accidental fright or a genuine fright.'[7]

The *Gaelic American* made no attempt at obfuscation. From a 'careful reading and sifting of the various dispatches', Devoy pieced together an accurate description of the attempt to kill the '*Lord Chief Butcher*'.[8] It was a 'military attack on a detachment of the English Army of Occupation which is carrying out a merciless Reign of Terror in Ireland.' Three weeks later, de Valera adopted Devoy's approach; the attack did not shock him any more than 'an attempt to assassinate General von Bissing by the Belgians would have shocked me during the war.'[9]

On learning of the shooting, Boland noted, 'French fired at. Missed.'[10]

Secession

Lloyd George, finally engaging with the Irish question after spending much of the year in Paris, set up a special Irish committee, whose first report expressed a preference for a two-parliament solution; one for the three southern provinces and one for Ulster, together with a Council of Ireland composed of members of the two Irish parliaments.

Lloyd George was mindful of American public opinion toward his proposals on Ireland. Messaging coming from London began to have an American flavour to it, equating Home Rule powers to those of State legislatures.[11] Some suggested that his urgency in getting an Irish government bill passed was to keep a promise to Sir Edward

Grey before he would accept his mission as British Ambassador to the United States.[12]

Three days after the attack on French, Lloyd George turned combative when formally introducing his two-parliament Home Rule proposal.

> Any attempt at secession will be fought with the same determination, with the same resources, with the same resolve as the Northern States of America put into the fight against the Southern States. It is important that that should be known, not merely throughout the world, but in Ireland itself.[13]

Recalling German submarine activity, and the strategic importance of Ireland's ports in the war, he declared that the severance of Ireland from the United Kingdom was an impossibility. 'If Ireland had been a separate unit … a hostile republic there … or even an unfriendly one might very well have been fatal to the cause of the Allies.' With less sound logic, he claimed Irish independence would be 'fatal' to Irish trade as Britain was Ireland's 'best customer'. In fact, Britain was Ireland's *only* trading partner because of restrictive trade policies. This would continue to be the situation under Home Rule. Britain would also retain control of income tax, customs and excise, monetary policy and banking regulation, as well as military, foreign affairs, navigation and all communication links.

Lloyd George cast his taxation proposals in an American light. 'It is proposed that each Irish Parliament shall have the taxing powers which, broadly speaking, are equivalent to those of State Legislatures in the United States of America.' Facing a huge post-war national debt, he proposed that a portion of the excess of taxes raised in Ireland over a lump sum returned to pay for her services would be deducted as 'a fair contribution to the Imperial service.'

Arthur Griffith dismissed the proposals when speaking to American reporters. 'They are not intended to be operative. They were made in order to affect and mislead public opinion in America. The English Premier is again today in need of American aid.' He handed reporters a list of acts of aggression made against the Irish people in the previous six weeks, including 2,829 military raids on private houses.

On 29 December, in the wake of the attack on Lord French and the prime minister's secession speech, a *New York Times* editorial justified a British military assault on Ireland.[14]

The first effect of the campaign of assassination ... *must be the pouring of reinforcements* into the country, already strongly garrisoned, to put an armed guard at every crossroads, and make an end of terrorism.

14

1919 CLOSES

In Washington, taking advantage of their presence at the Mason hearing, Frank Walsh presided over a meeting of more than twenty state chairman of the bond drive.[1] At this, he issued an optimistic assessment of the preparations in 'Good News Bulletin No. 1'.[2] On 16 December, bond headquarters published the names of thirty-eight state chairman (out of forty-eight states) and one for the District of Columbia.[3] State chairmen had been instructed to open *local* bank accounts in the name of de Valera and were informed that bond certificates would be issued from headquarters, a necessary change from an original plan that the state chairmen would issue certificates directly.[4] The reconciliation of money deposited in local bank accounts to copies of receipts sent by field workers to bond headquarters, required before bond certificates could be issued, would still be a mammoth task. Records of the issue would be kept in New York, Dublin and Paris.

Despite the optimism of Walsh, O'Mara was feeling the pressure. On 19 December, he sent 500 instruction manuals for the bond drive to Bourke Cockran, who had agreed to become state chairman for New York. 'I hardly need add that the sooner these documents are in the hands of those for whose use they are intended, the better, especially in view of the shortness of the campaign.'[5] O'Mara then sent a letter to Lynch, enclosing de Valera's tour expense accounts.[6] The campaign had built up a deficit of $12,400, which was the excess of costs of $32,400 over the two cheques of $10,000 that the FOIF had provided to cover the expenses.[7]

He was also in dire need of funds to launch the bond drive. Local committees had no money for marketing. In his desire to access funding from any source, he was dragged into the dispute between Lynch and McGarrity on the refusal of some FOIF branches to return their Victory Fund proceeds to headquarters. On the advice of McGarrity, O'Mara recommended to Andrew Gallagher of California to use the Victory Fund proceeds to carry on the bond campaign. 'I am quite sure that any expense which you may incur in the bond drive on which you may pay from the fund on hand, I am sure will be gladly ok.'[8] Days earlier, O'Mara had accepted an invitation to spend Christmas with the Lynch family.[9]

Lynch was busy finalising the audited FOIF annual report, which highlighted the two objectives of the organisation: 'save America and free Ireland.'[10] The report concluded: 'Strong in the hope that the coming year will witness the international recognition of the Irish Republic.' On 28 December, he attended the first meeting of a new bond advisory committee set up by de Valera, along with Cohalan, Devoy, McGarrity, O'Mara and Richard Dalton. According to Lynch, the 'distracting developments' of 1919 were not discussed at the meeting in the Waldorf.

De Valera spent Christmas with his mother in surroundings more attractive than Lincoln Jail where he had celebrated it the previous year.

Boland received a late invitation from Frank Walsh to spend Christmas Day with his family.[11] He was not the only revolutionary at the table. Muhammad Mahmud Pasha, the future two-time prime minister of Egypt, dined with them. After dinner, Boland went to see *Irene*, a play by Samuel Johnson, and later called on Devoy. The following day he answered correspondence and went over affairs with O'Mara, who had things 'in fine shape.'[12] On 30 December, Boland had a meeting with George Creel who introduced him to Joe Tumulty, President Wilson's private secretary.

On New Year's Eve, de Valera and Boland cut lonely figures in their hotel rooms; de Valera absent again from his wife and children; Boland pining for Kitty Kiernan. Neither expected to be in America so long;

the bond drive launch postponed to 1920 and recognition of the Irish Republic no closer. The younger man gave a poignant description of the year passed and the prospects for the year ahead.

The year has been one of great adventure for me and has given me 365 days of real experience. I feel that Ireland's cause has made wonderful progress. Hope the year we are entering on will see the triumph of Ireland. Go to bed early and am awakened by the passing of the Old Year to the usual accompaniment of bells, bugles, etc. find deV writing to wife, 'his first duty' in the New Year.

PART 2

15

LAUNCH

Knickerbocker

Three weeks after the launch, the bond drive had lost momentum. 'Can they but perfect an organization', James McGuire wrote hopefully to Cohalan on 8 February 1920. 'I am sure the $10,000,000 can be secured.'[1]

McGuire had spent the previous day, Saturday, at bond headquarters sending out telegrams and letters. He had reason for believing that $10 million could still be raised. One day in Washington he had written thirty letters to acquaintances across the country, most of Irish blood but not active, urging subscriptions to the bond and was 'amazed' to receive favourable replies from all. He was encouraged by the 'very wonderful reception' de Valera received in Worcester, where 6,000 people had marched through a heavy snow storm. Much work had been done in the past few years and the 'spirit of the people' was good.

McGuire did not have confidence, however, in the bond drive organisers. As the Irish campaign would be a 'protracted one', all involved would have to do 'some practical thinking along material lines', he commented to Cohalan. The focus had to be on the 'care, disposition and intelligent accounting and wise expenditure of the large sums of money collected.'[2] He recommended Cohalan meet the new trade consul sent from Ireland, 'who has a critical yet a constructive mind, *one of the few*.[3]

New Yorkers were enduring one of the worst winters in thirty years, during which influenza and pneumonia had gripped the city again. McGuire had been laid up for eight days, while Cohalan was recovering from a bout of influenza which had prevented him speaking at a large bond rally.[4] 'Mighty glad' to hear of Cohalan's improvement, McGuire expressed the hope that he would do no more out-of-town work for the remainder of the winter. 'You have had a most severe five years since 1914 and the nervous and physical strain added to your daily work is too much to endure'.[5]

Boland was also at bond headquarters writing messages home. McGuire had come to admire Boland's give-and-take style, his heart-on-sleeve approach and his fighting spirit.[6] Although twenty years separated the two men, they had become good friends. McGuire had brought Boland to the Metropolitan Opera to see *La Juive* by Halevy on the evening before.[7] It was the fifth performance of the season; Enrico Caruso in the role of Eleazar was in popular demand.[8] McGuire even arranged for Boland to meet the acclaimed tenor.

Before going to the opera, Boland had taken a call from the *Manchester Guardian*.[9] The reporter was looking for a comment on a new policy statement given in an interview by de Valera to the *Westminster Gazette*, an influential liberal newspaper in London. The statement had been important enough for Boland to note in his diary, 'Chief gives interview to *Westminster Gazette*, on England's security. *good stuff*.' [10] De Valera had left that morning on a short tour of New England.

Boland was facing into a busy week. Ordered by de Valera to return to Washington to monitor the renewed treaty ratification debate, he had agreed to fit in three meetings in Philadelphia to shore up the struggling bond campaign in the city.[11] On Sunday evening, he went to the Knickerbocker hotel bar with Seán Nunan.[12] On the corner of 42nd and Broadway, it was the place for two young men to be seen. Babe Ruth had recently signed for the Yankees at the Knick.[13] F. Scott Fitzgerald was a regular.

[Amory Blaine] awoke laughing and his eyes lazily roamed his surroundings, evidently a bedroom and bath in a good hotel. His head was whirring and picture after picture was forming and blurring and melting before his eyes, but beyond the desire to laugh he had no entirely conscious reaction. He reached for the 'phone beside his bed. 'Hello—what hotel is this—? Knickerbocker? All right, send up two rye high-balls—' [14]

Mayor

Three weeks earlier, the bond drive had finally been launched to much fanfare. 'Great day for New York. Chief receives Freedom of City. 69th in full uniform. Wild enthusiasm, cheers, band, songs … Banquet,' wrote Boland in his diary on 17 January. 'I dash for Broadway en route to Chicago to open Bond Drive.' [15]

Shortly after noon that day, a long line of cars had come down from the Waldorf Astoria to the front of the Municipal Building. A line of men from the 69th Regiment, with a large crowd gathered behind, awaited the first car, which included de Valera, Bourke Cockran, Cohalan, Devoy and Nunan. [16] Mayor Hylan's secretary took de Valera to the Aldermanic Chamber in the city council building, where Bourke Cockran presented him. 'Mr. Mayor, I have been asked by the Friends of Irish Freedom to discharge the very pleasant and honorable task of presenting to you … the President of the Irish Republic.'

Hylan praised de Valera's 'dignified campaign of education, coupled with a masterly presentation of safe and sane governmental policy.' He singled out the glorious old 69th which had been 'in the thick of the fighting on the Lorraine front, in the Champagne, at Chateau-Thierry, St. Mihiel, the Argonne and the River Ourcq'.

The *New York Times* criticised Hylan for receiving "President" de Valera in the same location that 'it seems only yesterday, the Prince of Wales heard so many nice things said to him.' [17] Ironically, the mayor had incurred the wrath of Devoy over the same reception, who accused him of being out of sympathy with the aspirations of the Irish people. The mayor, determined to represent all his constituents, issued a blunt riposte to Devoy.

You have put a petty and unwarranted misconstruction upon an official courtesy properly shown by me as a representative of this cosmopolitan city to the Prince of Wales and your state of mind concerning the British Government is no excuse for it.

My sympathies with Ireland are fully as deep and as great as yours. The fact that I have not made my living exploiting it is not necessarily a test of my sincerity.[18]

The Irish camp enjoyed a double high that day when news came through of the strong republican performance in the municipal elections in Ireland. Sinn Féin had won 31 per cent and Labour 22 per cent of the seats, and their combined total gave them control of nine of the eleven corporations, including Derry.[19] Wexford had a Labour majority, while Belfast remained under Unionist control. Cork and Limerick corporations immediately pledged allegiance to Dáil Éireann, and Dublin followed on 3 May.

The celebrations may have been muted that evening, however. *John Barleycorn* had died peacefully at the toll of midnight on the eve of de Valera's reception – New York had entered the prohibition era. A few enterprising restaurateurs held funeral ceremonies in memory of the deceased. The ironically named Daniel Porter, supervisor of the Internal Revenue Agents for the New York District, said he was preparing for a rigid enforcement of the law. Agent Porter was of the opinion that the penalties for violation were 'so severe that the people of New York would not attempt to violate the law'.[20]

A mass meeting at the Lexington Theatre the following day maintained press attention on the bond drive. Presided over by Bourke Cockran, the speakers included Nancy O'Rahilly, the New York born widow of *The O'Rahilly*, the most senior casualty during the Easter Week fighting. The chairmen of each borough made their pledges; Manhattan and Brooklyn were good for $1,000,000 each, $250,000 was achievable in the Bronx, Queens pledged $200,000, while Richmond (Staten Island) aimed for $100,000.

That evening, W. F. Quinn, a Republican alderman, issued a statement bitterly attacking the bond drive. 'The misty dream of a deluded

agitator is not and never can be called security for a bond issue.'[21] Proud
of his Irish ancestry, Quinn felt it was his duty to protest against the
financial appeal being made by the so-called president of the mythical
Irish Republic. For him, de Valera's plans for Ireland were ridiculous, but
'with $10,000,000 he may do enough harm to embroil the United States
in a war with Great Britain' and Mayor Hylan was a 'cheap pettifog-
ging demagogue' for allowing himself to become a party to a fraudulent
scheme. Two years later, Quinn would appear before Judge Cohalan on
a charge related to a separation suit.[22] In an affidavit, his wife, Gladys
Quinn, alleged that her husband's theory of married life was that 'beating is the only language a woman understands.' Affidavits from friends
stated that the alderman publicly beat his wife when displeased. He
denied all allegations against him.

Live for ever

Boland threw himself into the launch of the bond drive. On his return
from Chicago, he squeezed in a meeting in Philadelphia before going
with de Valera to Albany for a reception with Governor Al Smith, a
future presidential candidate and the first Roman Catholic to be nom-
inated by a major party. Boland noted that de Valera was 'very tired.'[23]

Back in New York City, after grabbing a few hours' sleep and catch-
ing up on shopping, Boland attended five meetings in five hours, driving
forty miles during a heavy snow storm.[24] He arrived with de Valera close to
midnight at a ball organised by the FOIF at the Central Opera House on
Third Avenue.[25] 'President De Valera, although very tired and hoarse from
prolonged speaking,' reported Devoy in the *Gaelic American*, 'delivered one
of the best speeches of his tour, dealing mainly with the bond drive and the
situation in Ireland, and received another ovation when he was through.'[26]
Lynch, who was also at the ball, believed the enthusiasm and unity displayed 'were a splendid augury for success, not merely for the Loan but for
the attainment of the main object of the Irish–American movement.'[27]

Nunan wrote enthusiastically to Collins on the launch of the bond
drive. 'I feel certain that *more than* the ten million will be realised.'[28] The

bond department was 'going in good style' and O'Mara 'sends his love.' Nunan listed their achievements, including de Valera receiving the freedom of the city, the meeting at the Lexington Theatre 'where $2,400,000 was pledged' and the passing by the New York assembly of a resolution approving the issue of the bond certificates. 'So you see things are going.'

On the last day of January, after an overnight train journey from Washington, Boland received the distressing news that Collins had been captured in a mass raid. Boland was disconsolate. 'All get very sad at news, feel so far away'.[29] Ironically, the previous week he had written in his diary, 'Micheál has had wonderful escapes, hope his luck will continue. I give it to Micheál, great man.'[30] The *New York Times* reported that the police had been searching for Collins for some time.[31] Boland remained defiant, 'thankful that we are here to carry on.' His month-end diary entry finished on a heroic note. 'Bond will go over. An Irish Republic will live for ever.' But he need not have worried about Collins, whose luck had continued. He had received warning of the raid. Collins had not been arrested. '[B]est of news – hurrah.'[32]

16

INTERVIEW

Figurehead

Drained, frustrated and tired from long days, frequently behind schedule, and enduring endless storms, de Valera was in a troubled state, emotionally and physically, not helped by the troubled bond drive. In Washington, Boland had noticed that de Valera 'was not in his usual form' and he was 'upset' at the 'small talk and knocking tactics of some'.[1]

He was in constant demand for speaking engagements which took him away from events in New York and Washington, and then, when back, there was little he could do himself. The 'President of the Irish Republic' was a political figurehead; the bond organisation was in the hands of O'Mara, the recognition campaign in those of O'Connell in Washington, while Cohalan successfully co-ordinated high-level political engagements.

De Valera was also 3,000 miles from the nation-building activities at home. A new pretender to his leadership had emerged in the form of Collins; eight years his junior and almost an unknown when de Valera left Ireland. He needed to deliver a successful bond drive and to show demonstrable progress in the recognition campaign before he could return home. A letter from Collins added to the pressure. 'The necessity for the money is now beginning to press.'[2] Collins gave instructions to de Valera to send the funds to trusted individuals in Dublin and London in amounts of £10,000, and he had arrangements in hand 'whereby very much larger sums may be received'.

Collins enclosed a memorandum on the bond drive in Ireland for pub-lication in America. Dublin Castle had censored the newspapers, but 'such an epistle coming from America might, as a result, secure publication in this country.' The update made difficult reading for de Valera. Collins con-gratulated him on the welcome news he had sent of the 'wonderful success' of the loan in America. Collins was sure of its 'final success' in Ireland, despite the intensity of the enemy campaign, which must 'at all costs pre-vent our getting the necessary funds.' English repressions against the loan were being carried out 'with a renewed determination and savagery.'

On a personal level, Collins reported to de Valera the arrest of Robert Barton, the director of agriculture and promoter of the new national bank. 'I am smarting under a feeling of great personal sorrow, as we had been in such close association on pretty well all things during the past difficult year'. Collins continued to make regular calls on Mrs. de Valera. 'She is standing the strain well.' He added a postscript, 'You will *of course* hand over the details mentioned above to whoever is dealing with the transmission of money.'

Bold policy

De Valera sought relevance in a bold new policy statement governing the future relations between an independent Ireland and England, which he trialled in a speech in Yonkers on 1 February, and which he had hoped would be picked up by the press.

> If you, in this country, had taken the attitude which England bears to Ireland, you would have annexed all of the small nations to the south of you. But you secured your own safety without infringing on the rights of other nations by your *Monroe Doctrine*. England could very well proclaim a Monroe Doctrine for these two islands.[3]

Arguing that an independent Ireland and England would be natural allies, and that a threat to one would be a threat to the other, he proposed a *military alliance* between a free Ireland and England.

England is less secure at present than she would be with an Independent Ireland. If England allows us to exercise our independence, then a threat at England might very well be construed as a threat against our independence. Free Ireland means a *natural alliance* with England.[4]

The proposal of an English Monroe Doctrine over Ireland, including a military alliance, represented a radical policy change. Many interpreted the Monroe Doctrine as giving the United States hegemony and a right of intervention in the central and south American republics. Such a policy would also reinforce England's control of the seas, potentially alienating Americans who supported Irish independence because it would weaken English naval power. A military alliance also raised the prospect of Ireland siding with England in a naval dispute between the superpowers.

Newspapers did not report on the statement. Instead, they focused on a verbal gaff de Valera made at a reception in the Bronx that afternoon in front of an audience of 3,000 people. 'So far as England was concerned,' the *New York Times* quoted de Valera, 'Ireland wanted Germany to win the war'.[5] The *Daily News* quoted him as saying that we of the Irish Republic 'are the *perpetual* enemies of England.[6] It was not the news cycle that de Valera desired as he attempted to assuage England's security concerns in the event of Irish independence. The *London Times* carried the story under the heading 'Ireland Wanted Germany To Win'.[7]

De Valera's comment was a reflection of the highly charged atmosphere at the Bronx meeting, chaired by a German-American. Boland noted in his diary, 'fierce talk from Chief. I also harangue the crowd.'[8] An exhausted Boland had failed to rein in de Valera; the night before he had attended a *Printers Mass* at 2.30 a.m; the previous night he had taken another overnight train from Washington. Boland returned to Manhattan after midnight 'tired and weary'.[9]

On the following afternoon, de Valera received the Freedom of the Commonwealth from the governor of New Jersey and spoke in front of the state assembly.[10] After dinner, he returned to Manhattan 'sick and tired'.[11] He awoke more cheerful, but was 'very much upset' by the newspaper reports on his Bronx statement.[12] After meeting Boland and Nunan at bond headquarters, he set about writing a reply statement to the newspapers.[13] A snow storm set in and continued all day, exactly one year since de Valera had escaped from Lincoln Jail.[14]

Snow continued falling the next day and there was no respite from his Bronx statement.[15] The *New York Times* published a witty and irony-laced piece on the 'Irelandization of Germany', a phrase used to depict the iniquity of the Treaty of Versailles, which opponents said placed Germany under the power of 'perfidious Albion'.

> If Germany were really Irelandized, the Kaiser would today be in possession of the freedom of New York City. The German cause would enjoy the formally expressed approval of any number of great deliberative bodies from the United States Senate down. An Irelandized Germany would have a propaganda bureau in Washington whose chief would … claim as German in race … every American citizen who has a drop of German blood in his veins.[16]

The columnist concluded that de Valera told a New York audience that Ireland wanted Germany to beat England, but 'leaves the audience to think out for itself *how the Germans could have beaten England without beating America, too.*' That evening de Valera and Boland sought the solace of poetry, music and drama at the Irish Literary Society.[17]

New York *Globe*

On 6 February de Valera embarked on his short tour of New England, determined to push out his new policy statement in a speech in Worcester that evening. He had given an interview to W. J. Hernan, the American correspondent of the *Westminster Gazette*, which would ensure his proposals for alleviating England's security concerns would be heard in London.

McCartan accompanied him on the tour, at de Valera's request.[18] After their formal welcome in Worcester, de Valera was granted the freedom of the city. Behind schedule due to the weather, the transport system paralysed and streets filled with deep snow drifts, he hurried to the Bancroft Hotel to address a meeting of bond workers. Irish Loan Week was due to open in Worcester a month after the public launch of the drive in New York.[19] It was late when de Valera retired to bed that night.

His German comment continued to haunt him the following morning. Just before receiving a doctor of laws from Holy Cross College, he was forced to issue a statement to the Associated Press.[20] In it, he denied that Ireland ever 'knifed' America in the back as British propagandists would have the American people believe.[21] It was an unfortunate choice of word that extended the news cycle. 'De Valera Denies Ireland "Knifed" America in War' reported the *Buffalo Times*.[22] A bad media week was about to get worse.

The New York *Globe* carried a report and an editorial comment on his interview; the only American newspaper to do so the day after it was given to Hernan.

De Valera Offers *Settlement* To England.
    Éamon De Valera, President of the Republic of Ireland, in an interview with the New York correspondent of the Westminster Gazette, divulged today, for the first time since his arrival in the United States, the *concessions* that the Sinn Féin, or Republican party, is willing to make to Great Britain toward reaching an amicable settlement of the Irish problem.

The *Globe*'s editorial praised de Valera and his proposal: 'Has a suggestion more nearly preserving both interests come from any authoritative source?'[23] But, for de Valera, it came to a devastating conclusion on his interview.

This statement introduces a new *principle* – the withdrawal by the official head of the ''Irish Republic' of the demand that Ireland be set free to decide her own *international relations*.'[24]

In the interview given to Hernan, de Valera had introduced two additional policy proposals by which England could ensure her security; one was problematic and the other was inflammable. He opened the interview by denying the assertion that England maintained her dominance over Ireland for her own security; her objective was to retain her commercial monopoly over Irish markets and to use Irish harbours to strangle commercial and imperial rivalry. De Valera was correct on the latter, but stating that England was not concerned about her security with an independent Ireland on her flank defied geopolitical reality. De Valera expanded that *if* England was genuinely concerned about safeguarding herself, she could make provision for it 'without the need to deny the same right to Ireland.'

He suggested four mechanisms by which this could be achieved: a Monroe Doctrine, a 'genuine' League of Nations and the two new policy options. The first of these, the least controversial, was the framing of an international agreement whereby England and other nations would guarantee Ireland's neutrality, similar to the case of Belgium. The second of the new policy proposals invoked the legal relationship existing between the United States and Cuba, a de facto *protectorate* of its larger neighbour. De Valera quoted the *first* clause of the Platt Amendment, part of the agreement that governed the Cuban–American relationship. 'The United States safeguarded itself from the possible use of the island of Cuba as a base for an attack by a foreign power by stipulating':

> That the Government of Cuba shall never enter into any treaty or other compact with any foreign Power or Powers which will impair or tend to impair the independence of Cuba, nor in any manner authorise or permit any foreign power or powers to obtain by colonisation or for military or naval purposes, or otherwise, lodgement in or control over any portion of the said Island.

Immediately after the quotation, de Valera casually stated, 'Why doesn't Britain do with Ireland as the United States did with Cuba?'[25]

De Valera did not mention the new proposals in his speech in Worcester that evening as planned. He had made a huge policy faux-pas. While his proposals on England's security were intellectually elegant, they were open to wide interpretation and he did not consider how they would be implemented in practice. In particular, they left open the right of military intervention by England, which was implicit in the Monroe Doctrine and exercised by America in Haiti five years earlier, and explicit in the Platt Amendment exercised by the American intervention in Cuba in 1906.

The *Globe* concluded that de Valera would accept Irish independence 'on the same basis' as the independence granted to Cuba by the United States following the Spanish–American War, by which Cuba had 'an autonomous government under the *virtual protection*' of the United States.

Reaction

The *New York Times* reported on the interview under the headline, 'For Erin Free *Like Cuba*'.[26] The *Chicago Daily Tribune* commented that de Valera outlined the 'concessions' which Sinn Féin was willing to make to Britain, including the granting of independence to Ireland on the same basis as the independence granted to Cuba by the United States.[27] Both papers published their comments the day after the *Globe*'s piece, as did the *Westminster Gazette* in London.[28] The latter's 'exclusive', from its own correspondent in New York, commented on the 'remarkable development of De Valera's views.'[29] He had endeavoured to remove one of the 'substantial fears' in regard to Ireland on 'practical and tested grounds.'[30] The *Gazette* reprinted the New York *Globe* editorial.

A cablegram sent from England echoed the same sentiment as the *Gazette*:

Reports of an announcement by President De Valera, of the Irish Republic, that he favored a British *protectorate* similar to that which the United States exercises over Cuba, were characterized by officials as 'the sanest utterance the President has yet made.' They saw in it a 'willingness to make concessions.'[31]

Nationalist reaction in Ireland to the interview was disbelief. On 9 February, the *Irish Independent* carried the text of the *Gazette* report, including the reprinted *Globe* editorial. A 'prominent Dublin Sinn Feiner' told a reporter that 'the utmost caution should be observed with regard to messages purporting to represent declarations of Irish leaders abroad'.[32] His advice to the paper was 'Wait and See.' *The Freeman's Journal* reprinted the *Gazette* report under the headline, 'Mr. De Valera's reported offer to Britain'.[33] A special section entitled 'The Status Of Cuba' commented on the leasing of Guantanamo harbour to the United States and the prior military intervention.

The *Morning Post's* Dublin correspondent reported back to London that, 'Many of the old Nationalists appear to think that it is something of a climb down on the part of the President'. The correspondent added, 'It is, at all events, significant to the extent it indicates an admission of the fact that Britain will not stand an "independent Republic" on her western seaboard, and that position has got to be reckoned with.'[34]

The *United Press* news agency reported from Dublin that 'Sinn Féin leaders were cautious in comment on the so-called Monroe doctrine interview, of President De Valera, who is now in the United States. They wished to get additional details from De Valera on his statement … before forming an opinion.'[35]

The unionist *Irish Times* commented that the interview was indicative of the 'instability' that afflicted de Valera, and his 'evident desire' to recede from a position regarded as 'hopelessly fantastic by every sane American'.[36] The 'encouraging whoops' of the Hearst media, the 'bravos' of the hyphenated-Germans, and the 'massed oratory' of the Irish–American vote hunters did not constitute public opinion in the United States. The paper honed in on de Valera's mixed messaging by contrasting his proposals with his poorly timed comments in the Bronx. 'A few days ago Mr. de Valera assured an American audience that Ireland always had sided, and always would side, with England's enemies.' The paper noted that the nominally independent republics of Latin America existed 'under the shadow of Uncle Sam's big stick and bigger purse.'

'Collins was critical of de Valera's action,' according to Patrick Moylett, a high-profile and successful Sinn Féin businessman, who met Collins and Griffith in the wake of the interview.[37] McCartan later reported that Countess Markievicz, minister for labour, Count Plunkett, minister for foreign affairs, and Cathal Brugha, minister for defence, were also all hostile to the proposals.[38] Griffith was more circumspect. 'We know the President better than we know the men who are *opposed to him* in America,' he wrote. 'It is our business to be perfectly loyal to him.'[39] Griffith believed that if something was to be done in reference to de Valera's statements, the correct means would be to summon him to a meeting of the cabinet.[40] But that option was not available. A diplomat could be recalled, but not the head of the young Irish government. An open split in cabinet would be ruinous; professed loyalty was the only option.

Speaking at a luncheon given by foreign press correspondents in London, Griffith supported de Valera's position – 'that Ireland was willing to accept a British Monroe Doctrine if she were granted *full* independence.'[41] Pressed by reporters for a more complete statement, Griffith insisted that such a guarantee 'was possible only after Ireland was free and could treat with Great Britain on equal terms.' He was unable to see a possibility of an agreement, however, after 'Premier David Lloyd George's recent declarations'.[42]

Car crash interview

McCartan *privately* believed the whole movement towards recognition 'was shattered' by the Cuban interview, which clearly intimated that de Valera was prepared to accept 'much less than complete sovereignty' and was willing to degrade the claim of Ireland to a 'domestic issue' of England.[43] He later claimed that de Valera consulted no one and had given no hint that he intended to issue the statement. 'It came as a thunderbolt to us.'[44] But, like the cabinet in Dublin, the only option available to him was professed loyalty. 'We had built up de Valera as the sovereign symbol of our cause in the United States ... [W]e had to defend him and to explain away that fatal interview'.[45]

He did so in the *Irish Press* by accusing American editors of pretending to see the basis of a 'compromise' in the interview; the 'Scotch editor' of the *Globe* discovered it, but failed to point it out in the statement. The interview was an assertion that Ireland was willing to negotiate a 'certain treaty' with England, 'just as France, Belgium or Germany might do and on the same status as these states would.' The paper printed a speech given by de Valera on 9 February claiming it included the text of the interview.[46] This 'correct version' included an edit to tighten de Valera's casual comment in the original: 'Why doesn't Britain make a stipulation *like this* [the *first clause* only of the Platt Amendment] to safeguard herself against foreign attack as the United States did with Cuba?[47]

William Maloney gave the 'best interpretation the interview would bear' to the newspapers, including *America* and *The Nation,* and in published letters.[48] Some editors came to de Valera's aid, if reluctantly; Joseph Gurn, the writer of a supportive editorial in the *Irish World,* 'hated the task.'[49] The *Irish Press* reprinted extracts from those newspapers that 'intelligently discussed' the interview.

De Valera issued a press release stating that the *Globe* had printed the article under a 'misleading headline.' The quotation from the Platt Amendment made it clear that de Valera had in mind 'that passage and nothing further.'[50] The statement created wriggle room by claiming that the interview was a 'condensation' of a full statement. In a further damage limitation exercise, de Valera granted a second interview to the *Globe,* despite having just accused the paper of publishing the first interview under a misleading headline.[51] He wanted to move the news cycle away from Cuba and the Monroe Doctrine, to the more generic international treaty proposal.

As an Independent National State, the Irish would, in my opinion, be quite ready to calm England's pretended or real fears by assenting to an *international compact* which would safeguard Britain from the possible use of our island as a base for hostile attack upon her by some outside power.

De Valera confirmed to the reporter that he was 'correctly quoted' in the first interview. But his meaning would have been expressed with 'greater precision' had he asked, 'Why doesn't Britain do THUS with Ireland?' [52] The edit in the *Irish Press* was not the 'correct version'. When the reporter asked de Valera to explain why no reference was made to the Cuban proposal in England, while the Monroe Doctrine received favourable comment, instead of deflecting to his core new message, de Valera's convoluted answer attributed blame on the *Globe*'s headline again. He also accused the paper of misinterpreting the interview. [53]

I might ask why it was that the Monroe Doctrine suggestion was not commented upon here whilst the Cuban one was? *A great deal depends upon the first newspaper headline.*

The cable as sent, and as quoted in your paper, expressed my ideas accurately. *Of course, your introduction and your comments are your own.* [54]

The *Globe* published the second interview on 14 February. Cuba was still in the news cycle.

Liberty like Cuba's Irish demand. That should he point-stressed in compromise offer, not Monroe Doctrine, De Valera says. President of Republic of Ireland regrets he did not make his meaning more precise. [55]

Forced into yet more damage limitation, the *Irish Press* attacked the credibility of the *Globe* with a story headlined, 'De Valera's Statement Furnishes an Example of How News is Doctored for the Public.' [56] The headline and introduction to the report gave a 'false interpretation.' The *Irish Press* claimed that the interview had not been pre-arranged; the reporter had 'called on' de Valera in reference to comments in the English newspapers.[57]

Devoy editorial

The *Gaelic American* did not comment on the interview until 14 February, eight days after the report in the New York *Globe*, seven days after the *Westminster Gazette* and five days after the first newspaper comments in Ireland. Devoy was reasoned and restrained in his comments. The *Irish World*, no friend of Devoy, noted he wrote with 'unwonted restraint'. Pressure had been put on him not to comment adversely on the interview. That was not quite possible on a matter he considered a 'vital change' to Ireland's national policy. Devoy made a plea for debate on the proposals in a 'frank, and friendly spirit' and 'without heat or passion', and 'with all respect to President De Valera'.

Devoy's primary concern with the interview was that the 'character' of the proposition opened the way for the discussion of a 'compromise, or a change in objective'. It will be hailed in England 'as an offer of surrender.' The *character* of the proposition amounted to a proposal 'for a self-governing Ireland under an English Protectorate, or some kind of an international guarantee.' Examining three conditions that England might demand of Ireland in the unlikely event of her agreement, unlike de Valera, he thought through the practical implementation of the proposals.

England would insist on '*control of Ireland's foreign policy and her national defence*', and insist on holding possession of the great harbours on the south and west coasts as naval bases. This would make it much harder for America to succeed England as the dominant power on the sea. America would have no incentive to offer recognition to an Irish Republic that did not control her own ports.

England would demand an 'offensive and defensive' alliance between the two countries. Ireland would have to expend her manpower and finance for the defence of the British empire. Being tied to an empire on the road to bankruptcy, and involved in constant wars for self-preservation, would see Ireland 'go down with England in the wreck and ruin.'

England could propose an 'Anglo-American Alliance' in return for Irish independence. The Irish in America, who were 'passionately loyal' to their country, would never consent to such an alliance, even in return for Irish freedom. They would not 'barter American honor and interests' for any possible benefit to Ireland.

Devoy outlined a scenario whereby de Valera's propositions would lead to the opening of unofficial negotiations that would eventually be put to the elected representatives of Ireland.

> Finding that President De Valera is willing to recede somewhat from the demand for a wholly Independent Irish Republic, they may offer a Home Rule Bill of larger proportions ... or they may be encouraged to persevere in their determination to partition Ireland.

Devoy acknowledged that the proposition, which came like a 'bolt from the blue', would appeal to Americans who saw Irish republicans as 'impracticables, if not lunatics', and to the portion of Irish–Americans, including Senators Phelan of California and Walsh of Montana, who believed that President Wilson would do something for Ireland. He warned of the potential collapse of the support of the Irish in America if the present movement 'metamorphosed into a demand for a free Ireland under an English Protectorate.'

Devoy had frequently railed against President Wilson's expansion of executive authority, and now he warned of the threat to democracy in the emerging Irish state if one man could unilaterally change the national policy adopted by Dáil Éireann on 21 January 1919.

> No man, not even the President of the Irish Republic, has authority to change it. It can only be properly changed by similar representative assemblies, if the very essence of Democracy and Representative Government is not to be destroyed among our people.

Devoy concluded with a plea for freedom of discussion.

As the proposition was made through an English paper and will doubtless be freely discussed in the British press, there is no good reason why Irishmen in America should not give their views, always provided that it be done in a frank, and friendly spirit.

According to Boland, de Valera was 'on edge' the day the editorial was published.[58] Devoy was causing him 'grave concern' and he was 'very sad', declaring 'Poor Sinead, 'twill break her heart'.

In an unusual move, Devoy had added a by-line to the comment and issued it under the headline 'JOHN DEVOY'S OBJECTIONS'.[59] He was aware that any disagreement with de Valera, however mild, exposed Cohalan to renewed attack from McCartan and Maloney. His caution was warranted.

17

PLOT

Creel

McCartan would later state that there was 'little Devoy said with which we could in our hearts disagree', and that de Valera had not given Devoy an adequate explanation of his proposals.[1] Despite this, McCartan and Maloney commenced an orchestrated press campaign against Cohalan and Devoy, designed to remove the former and discredit the latter. Their first move came on 8 February, two days after the *Globe* editorial.

'Cohalan is an infamous traitor,' shouted George Creel, the former head of the war time propaganda bureau, his face flushed.[2] Creel, another recent convert, had published a book on Irish nationalism. 'That's a lie,' a shout came from the middle section of the Ford Hall Forum in Boston. People half lifted themselves from their seats. The chairman pleaded for calm. 'I withdraw, and I apologise for losing my temper,' declared Creel, who still insisted on having the last word. 'All through the war I was hindered in my work by people who were not for America. Judge Cohalan was never for America in this matter.' One newspaper ironically commented, 'George Creel, whose expert analysis of mind control and training has been published in all the papers and magazines of the country, lost his temper in Boston the other day.'[3]

The League of Nations, Creel also declared, was the 'best hope' for the Irish, adding that no man in the United States feels the justice of the Irish question more than President Wilson.

Devoy responded to the attack on Cohalan in the *Gaelic American*. 'George Creel thinks that because he wrote a book favouring Ireland's right to freedom he is privileged to defame and insult every Irish citizen who refuses to worship Woodrow Wilson.'[4] He recalled that Creel had 'personally directed' the attack on Irish citizens by releasing the von Igol documents seized by the secret service. The Irish National Bureau called Creel's outburst a 'vicious attack' on Cohalan. The wide newspaper coverage was 'additional conclusive evidence that a *definitely planned scheme is being worked out with the object of undermining, if possible, the great leadership of Justice Cohalan.*'[5]

Trolling

Maloney arranged for a report to be planted in the New York *Sun*, a large circulation daily newspaper, that attributed the editorial comment in the *Gaelic American* to Cohalan, despite Devoy's by-line.

> The *Gaelic American* is the official organ of the Clan-na-Gael. Though Mr. Devoy is its editor, he is not generally credited in Irish circles with being the *directing force* on the paper. The policy of the *Gaelic American* is believed by many to be controlled in large measure by Justice Daniel F. Cohalan, of the New York Supreme Court.[6]

Maloney brilliantly undermined the credibility of any critical response from Devoy directed at him.

> One of his chief weapons in debate – and one which has brought him many victories – is to accuse his opponent of trying to cause division and dissension 'in our ranks'.

The *Sun* concluded that it was 'with feelings akin to consternation … that many readers of the *Gaelic American* this week saw what they regarded as a sign of a break between the "old man" and the leader of Sinn Féin.' Cohalan was cast as the cause of the split. The *Irish Press* reprinted the story. This was a step too far for some; not only did it give credence to the report and spread it to a wider Irish community, it also meant Devoy would have to defend his integrity, risking a rupture in the movement at a critical time.

Liam Mellows, who loathed Cohalan and disagreed with Devoy's stance on the interview, wrote to a friend, 'Of course the Press ought not to have printed the 'Sun' story. Whether McCartan was responsible or not I don't know but it was very wrong.'[7] Mellows was upset enough to complain directly to McCartan. 'You ought not to have quoted the Sun squib,' he wrote, 'it could have done no good; only harm'.[8] Mellows, who was organising the bond drive in the mid-west, had been watching 'with increasing anxiety' the events transpiring in the east.[9] He pleaded with McCartan, 'if it is not settled now, the bond Certificate campaign is going to be crippled. And you know how hard it is to keep things going – so few workers to do this particular work.'[10]

The *Irish Press* further provoked Devoy in a clever editorial dismissing him as a gossipy old fool; his comments on de Valera's interview reminded one of 'The Spreading of the News' by Lady Gregory. The principal character of that play, a deaf elderly female apple vendor, picks up gossip, redistributes it with her own misinterpretations, picks it up again and recycles it with further flourishes.[11] Devoy, whose deafness was legendry, was the old woman, and the analogy superbly, if brutally, diminished the credibility of his analysis of the interview. Ironically, the editorial concluded, 'If the President cannot depend on the intelligence of his friends, public discussion of vital issues would become well nigh impossible'.[12]

The campaign of attack continued in the New York *News*, which published an exclusive despatch from Washington with a front-page headline, 'Devoy And Judge Cohalan Open War On D'valera [sic]'.[13] They had assailed and charged him with hauling down the Irish flag. Devoy had even advised the leaders in Ireland that de Valera had 'deserted the cause'. The Irish president was 'standing pat' in the belief that they represented only a small faction. The paper printed a cablegram sent by de Valera to Griffith clearly worded for publication.

Now, a word to the wise is enough. The Irish people are too wise to allow themselves to be disturbed by misrepresentations, no matter how adroit, no matter how cunning, *no matter whence they emanate*. This is not the time to sidetrack our advance into the by-paths of a profit-less discussion based on a series of 'ifs.' My attitude is, of course, the same as ever. All is well.

Possibly attempting to bring balance to the story, the reporter observed that the previous edition of the *Gaelic American* 'appeared to be still friendly to Mr. de Valera and his cause and, in special correspondence and otherwise, featured and supported the tour of the Irish president and his campaign in this country'.

Any balance, however, would disappear in a follow-up report the next day. Cohalan and Devoy 'were in a fight' against de Valera's leadership according to an 'insider'.[14] Almost comically, failed diplomatic ambitions on Devoy's part were given as the reason for his supposed antagonism towards de Valera.

> Ever since the arrival of De Valera there has been bitterness because he refused to follow the councils of the fiery editor of the '*Gaelic American*'.
>
> It was well known that Devoy expected to be appointed as Ambassador of the 'Irish Republic' to the United States. Dr. Patrick McCartan was sent in his stead.
>
> Ever since the appointment the spark has been smouldering.[15]

Boland was quoted as telling the reporter that there would be no statement issued on the break, but the story ended with surprising detail.

> The cooler heads, *it is said*, will be with De Valera, and it is *quite likely* that in this camp will be found Bourke Cockran and ex-Governor Dunne, of Illinois; Joseph Scott, of Los Angeles; Eugene Kinkaid, of New Jersey, and other leaders of the Irish fight for freedom.[16]

Devoy mocked Boland in a letter to Cohalan; he 'tries to cover his tracks by saying he has nothing to say - *after* saying it'.[17] He informed Cohalan of another McCartan 'inspired' editorial in the *Philadelphia Record* that commended de Valera 'for getting rid of you and me'.

The *Gaelic American* described the despatch in the *News* as a 'rigma-role'; there was 'no doubt whatever about its origin.'[18] It questioned the genuineness of the cablegram sent to Griffith; if genuine it showed that the entire report was given out by some person '*very close*' to de Valera.'[19]

The press attacks came two months after de Valera had told the National Council meeting that Cohalan and Devoy had given him 'every assistance in their power', and after his appeal for unity had evoked strong applause.

Coinciding with the attacks, the Irish Progressive League issued a statement reaffirming its support of de Valera as the president of the Irish republic *and* 'chosen leader' of the Irish Race.[20]

Devoy defends himself

'What I said was mild, fair and friendly criticism of a public proposition involving the vital interests of the Irish National Cause on which every Irishman has a right to express an opinion,' wrote Devoy in a second editorial on 21 February. 'I claim no more and will accept no less than that common right.'[21] He denied he had attacked de Valera. '[Are] we to be shut off from expressing an opinion on the ground that any criticism is to be treated as an "attack"'? Continuing, Devoy explained that he saw nothing in the official statement issued by de Valera that addressed his objection to the proposals; you cannot cite the Platt Amendment 'without bringing in the whole text of it', and a Monroe Doctrine amounted to an 'Anglo–Irish Alliance' that could align Ireland against the United States in war. While calling for de Valera's proposals to be dropped and the 'regularly adopted policy' reaffirmed, Devoy also challenged the assertion that he was opposed to de Valera; his stance on the interview was principled.

There is no man in America who worked harder to prepare the way for Éamon De Valera's coming here and, subject to some handicaps due to infirmities of age, has supported him more loyally or energetically since he came. But I cannot, and will not, support him in the radical change of policy which he now proposes.

The storm is up, and all is on the hazard

On 11 February, three days before Devoy published his first editorial, Boland noted in his diary that Cohalan had called to the Irish National Bureau, but had not come to see him, 'Tá fath le gach nidh' [There is reason for everything].[22] Boland was ready to hit out. 'John Devoy out for trouble. Hopes to bring de Valera to heel for Cohalan. John my son you have your hands full'.[23] All prior thoughts of unity were out the window, with seemingly no consideration for the bond drive, the recognition campaign and the approaching League of Nations vote.

Boland was in a fight for control of the Irish movement. 'Shall America dictate? that's the question. I have no fears of the result. Sorry the "old man" is firing the balls for Cohalan.' On the day of Devoy's first editorial, Boland's pugilism soared. 'I can see what is to come. I prophesy here that we will win out.'[24] He quoted Cassius on the eve of battle from Shakespeare's *Julius Caesar*: 'Blow wind, swell billows, float Barque'.

Boland undertook an eight hour journey to Boston to address a bond meeting, returning on the overnight train.[25] Understandably irritable the following day, a visit from Larry Rice resulted in a heated encounter. The New York Clan-na-Gael leader apparently attempted to 'dictate' to Boland to 'quit the Chief'. Boland reacted as expected. 'Sorry I did not kick Larry out. [D]one next best thing.'[26] Another day trip to Philadelphia saw Boland return to New York at 1.30 in the morning, at which point he noted in his diary that a 'momentous decision' had been made, and that '[McCartan] and I fix up journey of moment.'[27]

On 17 February Boland attended a meeting with Frank Walsh, Bourke Cockran, McGuire and Eugene Kincaid. 'All stand up with Chief. Out of evil cometh good. We will clean the Augean stable yet'.[28] But Boland had read at least some of the room wrong. Although McGuire saw 'no serious objections' to de Valera's statement, he was not against Cohalan. McGuire judged that de Valera had not committed himself beyond the specific article of the Platt Amendment quoted.[29] McGuire had travelled to Cuba in 1897, just before the Spanish–American War, and had been there often afterwards. 'This small state today is probably the wealthiest in the world,' he wrote to Cohalan. 'Americans claim great credit for saving it and I think people generally like to compare free Cuba with the possibilities of a free Ireland'.[30]

Cohalan was not short of supporters in New York. On the day Boland was ready to clean the Augean stable, Cohalan was appointed Grand Marshal of the St. Patrick's Day parade at a meeting of the United Irish organisations of the five boroughs. At first, he had declined to serve, 'but yielded to a committee which assured him he was the unanimous choice of the meeting'.[31] Roderick Kennedy, Cohalan's personal attendant, who was appointed chairman of the arrangements committee, hoped 25,000 marchers would be in line. They expected no rival parade; the celebration would be as harmonious as the previous year when all factional differences had been merged because of the war.

Ireland frontline

The battle against Cohalan and Devoy was moved to Ireland. So concerned was de Valera with the reaction to the interview there, he sent McCartan home to explain the situation to the cabinet. McCartan may have privately disagreed with de Valera's proposals, but he was sure to be on point on the supposed opposition of Cohalan and Devoy to de Valera and the Irish mission.

De Valera prepared the way for McCartan's visit in a letter to the cabinet, in which he called Cohalan and Devoy, who had fought for the Irish Republic for decades prior to de Valera's arrival in America, the 'enemy', 'mischief makers' and 'malicious persons.'[32] There was a 'movement now on foot' that could lead to 'possible serious consequences.'

Cohalan and Devoy were accused of making a '*deadly attempt* to ruin our chances for the bonds and for everything we came here to accomplish.'

To fully discredit them, de Valera first had to negate the contents of a letter Boland had sent to Dublin two weeks earlier, when the latter wrote that Cohalan and Devoy 'have all their lives been strong and active supporters of the Irish Republic, and I want to say right here that to-day they stand exactly as they always stood'.[33] De Valera explained away the letter as a 'desire on our part not to appear to be unjust', and to balance 'our accusatory impressions with corresponding statements as to the virtues of those we had to accuse.'

With no evidence to back up his accusations, and with no obvious motive why Cohalan would want to do the things attributed to him, de Valera declared, 'The trouble is purely one of personalities'. He invented 'ulterior motives' for Cohalan's actions.

(1) To drive me home – jealousy, envy, resentment of a rival – some devil- ish cause I do not know what prompts, or,
(2) To compel me to be a rubber stamp for somebody.

Cohalan, a judge of the Supreme Court of New York, secure in his Americanism and proud of his familial roots, had no reason for jealousy, envy or resentment of a rival. He was confident in his opinions, seldom made mistakes and rarely had to explain himself. De Valera, by contrast, found himself constantly justifying his actions, either to the press or to cabinet, as he did in the letter.

To ease the mind of everybody I want you to know at all times that I never in public or private say or do anything here which is not thor- oughly consistent with my attitude at home as you have known it. That will enable you to judge whether anything I may by newspapers be reported to have said is true or false.

Never forget that the Press is an instrument used by the enemy – *gar- bled statements misleading headlines etc.* You know the press and a word to the wise ought be enough.

Boland took his cue from de Valera in a letter to Collins a week later. Cohalan became a 'low down, cheap Tammany Hall politician, who cannot even run straight with his own people'.[34] Acting with Devoy, they were '*prepared to knife* every man who comes from Ireland if they attempt in the slightest way to guide the movement for Irish freedom in this country.'

Bait not taken

On 18 February Boland returned to Washington arriving in the late afternoon.[35] He went to the Irish National Bureau to clear up outstanding items and there met Kathleen O'Connell, de Valera's private secretary, who he noted was a 'very good girl could not manage without her'. She had joined de Valera in the previous October to support him on the tour.[36] Just a year younger than Boland, she had embedded herself in all aspects of the national movement since emigrating from Kerry in 1904, working at various stages with the Gaelic League, FOIF, Clan-na-Gael and Cumann na mBan. On a brief visit to Ireland in 1915, she brought money and messages from Devoy to the Irish Volunteers in advance of the Easter Rising.

Within hours of his arrival, Boland was ordered back to New York after receiving an advance copy of Devoy's second editorial.[37] Arriving off the overnight train, he went for a walk along the river in the snow with Nunan, before going to meet Lynch to discuss Devoy's article.[38] 'Diarmuid knows DeV is right', he seemed to convince himself.[39] Boland then called on Devoy himself; 'take him easily.' Boland had a blazing row with a 'Mr. O'Reilly' who had accused de Valera of lowering the flag. He later regretted calling him a 'blasted liar.' He returned to Washington on another overnight train.[40]

When he reached the hotel the following morning, Boland found that de Valera and Diarmuid Fawsitt, the trade consul, were both still in bed. They went to the office, then for a walk over the Potomac, during which they made a 'final decision' – they would get Cohalan, who had not publicly reacted to the accusations in the *Sun* and *News*, 'in open if possible'.[41] De Valera would write him a letter, in the hope that the reply, which they would publish, would somehow expose Cohalan.

De Valera and Boland returned to New York on another overnight train so that they could hand deliver the letter due to its sensitive content. 'Some journeyings this week to be sure', Boland noted wearily. 'Tis in vain for soldiers to complain'.[42] When they arrived at Penn Station, de Valera was mistaken on the platform by a police escort waiting for Sir Ronald Lindsay, the most senior official in the British Embassy. 'De Valera fell back a pace, while his followers gasped,' reported the *New York Times*. 'Then he laughed heartily and said: "Oh, no my good man. I am the President of the Irish Republic."' [43]

That afternoon, Boland carried the letter to Cohalan. Amazed and stunned at the contents, he read the letter in front of Boland in 'painful silence'.[44] Cohalan was given two days to reply. However, the letter was too obvious in content and tone to belie its intent of drawing him out. Devoy called it the 'most astonishingly foolish letter … written by a public man in my time'.[45]

Dear Justice Cohalan,

After mature consideration, I have decided that to continue to ignore the articles in the 'Gaelic American' would result in injury to the cause I have been sent here to promote.

The articles themselves are, of course, the least matter. It is the evident *purpose* behind them, and the general *attitude of mind* they reveal, that is the menace.

I am answerable to the Irish people for the proper execution of the trust with which I have been charged. I am definitely responsible to them, and I alone am responsible. It is my obvious duty to select such *instruments* as may be available for the task set me. It is my duty to superintend every important step in the execution of that task. I may not blindly delegate these duties to anyone whomsoever. I cannot divest myself of my responsibilities.

I see added force being applied, day by day, to the power end of the great lever of American public opinion, with which I hope to accomplish my purpose. I must satisfy myself as to the temper of the other end of the lever.

The articles of the 'Gaelic American,' and certain incidents that have resulted from them, give me grounds for the fear that, in a moment of stress, the point of the lever would fail me. I am led to understand that these articles in the 'Gaelic American' have your consent and approval. Is this so?

The Friends of Irish Freedom organisation is an association of American citizens, founded to assist the Irish people in securing the freedom the Irish people desire. By its name, and by its constitution, it is pledged to aid in securing recognition for the established Republic. I am convinced it is ready to cooperate to the full with the responsible head of the Republic, who has been sent here specially to seek that recognition.

You are the officer of the Friends of Irish Freedom, who, de facto, wields unchallenged the executive power of that organisation. You are the officer through whom its several resources are in the main applied. You are the officer who has accepted its most important commissions, and spoken, not merely in its name, but in the name of the whole Irish Race in America. It is vital that I know exactly how you stand in this matter.

The whole question is urgent, and I expect you will find it possible to let me have a reply by Monday. To avoid all chance of miscarriage, I am having this delivered by Mr. Boland, personally.

I remain,

Very sincerely yours,
ÉAMON DE VALERA.[46]

Boland walked back to the office, where, on hearing Cohalan's reaction, de Valera was 'very upset and disgusted'.[47] A conference of de Valera, Boland, O'Mara, Nunan and Fawsitt discussed the situation. The following day, Boland addressed a bond meeting in New Rochelle, after which he spent the evening with McGuire discussing the 'pros and cons' of the situation and they decided a 'plan of action'. An over-tired Boland was stressed and emotional. 'The more I see of this scandalous affair the more disgusting it becomes. The Rice attempt on me was most dastardly. Cohalan an evil for Ireland'.[48] When Boland returned to New York, the 'sole topic' of conversation was Cohalan and Devoy.

Devoy handed the reply letter to Boland on the evening of 23 February, who made a calculated decision: 'do not give letter to Chief till morning. [S]leep more important'. Boland considered the letter to be a 'dirty clever police court lawyer's reply', but it was well-crafted and to the point, as would be expected from a judge, and included a hint of derision towards de Valera. Devoy considered it the 'finest thing' Cohalan had ever written.[49]

The letter offered no advantage in publication. Cohalan wrote that he refused to be drawn into any controversy de Valera had with Devoy. He touched on a number of areas: freedom of speech ('I assume you will grant'), his Americanism ('only allegiance is to America') and the British Monroe Doctrine ('Ireland the ally of England'). Cohalan cautioned de Valera against endangering the unity of action in America, 'which you found here amongst us when you came'.[50]

Dear President De Valera,

Your communication, dated February 20th, was handed to me by Mr. Boland on Saturday afternoon.

I was amazed at its contents. In spite of its tone, and because of the position which you occupy, I am responding to it.

The 'Gaelic American' is edited, as you know, by Mr. John Devoy, for whose opinions and convictions I entertain the highest respect. I control neither him nor them.

That he has the right to comment upon, or discuss your public utterances, or those of any man who speaks for a cause or a people, I assume you will grant. In any event, it is recognized by all Americans as one of our fundamental liberties. We have no law of lèse-majesté here, nor, as far as

I can judge, is there talk of having one in the democratic and free Ireland in which we believe.

Into any controversy you may have with Mr. Devoy, or others, I refuse to be drawn.

May I venture to suggest that you evidently labour under a serious misapprehension as to the relations which exist between you and me.

I know no reason why you take the trouble to tell me that you can share your responsibility to the Irish people with no one.

I would not let you share it with me, if you sought to do so. That is a matter between them and you.

What I have done for the cause of the independence of the Irish people, recently and for many years past, I have done as an American, whose only allegiance is to America, and as one to whom the interest and security of my country are ever to be preferred to those of any and all other lands. What the extent and effect of that work may be will be [sic] decided by the members of the Race and by general public opinion.

I have no appointment from you or any other spokesman for another country, nor would I under any circumstances accept one.

So long, and just so long as I can continue to work thus, I shall exercise such influence and talent as I may have in the same way, and for the same ideals as in the past.

The people of Ireland have placed themselves unequivocally upon record as favouring complete independence for their country, and, unless and until they by vote reverse that decision, I shall regard it as final, no matter what any man or set of men may say to the contrary.

With their demand for independence I am confident all Americans will finally agree, as it is not alone just, but in line with the ideals and best interests of our country, and essential to the permanent peace of the world, that all nations and peoples should be free.

If Ireland were to change her position, and to seek a measure of self-government that would align her in the future with England as an ally, in what I regard as the inevitable struggle for the freedom of the seas, that must shortly come between America and England, every loyal

American will without hesitation take a position unreservedly upon the side of America.

A British Monroe Doctrine, that would make Ireland the ally of England, and thus buttress the falling British Empire, so as to further oppress India and Egypt and other subject lands, would be so immoral, and so utterly at variance with the ideals and traditions of the Irish people, as to be as indefensible to them as it would be intolerable to the liberty-loving peoples of the world.

I believe the people of Ireland were in deadly earnest in declaring for absolute independence, and no voice but that of the people themselves can convince me that they intend to take a position which will put them in hostility to America.

Should they, however, take such a step – as a free people undoubtedly have the right to do – I know that the millions of Americans of Irish blood, who have created this great movement in favour of Ireland's independence, which you found here upon your arrival, will once again show with practical unanimity that we are for America as against all the world.

Are you not in great danger of making a grave mistake when you talk in your communication of selecting 'instruments' in this country, and of 'levers,' and 'power end,' and 'other end of the lever,' through which you hope to accomplish your purpose here?

Do you really think for a moment that American public opinion will permit any citizen of another country to interfere, as you suggest, in American affairs?

Do you think that any self-respecting American will permit himself to be used in such a manner by you?

If so, I may assure you that you are woefully out of touch with the spirit of the country in which you are sojourning.

You point out that I have on occasion been called upon to speak, not merely in the name of the Friends of Irish Freedom but in the name of the whole Irish Race in America. May I call your attention to the fact that it was always as an American, and for my countrymen, that I spoke?

You might have added that at those times, as at others, I have said nothing that took from the self-respect or dignity of those whom I represented,
or that left any doubt upon my hearers that I believed many millions of
Americans sympathised with that demand of the people of Ireland for
absolute independence, which you come here to voice.

I respectfully suggest, in closing, that you would be well advised if you
hesitate before you jeopardise or imperil that solidarity of opinion, and
unity of action, among millions of American citizens, which you found
here amongst us when you came, which have been the despair of England's
friends, and have already accomplished so much for America and Ireland.

Those millions do not desire to see a return of the conditions which,
under the late Mr. Redmond, made political activities in Ireland a football
in English party politics.

Yours very truly,
DANIEL F. COHALAN[51]

'Chief in a rage.'[52]

Hearst

To shore up de Valera's reputation, a meeting with newspaper magnate
William Randolph Hearst was arranged, possibly through McGuire,
who had been politically allied with him since 1905, when Hearst unsuc-
cessfully ran as a reform candidate for mayor of New York City.[53] Boland
had expected him to be a 'forceful aggressive type', only to find him
'quite thoughtful and very fine towards Chief'.[54] He agreed to help them.
Within days, Frank Walsh made an appointment with Philip Francis, the
leading editorial writer in the Hearst group, 'for broadside'.[55] Francis was
also one of the speakers, with Walsh and de Valera, at a dinner in support
of Indian independence the same week.[56]

Cohalan and Hearst may have been closely aligned in their dislike of
British imperialism, but there was no love lost between them. In 1910,
the *American*, one of the Hearst newspapers, had falsely accused New
York mayor William Gaynor of making an illegal payment to Cohalan.

The paper published a draft for $48,000 on its front page, but excluded the stamp showing it had been audited as a valid claim against the city.[57] At a joint banquet of the Associated Press and the American Newspaper Publishers' Association at the Waldorf Astoria, in front of 600 editors and publishers from across the country, Gaynor displayed the Hearst facsimile and the original warrant. 'The truth is I am assured that the dates were actually cut out of the plate with a routing machine'. Many members of the press welcomed the opportunity to attack Hearst's brand of 'yellow journalism'.

The Hearst newspaper group had become more antagonistic towards Britain as the League of Nations vote approached. An editorial in the New York *Nation* addressed British misunderstanding of the cause of America's increased hostility.

> The chief, or at all events, the immediate, cause of American ill-feeling, we are invariably told is Ireland. We admit that the Irish imbroglio has a great deal to do with American feeling toward England; but the Englishman who imagines that, having mentioned Ireland he has told practically the whole story, is in need of enlightenment.[58]

That enlightenment came in an editorial penned by Hearst in the *American* on the reasons people distrusted the British government, in particular its attempt to influence American opinion 'by biased propaganda.'[59] He listed the actions that England could take to improve her popularity: create its own army and navy and not expect America to pay for weapons 'which may at any time be used against us'; admit that it is not entitled to six times the representation of the United States in a League of Nations; stop 'hypocritically' declaring that 'blood is thicker than water' when making treaties 'with nations of Oriental blood like Japan'; and stop 'tallying sentimental nonsense' when 'American hands are always expected to be stretched out generously full of gifts and benefits.' Hearst concluded that Americans 'very generally have come to doubt whether England really wants a friend among nations which it cannot use entirely selfishly and to its own advantage.'

The *American* reported on the seizure of newspapers that had arrived in Dublin. The papers had been carried to Dublin Castle, where the wrappers were cut and the contents searched before releasing them for distribution.

> Britain's 'shadow service' in Ireland, which long since has paid conspicuous attention to all things American, took a new form when a squad of special agents descended upon the Dublin Post Office and seized tremendous batches of American newspapers mailed hither.[60]

Despite the successful outcome of the Hearst meeting, de Valera was 'not in good form' that day. Over the previous ten days, Boland had described him being on edge, very upset, disgusted and in a rage. He would have been in worse form that day if he had seen *Punch*, the satirical London magazine, which published a poem on the 'Cubanisation' of Ireland.

> When Ireland is treated like Cuba
> As great DE VALERA suggests,
> And the pestilent loyalist Pooh-Bah
> No longer our island infests,
>
> The militant minstrels of Tara
> Will change their war-harps for guitars,
> And Clare, to be called Santa Clara,
> Will grow the most splendid cigars.

Boland made a trip to Washington to collect letters from home and answer outstanding correspondence. He replied irritably to a letter from a Thomas J. Lynch, who opposed de Valera's views on the Monroe Doctrine.

> I *resent* you, or any other person, suggesting that a man of President de Valera's record would compromise Ireland's sovereign claim.[61]

Boland also answered a letter from Charles Rice, a lawyer who had emigrated from Ireland in 1908 and had served with the US army during the war. He would later serve as president general of the American Irish Historical Society.[62] Although polite, Boland made it understood there was no room for debate.

> President De Valera knows he cannot please everybody, and does not intend to try the impossible. He is responsible for his actions to the Irish Congress, and to the Irish people. He will render an account to them, and to no others.

The fallout from the *Gazette* interview upset the Irish National Bureau staff. Boland had to calm the 'ruffled brow' of Willard de Lue, chief of the section of information, who was 'uneasy' about the articles.[63] Two weeks earlier, Captain O'Connell had announced that he was leaving Washington to resume his law practice. His loss would be a serious blow to the Irish movement; although he was firmly in the camp of Cohalan and Devoy, Boland thought he 'did good work'.[64] Before his departure, O'Connell gave Boland 'some advice' for de Valera. Never good at delivering difficult news, and not wanting to be the messenger shot by an increasingly agitated de Valera, Boland took 'refuge' in asking O'Connell to ring up de Valera himself. The call between the two did not go well. '[R]esult Fireworks.'[65]

Boland wrote a long letter to Collins and then went to the movies, 'Forget Chief, Cohalan and Devoy'. He also noted in his diary that de Valera was 'determined to join issue in the function of F.O.I.F.' Returning to New York the evening of 27 February, he found de Valera sick in bed, where he had been for two days, 'looks bad'. Boland's diagnosis, 'this Devoy business has done him no good'.[66]

England's Hidden Hand

Devoy responded to the *Irish Press* attack in a third editorial in the *Gaelic American* on 28 February, naming McCartan and Maloney for the first time, and again calling for a 'free and fair discussion.'[67] Making no mention of de Valera, he continued to cover his speaking engagements with front-page headlines: New Bedford Gives De Valera Great Welcome; and Fall River Gives Irish President Great Ovation.

Devoy called out the 'particularly mean and contemptible' reprinting of the *Sun* report, which he said was done for the deliberate purpose of 'affording a false pretext' for action against Cohalan because McCartan 'had not the *manhood* to make the statement on his own responsibility.' The action was part of an 'organised plan' to give the impression to the public that Cohalan was 'attacking De Valera'. The allusion to the Lady Gregory play was McCartan's 'manly way' of putting the whole 'misunderstanding' of de Valera's very plain words on Devoy.

He went on to accuse Maloney of carrying out the plan made at the British Embassy in 1917 in the presence of Shane Leslie and Lord Percy to break up the Irish movement and destroy Cohalan. The plan was carried out through the 'hypnotized' McCartan, so that his 'weak will and over-wrought nerves' were under the domination of Maloney. Expecting the final blow to fall on Cohalan within a few days, Devoy issued a warning to his opponents: 'God help the men who provoked and deliberately planned the fight when the Irish manhood of America is through with them.' He was ready for battle, 'the best laid schemes of mice and men gang aft agley'.

Devoy penned a separate editorial explaining why leadership of the Irish movement needed to remain in American hands; otherwise, he argued, they would be accused by opponents of acting on Irish rather than American motives.[68] 'The sooner these basic facts of the situation are understood and accepted by all concerned, the better.' The Irish in America acted in the good of the United States; they opposed the League of Nations as American citizens. 'That their efforts, if successful, would benefit Ireland goes without saying, and they are glad of it, but benefit to Ireland is not their main motive.' He added that there was a 'quiet effort' being made to placate President Wilson 'by sacrificing certain Irish leaders whom he hates'.[69]

Devoy elaborated on these views in a letter to John McGarry in Chicago. 'American citizens controlled in their public actions by orders from outside the U.S. What a spectacle it would make of us and what a text for attack by our enemies.'[70] He believed de Valera's actions since his arrival were the 'deliberate preparation' to implement his new policies, 'which he knew we would not stand'.[71] De Valera had filled the ACII 'with enemies of ours' who made no concealment of their hostility. And they 'represent nothing.'

Devoy was particularly upset at accusations of fraud made against Cohalan and himself, which he contrasted with the excessive expenditure of the Irish mission.

> They are squandering money recklessly, giving big salaries to men beyond anything they have earned. The expenses of the Bond Bureau are over $1600 a week, and I don't know the exact figure of the Waldorf Astoria, but it is certainly very big … while some of his friends are openly saying that "Cohalan and Devoy have made way with the Victory Fund".

March comes to us like a lion in snow and frost.

As he rose to speak, Cohalan received a tremendous ovation reported the *Boston Globe* on the front page. 'I come not as one of Irish blood though there is not a drop of any but Irish blood in me,' he declared to the Boston audience on 29 February, 'but as an American that loves liberty for all races.'[72]

In presenting Cohalan, the chairman of the meeting contrasted the apathy to the Irish cause fifteen months earlier to the 'energetic activities' of the present due to the 'sustained campaign of education evolved in the heart and brain of Judge Cohalan.' He was 'a lion-hearted leader of an old and unconquerable race'. On his part, Cohalan declared that the bond campaign in Massachusetts had become an inspiration. That evening, he also spoke at a bond meeting in Providence.[73]

The same Leap Day saw Boland filled with optimism. 'The Bond drive now promises to be a success, earnest workers are in line in many States,' he wrote. 'The office under Jas. O'Mara's direction goes splendidly. Seán Nunan Manager tip top.'[74] February had been the 'most fruitful' month since he arrived. His month-end diary entry was a rallying cry.

> The Treaty is nearly finished and a grand healthy anti-British sentiment is abroad. Ireland is fighting magnificently and Russia is victorious. We all are confident that the future is ours. Ireland is now out in the sun and can never go back into the shadows of English Imperialism. We will yet place that crown on her 'dear dark head'. *March comes to us like a lion in snow and frost.* We go forward confident in our cause, having accomplished more in our few months than ever had been dreamed of by our late leaders. $300,000 to Ireland and ten million *in sight*, and Recognition not impossible. The gallant men in Ireland carry on cheerfully knowing that 'The very subtlest eloquence injured man can shew [show] is the pathos of a pike head the logic of a blow.'

He sensed that they had the upper hand in the conflict with Cohalan and Devoy. 'Seems to me that our friends are feeling sick with themselves, from the gossip I gather that they are uneasy, *we will keep them so*'.[75]

Across the divide, however, leading Irish-Americans had had enough.

Peace

Devoy had shown himself capable in the past of working with leaders that had come from Ireland, but with de Valera it was different. He had come to form a low opinion of the Irish president, which he expressed in a letter to McGarry.

> [H]is judgement is very poor ... he is filled with the idea ... that the great ovations he got are for him personally and practically gave him a *mandate to do what he pleases.*
>
> His head is turned to a greater extent than that of any man that I have ever met in more than half a century ... He is not a frank man nor a really

strong one. His strength is cardboard which cracks on pressure … we have to deal with a man gone mad with egotism.[76]

De Valera's unilateral use of his executive authority concerned him. 'If he can take that action now without consulting anyone, what is there he cannot do.' Devoy was not willing to sacrifice the 'fundamental principle' of the movement to avoid a fight, noting, 'we'd be worse off in the end than if we fought it out now.'

Devoy was not impressed with McGuire writing to Cohalan advising a delay in responding to the provocations, 'if James K's ideas of temporizing, as revealed in his letters to Dan are carried out, the situation will be made worse'.[77] But McGarry also had written to Cohalan urging restraint and Devoy also challenged him. 'I have read two of your letters to the Judge and it seems to me you go too far in your amity to avoid a break with De Valera'.[78]

Although appearing belligerent, Devoy was circumspect about starting a fight, proposing 'no drastic action' and wanting 'to avoid an open rupture.' Continuance of the present situation could lead to 'very serious danger' to the cause, but he recognised that the 'scandal of a fight' would be 'very bad'. He believed they were in a strong position, though understood a large number of people would stand by de Valera, either believing in the new proposals, for the sake of unity, or out of enmity to 'the old sorehead'.

McGuire had expected the *Gazette* interview to be forgotten within a week.[79] As March approached, and with no sign of resolution, he was determined to end the impasse, as were other senior Irish–Americans who asked him to use his influence to prevent a split. At a meeting on 28 February that he had arranged, all were 'absolutely' against a break with de Valera and 'warned against the danger of trying to ignore him.'[80]

The evening before the meeting, McGuire had a four-hour conference with John T. Ryan, a forty-six-year-old lawyer and former captain in the US army who had served during the Spanish–American War. Ryan was a fugitive from the law; on 21 January 1919, the same day that Dáil Éireann met for the first time in Ireland, he had been indicted by a grand jury for conspiracy to commit treason with German agents *after* America entered the war.[81] He had been in communication with Maria K. de Victorica, a German agent to whom he had paid $4,500, and had conspired with other German agents in Europe and South America. The authorities had lost contact with him in May 1918. Federal agents believed he had escaped to Mexico, but he was in hiding in America.[82] Ryan operated under different codenames, including Philippine Island Bill, Buffalo, and Jetter when smuggling arms for Clan-na-Gael.[83] He was a member of the Revolutionary Directory and had been on the FOIF executive committee.

McGuire sent copies of the correspondence that passed between Cohalan, Devoy and McGarry. McGuire and Ryan were in agreement on what needed to be done to resolve the situation. Both were sympathetic to de Valera, but the loss of Cohalan and Devoy to the Irish movement would be catastrophic, 'the situation locally would be destroyed'. Ryan believed that a fight was 'not only foolish but absolutely unnecessary.' And both agreed that Cohalan and Devoy 'would lose in the fight'.[84]

Ryan recommended a practical solution to McGuire, 'the thing to do was to have peace, help finish up the work the Chief was doing and *get him and his friends out of the country*.' He believed that this strategy would appeal to Cohalan and Devoy. Ryan, whose main objective was to see the bond drive a success, feared that a 'division would injure the loan – which is the big thing just now – after that is out of the way other matters can be considered.'[85] Ryan sent a letter to McGarrity in Philadelphia, summarising the discussion and enclosing copies of the Cohalan, Devoy and McGarry correspondence.

On 5 March Boland wrote to Collins.

I am happy to say the controversy seems to be ended, *at least publicly*. The attitude of De Valera the whole time has been excellent. He has not discussed the matter publicly [Boland made no reference to McCartan and Maloney], and this week's issue of the "Gaelic American" is back to normal.[86]

The following day he appended a note to a letter from de Valera to Ireland. 'I find on arrival [back in New York] that the word has gone out that Devoy & Cohalan to cease talking and I consider the incident now closed.'[87] McGuire received a note from Devoy notifying him of an upcoming event. A handwritten addition noted, 'no fight'.[88]

PART 3

18

TO DELVE INTO THE
REASONS WOULD
BE USELESS

No more banquets

On 6 March 1920 de Valera informed the cabinet that subscriptions to the bond drive were proceeding 'fairly satisfactorily.'[1] The reality was different. On the day before, Boland had written to Collins that 'much harm' had been done in the wake of the interview, and that it 'must be admitted that the criticism has effected the Bond Drive.'[2]

But the fallout from the *Gazette* interview was not the only factor impacting negatively on the campaign. Seven days before the launch of Irish Loan Week, the ACII issued a statement from the Waldorf that preparation in every state was not in the 'same degree of perfection.'[3] Several state chairmen postponed their campaigns to the early weeks of February. The organisation had not been perfected.

De Valera was providing little impetus to the campaign. After his visit to Worcester, he left for Springfield on 7 February, where he was welcomed by the usual reception committee and marching bands, the large crowd waiting patiently in a snow storm for his delayed arrival.[4] In an address to local dignitaries at the Hotel Kimball ballroom, he said, 'The *least important* part of my visit is to raise money for the legitimate expenses of the Republic as authorized by the people's congress'. Two days later, to an audience of New Bedford bond workers who had braved sloppy streets and mountainous banks of snow to hear him, he declared, 'I do not wish to have this work overshadow the more important achievement of official recognition by the Government of the United States. Our main objective is to secure it, and to detract or turn away public attention from that fact would be a grave mistake'.[5]

On the train to New Bedford, the setting for Herman Melville's novel *Moby Dick*, de Valera had been introduced to H.C. Hathaway, a police captain and former whaler, whose advice Devoy sought when he was organising the Catalapa rescue.[6] On the following morning, with snow falling softly, de Valera laid a wreath on the grave of George Anthony, the captain of the Catalapa, who Devoy had convinced to undertake the mission.[7] The *Gaelic American* reported de Valera's graveside words. 'We cherish in a special manner the Irishmen of the past generation on whose work we are building and the Americans who helped them are in a very special sense dear to us.'

Bond headquarters issued a statement calling a halt to banquets. 'Hereafter when a society or city wants to pay its respects to the representative of the youngest republic, the celebration must take the form of a rally for Irish Republic bond certificates.'[8]

Strike!

State chairmen and local organisers started to receive complaints. Word got about that subscribers who had given their money to bond workers were not receiving their certificates. On 2 February, O'Mara wrote to McGarrity.

We have received today a *very urgent* request from Mr. John D. Moore, Acting Chairman for the Borough of Manhattan, for delivery of the Bond Certificates. He holds it to be important in the interest of the Campaign that these should be available. Will you kindly let us know the earliest date at which we may expect the Certificates.[9]

O'Mara added a handwritten note. 'In a bad way for Bond certs. Hurry them up.' The credibility of the bond drive was at stake. The inability of headquarters to issue bond certificates to subscribers exposed local organisers to accusations of inefficiency and misappropriation of funds.

McGarrity was not in a position to fix the problem, however. He had secured the services of a specialist printer six days *after* the launch of the bond drive. Under the terms of the contract with E. A. Wright of Philadelphia, 478,300 bond certificates at a cost of $13,492 would be delivered in mid-March, seven weeks after the launch.[10] This expected delivery time would have been two weeks shorter if bond headquarters had returned the design proofs within the time specified in the contract.[11]

On 5 March Boland noted in his diary, 'Bond Cert. trouble with Printers. I get busy.'[12] Incredibly, Boland had made a complaint to E. A. Wright about their employment practices. The company issued a formal reply to McGarrity, stating that it ran an 'open Shop' that did not discriminate against the employment of union labour, and that the presses operated for the printing of the bonds were manned by union labour.[13] The company was 'ready to start deliveries as soon as you advise.' But Boland had stirred up a hornet's nest. Two weeks later, the International Steel and Copper Plate Printers Union informed McGarrity that it had entered a protest against E. A. Wright.[14] McGarrity immediately contacted the union, which agreed not to enter any further protest; it was not its desire to 'embarrass or inconvenience' his work on the bond drive, and the contract had been signed and two-thirds paid.[15]

Another design alteration resulted in a further delay to certificate delivery. On 26 March, the company wrote to McGarrity. 'We hope that you will be in position to let us know about delivery of the bonds in the *very near future*.'[16] Finally, on 26 April, bond headquarters sent out its first certificates.[17] The ACII apologised for the 'unavoidable delays' in the preparation and engraving of the certificates.[18] But having the certificates did not solve the problem of getting them into people's hands. The ACII was also experiencing an 'unavoidable' delay in the registration of subscribers. They had records of the money deposited into local bank accounts by organisers and application forms submitted by them, but reconciling one to the other was proving to be an enormous problem. The ACII said that certificates would be forwarded 'as expediously as the necessary work of registering allows.'

Then Boland received the bad news that McGarrity had become seriously ill. 'Doctors say Joe will not recover for a year. Terrible loss to us. I have no doubt that Joe's breakdown has been brought on by overwork.'[19]

Everything's fine – but we must have more help!

Philadelphia had raised just 20 per cent of its quota six weeks after the launch of the bond drive.[20] On 8 February, McGarrity had told Boland that he was not satisfied with arrangements in the city.[21] Leading by example, he subscribed $5,000 to the drive.

Two days later, Judge Bonniwell, the state chairman, declared 'Everything's fine – but we must have more help!'[22] It turned out that raising funds was not a *relatively simple affair* as the *Irish Press* had declared two months earlier.[23] State readiness had not been 'perfected down to the smallest electoral unit'.[24] Bonniwell expected the drive to be fully under way 'as soon as the ward and county chairmen have completed their lists of workers.' He complained that newspapers had failed to support the drive in the way they had supported those of other European peoples.[25] Bond organisers were also combating influenza, pneumonia and recurring blizzards. Illness had 'almost decimated the ranks.'[26] The wife of the city chairman in Scranton had died in the epidemic.[27] It was not possible to set a date for concluding the campaign.[28]

The *Irish Press* endeavoured to maintain morale. Bonniwell, the 'peppery jurist', was looking for a 'handsome oversubscription' and was as sure of success as he was a few weeks previously.[29] An editorial made the rather incredible claim that the Irish bond was impacting the sale of English bonds by J.P. Morgan. 'From all over the country there are reports of *mild* complaints made by bankers that the success of the Irish loan seems *somehow* to operate against the banks' ability to clear out of their strong boxes these British securities which they would like the investing public to take off their hands.'[30]

The status of the bond drive in Philadelphia became critical in late February. For the *Irish Press* it was convenient to run the headline, 'To delve into the reasons would be useless'.[31] The paper praised the beleaguered troops. 'Faced by almost every conceivable obstacle, the workers and chairmen have plunged ahead to the best of their ability. They have met with illness, bad weather, controversy prompted by the Ulster mission [a unionist delegation that had been sent to counter de Valera] and numerous other factors that have hindered them.' State organisers estimated they needed at least 10,000 workers to continue the house-to-house canvass.

De Valera was drafted in to speak at the Metropolitan Opera House in Philadelphia on 7 March to mark the 'reinauguration' of the bond drive.[32] A campaign had been launched to reach $500,000 before his arrival. Bonniwell adopted a new slogan – *Half a Million for De Valera*. 'With $500,000 in hand,' declared the *Irish Press*, 'it will be *easy* to obtain the other half million'.[33] Within days, however, Bonniwell said the slogan 'should not be too strictly interpreted.'[34]

The bond promotional film produced in Ireland was shown in the city.[35] Michael Collins and Diarmuid O'Hegarty, the secretary to the cabinet and senior officer in the Irish Volunteers, were seen taking subscriptions from a who's who of Irish revolutionary figures. Collins later reported to the Dáil that the seven-minute film, which was intended for use principally in America, had done 'very great service' there.[36] Harry Boland saw the chance to poke fun at his friend. 'That film of yourself and Hegarty selling Bonds brought tears to my eyes. Gee Boy! You are some movie actor. Nobody could resist buying a bond and we having such a handsome minister of finance.'[37] The film had been shown a good deal in Ireland too, where some cinemas may have been forced to show it at gunpoint; 'it was planned for a few volunteers in fast cars to visit certain cinemas, rush the operator's box, and, at gun-point, force the operator to take off the film he was showing, and put on the Loan film.'[38]

New York holding its own

The bond drive had gotten off to a reasonably good start in New York City, helped by Devoy's mobilisation of Clan-na-Gael. By the end of the first week $315,000 had been raised.[39] Although well short of the enthusiastic pledges made at the Lexington Theatre, Devoy never considered feasible the plan to raise the entire funds in a single week. The New York organisers faced the same difficulties as those in Philadelphia. Mobilising voluntary bond workers, even in the cause of Irish freedom, proved difficult in freezing weather conditions and during the influenza and pneumonia outbreaks. The *Gaelic American* issued a call for more volunteers.[40]

By late January, the daily total number of influenza cases in the city was more than the corresponding period during the 1918 pandemic, though official reporting had not been fully implemented at that time, and the mortality rate was now lower.[41] The city implemented regulations changing business hours to spread traffic over a longer period of time and to prevent overcrowding on the transportation lines, though the winter storms caused havoc with the traffic relief plan. Transport workers were encouraged to stop spitting and complaints were received about the lack of ventilation and overcrowding in buses. There was very little sickness in the schools, where special instructions had been issued to management, but there was a 'pressing need' for more nurses. The mayor's office was looking to see if something could be done to stop the tenant evictions.[42]

At a large rally for bond workers in Manhattan in early February, which went ahead despite the 'most terrible blizzard since 1888', it was conservatively estimated that Manhattan had passed the half-million dollar mark.[43] It was commented on, however, that affluent Irish–Americans had been alienated, and only the 'least wealthy' had subscribed to the drive.[44]

William Butler Yeats arrived in the city on 24 January for a lecture tour of the United States and Canada. 'For my part, I only know in a general way the big political issues, for I am not a politician,' he told waiting reporters anxious for his comments on the situation at home, 'but I do know that something must be done in Ireland.'[45] Yeats had no opinion on the bond drive, explaining that he 'always kept clear of high finance.'

Midwest blues

The bond drive is 'slow and hard and wearisome' wrote Liam Mellows on 9 March from the Hotel Sinton in Cincinnati.

> In Chicago they had no organisation to handle it – haven't had a real organisation for years, but they mean well ... I've been through many towns in *Illinois* speaking, but they are not ready for bond cert buying because they didn't know the first thing about Ireland. Reason – no organisation: no attempt made to organise. In *Ohio*, it is much the same. Such ignorance – even among the 'saved' – you never saw.[46]

The 27-year-old Mellows, a 1916 veteran who had been elected to the Dáil in absentia in 1918, had a troubled time since his escape to America. Until the previous summer, his life was 'misery night and day ... I wished Oh dear God, a thousand times that I'd never survived the Rising.' [47] He had just recovered from a mild recurrence of influenza. Believing that the situation in New York was partly to blame for his illness, he was 'horrified beyond measure' at Devoy's editorials, though he also rebuked McCartan for publishing the *Sun* article.[48] In a detailed analysis of the *Gazette* interview, he strongly defended de Valera. Having initially counselled restraint he now wondered 'whether a definite break or a tiding over was the best course.'[49] But he had a sense of sorrow that matters had reached this stage with Devoy, noting, 'the old man can never be the same to me. I regret it for it pains me.' There was no sympathy for Cohalan, however. 'As to the Judge – well, the least said, the soonest mended.'

Mellows was at the coal face of the bond campaign. 'John Devoy spoke of the country being splendidly organised before Dev came. How Silly! There was and is practically no organisation. The NY gang had done nothing to help the drive, but everything to hinder it'.[50] But Mellows had seen the poor organisation in Illinois and Ohio when on tour with de Valera five months earlier, and Boland knew then that Chicago would not come up to expectation in the bond drive.[51] The ACII had done nothing to rectify the situation in the intervening time.[52]

Mellows appeared out of touch, or deliberately coy, on the political machinations going on around him. He wrote that there was not the same situation in Chicago as in New York 'and for the most part all mean very well.' But John McGarry had warned Cohalan in January that he greatly feared for the success of the bond campaign in Chicago because of 'back-firing all the time.'[53] Mellows' own appointment had been made to block a troublesome local organiser getting the role.

When the bond campaign had launched in Cincinnati on 7 February at the Sinton Hotel, the *Irish Press* claimed it was a huge success. 'Seldom has an Irish meeting been held in the city at which such a fine spirit of enthusiasm was displayed', it reported, adding that 'upward of $10,000 was subscribed in a few minutes.'[54] The reality was very different. The main speaker that evening was Peter Golden, leader of the Irish Progressive League. Two days earlier, Golden had informed Frank Walsh that he was having trouble organising support for the campaign in Cincinnati.[55] Helen Golden, one of the founding members of the Irish Progressive League, wrote to her husband, 'Of course we've known the split would come, but *too bad* it had to come during the bonds.'[56]

Across the mid-west, the bond campaign was in trouble. The chairman in Indianapolis resigned less than two weeks after the campaign had commenced. A replacement could not be found because those interested in the role had refused it because 'so and so is taking an active part.'[57] The Iowa state chairman was 'disappointed and disgusted' with the lack of interest shown by Irish–Americans in the campaign.[58] Complaining to Frank Walsh about the poor organisation, he said, 'The so-called Irish leaders that I have personally met and who were shooting off the hot air during this entire campaign to my mind could not successfully run a ward caucus.'[59]

Opposition

State Department officials called for a 'firm policy' against the sale of the bonds to prevent United States territory being used 'to further rebellion against a friendly nation.'[60] The administration was urged to take action notwithstanding the misgivings of 'politicians on the eve of the election'. On 7 February, the secretary of agriculture, David F. Houston, wrote to Frank Walsh demanding that the exchange of Liberty Bonds for the Irish bonds be stopped.[61] Around the same time, the *New York Times* published a letter quoting the full text of Section 13 of the Criminal Code, 'Organising military expeditions against friendly power'.[62] The paper carried reports on the bond campaign next to stories on violence in Ireland: 'IRISH POLICE BARRACKS ATTACKED BY 100 MEN, Repeated Rifle Volleys Riddle Buildings in County Galway - Bombs Demolish Walls.'[63]

Financial newspapers lay into the bond drive with vigour. *The Street* displayed its opposition in an editorial with racial undertones. 'The new so-called "Irish loan" is very Irish in its confusion of terminology, and has all the originality, the bright disregard of common sense characteristic of the Irish.'[64] It regretted that the federal authorities lacked the 'political courage to stop the absurd but dangerous Irish loan swindle.' The newspaper was concerned that de Valera's 'worthless' certificates would bring all foreign stocks and shares into disrepute in the public mind. A valid criticism, but the editorial went on to attack 'mongrel' American politicians indorsing the bond through fear of the 'hypothetical' Irish vote, and the 'assorted collection of cranks, socialists, pacifists and former pro-German traitors to this country.' The *New York Times* covered the editorial in its columns.

The *Wall Street Journal* criticised the so-called "Bonds" of the "Irish Republic". 'Are these being sold to Irish domestic servants, and others of a like or lower standard of intelligence, as a legitimate investment for money in the savings banks?'[65] Politicians were 'too cowardly' to tackle the sale of a bond directed against a friendly nation, and the paper asked it there had ever been 'any accounting' of the 'hundreds of millions of dollars subscribed to Irish agitation in this country in the past eighty years.'

Bombshell

'What on earth is wrong with Mr. O'Mara?' Collins wrote despairingly to Boland on hearing that the head of the bond drive had submitted his resignation and asked to be relieved of his duties at the earliest possible date. 'There always seems to be something depressing coming from the U.S.A.,' he added.[66] He recognised that O'Mara's resignation would be a serious blow to the bond campaign and to the credibility of the entire Irish mission. 'Mr. Griffith is writing to Mr. O'Mara appealing to him to re-consider the question,' Collins informed Boland, 'as his action, if persisted in, would have a really bad effect here – very much worse than the Gaelic American difference.'

Collins was worn out. 'I cannot tell you how despondent this particular incident has made me. No doubt I am over touched in this matter, but yet, after a pretty hard year, every little divergence tells heavily.'[67] In addition to his financial responsibilities, Collins was conducting an intelligence war and, in the first three months of the year, had authorised the shooting of Assistant Commissioner Redmond, who had come within a hair's breadth of capturing him, three undercover British agents, and Alan Bell, a near-retired resident magistrate and former detective.

Bell had been appointed by Lord French to go after the loan funds that had been laundered into the commercial banks. He set up a criminal bank inquiry under the Crimes Act 1887, forcing Collins to delay dealing with a $200,000 bank draft that had come from America. On 20 March, Collins wrote to Nunan, 'Oh yes, I am fully aware of all the little troubles you have had in the New World, but the little troubles here are so absorbing that one is inclined to forget them.'[68] Six days later Alan Bell lay prone in front of the railings of the Royal Dublin Society, his shooting making the front page of the *New York Times*.

O'Mara's decision to resign was difficult to comprehend, and Boland considered it a 'very severe blow', noting that 'some serious crisis has overtaken Jim.'[69] He endeavoured to change his mind. 'I have long chat with him. Use all my persuasive power.'[70] In a private note asking Boland to hand his resignation letter to de Valera, O'Mara assured him that the root cause went 'away and beyond either the position at the moment or indeed the struggle at all.'[71] O'Mara had also requested to be replaced as a trustee of the Dáil loan funds and for a replacement to be found for him in his South Kilkenny constituency. He was retiring from all public life. In a letter home addressing his decision to resign as a trustee, he explained that his action was due to 'circumstances which I have been unable to control, it is impossible for me to continue in office.'[72]

O'Mara's daughter Patricia described him as being 'irritable and on edge and crotchety.'[73] His wife had not succeeded in securing a passport to follow him to New York. De Valera noted the 'strain which I have seen only too clearly has been affecting your health.'[74] In his resignation letter, O'Mara offered no explanation but justified the timing. He had 'succeeded in setting up the organisation for the issue of the loan; all the machinery of which is running smoothly and the work largely routine.'[75] In his short time in New York, O'Mara had done much to enhance the poor organisation structure he had inherited, but there was still work to be done.

De Valera was concerned that blame for O'Mara's resignation would be put on him. Having admitted to his own stubbornness, and ascribing his difficulties with Cohalan to personality issues, he had to reassure Griffith on O'Mara's resignation. 'It is purely on private grounds. We have worked together in the greatest harmony, and his services have been invaluable.'[76] One contemporary view disputed de Valera's explanation to Griffith. 'This statement was certainly misleading,' wrote Piaras Béaslaí. 'Mr. O'Mara had decided differences of opinion with Mr. De Valera, and resigned because he did not feel able to continue to work with him.'[77]

De Valera bought time by waiting until April to send the resignation letter to Dublin, along with his own correspondence to O'Mara, in which he attempted to guilt O'Mara into staying, by writing that 'if you leave me now I must cancel the tour [of the southern states] which would be a serious loss.'[78] He was more concerned about the optics. 'Your resignation would be misrepresented and misconstrued. Certain persons are, as you know, but waiting for a vantage point to attack. I hate to make it so hard for you but you know I am stating the conditions as they are.'[79]

In another letter, which he knew would be read at home, de Valera resorted to a base attempt to persuade O'Mara, who had given a lifetime of service to Ireland, to remain in his role. 'Your decision to leave at once will *let us down badly*.' This was followed by an empty threat that he would have to withdraw from his political activities 'so as to devote myself entirely to the winding up of the Bond campaign.'[80] De Valera commented that O'Mara's health 'seems to stand the strain pretty well now.' He made a final personal entreaty to defer his departure for a month or two, noting 'you know the campaign that has been taking place underground – and how every opportunity will be seized.' He then reminded O'Mara, who needed no reminding, of the difficulties under which those in Dublin functioned 'and the way every incident here will be exaggerated and distorted in the public eye under these circumstances.'

'At last de Valera broke Dad's resistance,' recalled O'Mara's daughter, 'perhaps against his better judgement.'[81]

Funding fight

De Valera had interfered with O'Mara's attempts to source much needed funds to launch the bond drive. On 29 December, O'Mara had sent a letter to the FOIF requesting a *further* loan of $100,000 towards the expenses of the campaign.[82] The FOIF had agreed to the additional loan on condition that a written request was received from de Valera, but he did not want to take another loan from the FOIF, even if O'Mara was in desperate need for funds.

At a meeting of the bond advisory committee at the Waldorf, de Valera 'emphatically stated' that all expenses incurred in connection with the bond campaign should be borne from the receipts of the drive, 'as the financing of the issue was properly a matter for the Government of

Ireland'.[83] At the 9 January meeting of the National Council, O'Mara withdrew his request for a further loan.

> I am now *hoping* that the loan of $100,000 so gladly placed at the disposal of President de Valera for preliminary expenses of the Irish Loan … *will be sufficient* for the purpose – and will be promptly repaid as desired by your executive.[84]

Lynch later denied that prompt repayment had been requested. Instead, the National Council converted the first $100,000 loan given to the ACII into a subscription to the bond. It also confirmed as a gift the $26,748 paid towards the expenses of de Valera's tour.[85] O'Mara thanked the Council.[86] To a motion expressing appreciation of Cohalan's performance at the Mason Bill hearing, O'Mara 'added his congratulations to the Irish Race in America on having Justice Cohalan as their leader.'

In his quest for funds to launch the drive, O'Mara was dragged into the dispute between Lynch and McGarrity on the retention of the Irish Victory Fund proceeds by some FOIF branches. Although the bulk of the proceeds of the fund had reached headquarters, $150,000 remained at branches.[87] De Valera irritated O'Mara when he promised to assist Lynch in getting the funds transmitted to the FOIF headquarters, and irritated Lynch when he failed to deliver on the promise.[88] On 15 January, with no sign of intervention, Lynch wrote to de Valera complaining about the growing number of branches in San Francisco, Chicago, Boston and other cities not forwarding their funds. 'At the time of your arrival in America the only city that raised a question about sending the proceeds of the Irish Victory fund to the National Treasurer F.O.I.F. was Philadelphia.'[89] Lynch wrote to O'Mara asking him to advise if similar arrangements had been agreed with other local branches.[90] He did not receive an immediate response.

The relationship between O'Mara and Lynch disintegrated further when the Irish mission attempted to take control of the entire proceeds of the Victory Fund. O'Mara first requested an update on the 25 per cent of the fund allocated to the bond drive as voted by the National Council on 11 June 1919.[91] Lynch replied that until the outstanding balances reached the national treasurer, it would not be possible to determine what 25 per cent of the total proceeds would amount to.[92]

On 10 April O'Mara addressed another letter to Lynch, in which he claimed that the 'entire proceeds' of the Victory Fund, not just 25 per cent, belonged to Ireland and he asked for a breakdown of the receipts and expenditures to date.[93] Lynch believed the 'decidedly provocative' request was made on the expectation of refusal to give foundation to charges against Cohalan on misuse of the Victory Fund proceeds.[94] Three days later Boland took O'Mara to meet Lynch, 'hell of a row ... O'Mara goes off at Lynch in great style. My efforts at peace-maker fail.'[95] Boland was 'reluctantly forced to the opinion that Lynch thinks more of Cohalan & Co. than of Ireland.'

The National Council adopted a resolution asserting that O'Mara's 'misunderstanding' of the situation was 'detrimental and should be cleared up'.[96] It stated that an amount in excess of the designated 25 per cent of the Victory Fund had already been sent 'directly and indirectly, to or for the account of our friends in Ireland.' The FOIF had given more than $115,000 for transmission to Ireland since July, before any bond drive funds reached home.[97] The amount increased to more than $250,000, or 25 per cent of the Victory Fund, including the $100,000 contribution to the bond drive and the money gifted to cover de Valera's tour expenses.

The resolution further stated that as proceeds from the bond drive were accumulating and because there was a need for 'sustained educational work' in America on behalf of Ireland and the United States, it needed to maintain a strong treasury. There was logic to this stance. The Irish mission and the government at home did not need access to the FOIF funds. Within a month of the meeting, $3 million had been raised for the bond drive, of which only $235,000 had been sent to Ireland.[98]

19

TE DEUM

Protest too much

Following the McGuire and Ryan peace efforts, de Valera updated the cabinet in a letter from Washington on 6 March.[1] 'The public misrepresentation here has ceased, but there is a good deal of private undermining going on that cannot be stopped, but it may be rendered comparatively innocuous.'[2] Ironically, he continued his own private undermining, enclosing a heavily annotated copy of Cohalan's reply letter to him, which he labelled 'a wilful misrepresentation of my whole attitude', and which 'of course' was written for the American public.

The line-by-line annotations on Cohalan's letter accused him of taking refuge behind Devoy like 'the General who puts the women and children first'. He had been antagonistic from the 'first hour we met', driven by ego and jealousy. 'Alone, with no one to share the credit with him in the public eye, the Judge would have worked wholeheartedly and enthusiastically.' De Valera had even considered returning home or going elsewhere. 'I realised early that nevertheless, and big as this country is it was not big enough to hold the judge and myself.' But he was 'determined' to stay on. De Valera also enclosed a supportive editorial published by one of the Hearst newspapers.

But he still did not feel secure enough in his position. 'I hate "votes of confidence",' wrote Boland to Griffith, 'yet fancy that a vote from the Cabinet would be of service just now to the Chief'.[3] The letter received was not as supportive as de Valera might have hoped. The government

of Ireland was '*gratified* at the success of your great work in indissolu-
bly cementing the bonds of friendship between the Irish and American
Nations.'[4] The annotated letter, the Hearst editorial and the vote of confidence request were still not enough to allay de Valera's insecurity.

He sent another letter four days later, this time from the Waldorf,
entirely devoted to the takedown of Cohalan and the justification of the
Gazette interview.[5] Cohalan had 'pooh poohed' the idea of bonds in any
shape and he had to be carried in the bond matters 'as a *dead weight*' (ten
days earlier Cohalan was in Massachusetts and Rhode Island promoting
the bond). He 'wouldn't play fair … was going around talking behind
our backs.' He didn't want him 'to go near the political end at all.' He
twisted the *Gazette* interview 'out of its plain and obvious meaning' to
'light a fire' that would force him back to Ireland. He had wanted him
sent home with three quarters of a million dollars, 'The biggest sum
any Irish leader ever brought to Ireland'. Cohalan (and Devoy) were
motivated by 'purely personal triumph.' Three months earlier de Valera
stated at the National Council meeting that they had given him 'every
assistance' and 'always found them ready with advice and help.'[6]

De Valera then proceeded to justify his own actions on the management of the bond drive and the *Gazette* interview. He chose the ACII
to manage the bond drive because the FOIF was 'quite inadequate' to
the task. He quoted the first article of the Platt Amendment because
it was germane to the point; 'if I accept one or several even of the 39
articles of the Protestant creed surely it cannot be said that that means I
must accept them all.' The interview would not have been 'misconstrued'
only for the cry raised by the *Gaelic American*, 'the judge really.' It was
'disgusting' to him to have to write this letter. 'I only ask you at home to
remember that I never say anything here which I would not say at home.'

De Valera touched briefly on the recognition campaign, the Mason
Bill and a proposal from Fawsitt, the trade consul, for the Irish government to acquire a 50 per cent stake in four trading ships. He
complimented the military action at home. 'What you are doing is
magnificent. Especially the guerrilla warfare making the enemy forces

concentrate … The Americans are beginning to realise how wonderful your resistance is.'

He concluded by stating that he was 'more optimistic' than when he had arrived. In case his message had not been clear enough, he added a postscript. 'We have some magnificent men here … in fact, except the *one,* I have never met one who isn't with us.'

De Valera asked the cabinet to consider sending McCartan to Russia to ask for official recognition from the Soviet government.[7] 'I hope to get in a day or two a letter of introduction for him from Mr. Martens.' De Valera believed it was worth trying to gain recognition from Russia 'before they settle with Britain', but Moscow was unlikely ever to recognise Ireland ahead of the signing of a crucial trade agreement with the British empire. The cabinet agreed to send a delegation to Russia, but rejected seeking recognition there before it was received in America.[8]

On 13 April Boland noted in his diary, 'Larkin on trial for Criminal Anarchy.'[9] The following day he met with Santeri Nuorteva, the Russian envoy, who asked him for financial assistance. After conferring with O'Mara, Boland wrote cryptically in his diary, 'Enter a new line of ladies' ornaments for security.'[10] The next day O'Mara drew a cheque for $20,000 for a loan to the Soviet government. Boland met Nuorteva again, 'make him happy.'[11] Collateral for the loan were Russian jewels, which Nuorteva told Boland were worth $25,000.[12] Later in the year, de Valera wrote to Boland authorising him to advance another $20,000 to the Russians.[13] No jewels were offered for security this time, but the loan was given on condition that an equivalent amount would be made available to representatives of the Irish government in Moscow when required. The jewels were restored to the Russian government in 1949 on repayment of the original loan. A valuer had advised the Irish government that it 'would be lucky' if they got £2,000 for them.[14]

Gerry Reservation

Cohalan continued to direct the FOIF campaign against the League of Nations, which had assumed a new urgency after Britain and France approved the Treaty of Versailles in January.[15] 'I am naturally happy that peace has finally become effective,' declared Baron Kurt von Lersner, head of the German peace delegation. 'My great regret is that the United States is the only country with which Germany is still in a state of war. I hope, however, that this situation will soon be changed.'[16] Von Lersner regretted that the treaty imposed on Germany the 'heaviest sacrifices ever borne by a nation in modern times.'

The Senate remained polarised on ratification of the treaty. President Wilson, now incapacitated following a stroke, was increasingly reliant on the First Lady, Edith Wilson, who had taken on a 'stewardship' role, with some believing that she was exercising executive authority. True or not, Wilson was uncompromising in demanding his senators oppose any changes to the terms signed in Paris. But a group of 'mild' reservationist Democrats expressed willingness to accept changes to the treaty in the hope of winning over wavering Republicans. On the other side, Henry Cabot Lodge demanded radical changes as specified in his now four-teen reservations. But under pressure from the Republican leadership to get the treaty off the political agenda before the presidential election, he had set up a series of bipartisan conferences. Senator Borah, leader of the small but powerful Irreconcilables, helped scupper any hopes of compromise by threatening to 'no longer respect or co-operate with the [Republican] party organization in the Senate.'[17]

On 17 March, two days before the final vote on the treaty, Senator Peter Gerry of Rhode Island introduced an unexpected fifteenth reservation that when the Irish people attained a government of their own choice 'it should promptly be admitted as a member of the League of Nations.'[18] Gerry, a freshman Democrat with no Irish heritage, was the great-grandson of Elbridge Gerry, the fifth vice-president of the United States, after whom the practice of gerrymandering was named.

The Gerry reservation lead to a heated Senate debate that examined various other reservations covering the independence of Egypt and Korea, and self-determination for all subject peoples, including the Philippines, Puerto Rico and Hawaii. The exchanges grew 'sarcastic and denunciatory'.[19] The Gerry reservation was finally carried by a vote of forty-five to thirty-eight the following day. De Valera immediately cabled Griffith believing he had achieved the great political victory he desperately needed to bring home. 'A Te Deum should be sung throughout all Ireland...*Our mission has been successful.*'[20] But he had jumped the gun.

The next day the Senate voted against ratification of the treaty. America would not be joining the League of Nations. The Gerry resolution had passed only out of political expediency. Boland noted in his diary, 'Irish Reservation was very clever move on Democrats part.'[21] The *New York Tribune* reported that the reservation had been proposed to make the treaty defeat 'certain'. Most observers had expected the *clean* treaty to be defeated. Democrats wanted to ensure that the treaty including the Lodge reservations also failed in the Republican-controlled Senate, avoiding Wilson having to apply his presidential veto, and thereby being blamed for America's rejection of the treaty.[22] Sixteen senators who voted in favour of the Gerry resolution voted against the treaty.[23]

If the Gerry resolution was an almost victory for de Valera, the final defeat of the League of Nations was another triumph for Cohalan. On 2 February, he had written to Senator Borah that 'reports from all over the country are entirely satisfactory as to the rising state of popular opposition to the whole British scheme'.[24] Two weeks later, at the monthly meeting of the National Council, Cohalan updated those present on the 'steps taken' in support of senators opposed to the League covenant.[25] Lynch sent telegrams across the country encouraging the holding of public meetings to demand the rejection of the League and to support senators 'who were standing up for true Americanism.'[26] In early March, Cohalan expressed his confidence to Borah. 'I believe a final triumph for America is in sight.'[27] After the vote, Cohalan wrote to Senator Hiram Johnson to congratulate him on the 'splendid work' he had done for the country in helping to defeat the League.[28] The *Gaelic American* endorsed Johnson for president.

Mason 'Resolution'

The Mason Bill, providing an appropriation for salaries for a minister and consuls to the Republic of Ireland, had remained stuck in committee for months; a political hot potato that neither party wanted to touch. De Valera had come around to the view that a *resolution*, which would be non-binding, rather than a bill, was the best that could be achieved. He gave a copy of his new resolution, which still referred to the Irish Republic, to Boland to give to Congressman Mason. In a letter to Griffith on 6 March, de Valera informed the cabinet of his decision.

> The Mason Bill has no chance of passing, for difficulties will be raised on purely technical grounds [Congress encroaching on Executive power to recognise new states] … In order to avoid the constitutional difficulties I suggested the enclosed. It is not of course quite as good as the Bill would be, but as there was no hope whatever that the Bill would pass, and as *time is pressing* all our friends here, *even the Judge*, consider this move wise.[29]

On 27 May the original bill, voted on as part of procedure, was defeated in committee by a vote of fifteen to five. De Valera's resolution was defeated thirteen to seven. But a backup had been prepared; five days earlier, at a meeting in the Irish National Bureau in Washington, de Valera had accepted that a flat defeat of his substitute resolution was politically unadvisable. In front of three congressmen and Captain O'Connell, he dictated an alternative resolution to Cohalan, this time making no reference to the Irish Republic.[30] The resolution was an expression of *sympathy* for the aspirations of the Irish people for a government of their own. The House committee on 28 May adopted the non-binding concurrent resolution.

The watered-down resolution was attacked by those in the Irish movement not privy to the smoke-filled back room committee negotiations. At a meeting of the National Council, Cohalan confirmed that de Valera had dictated and revised the draft resolution. McCartan challenged him on this, stating that de Valera had denied to him that he had drafted it. In response, Cohalan produced the document on which the resolution had been taken down with revisions in de Valera's handwriting. McCartan later described his version of what happened.

Cohalan openly affirmed that de Valera had drafted it. Instantaneously I denied this charge. Cohalan confounded me by drawing from his pocket a manuscript of the resolution — the first part of which — and the only part I looked at — was beyond doubt in de Valera's handwriting. I went straight to de Valera. He explained to me he had tried to draft a suitable resolution, and, having failed, threw the paper on the table, and that *evidently* Cohalan had finished it.'[31]

20

FINAL ROLL OF THE DICE

The Plank

De Valera returned from a troubled tour of the southern states in early May, where he had been greeted by smaller crowds and had met increased opposition, fuelled by anti-Catholicism, a rejuvenated Ku Klux Klan and some disgruntled American Legion members. He was desperate to return home, or at least leave America, and had even mooted a visit to South America.

The anniversary of his arrival in America was approaching; he needed a victory, and saw an opportunity for one in the Republican convention opening on 8 June in Chicago. He was going to stake everything on a convention strategy that even his closest advisers, including Frank Walsh, opposed.[1] He planned to go to Chicago himself, despite being advised that overt meddling in domestic politics by foreign representatives was deeply frowned upon. He was going to secure a plank recognising the Irish Republic by a direct appeal to delegates through a 'brass band' campaign of torchlight parades, marching bands, circus posters and banners.

While de Valera was on tour, the FOIF had set up a convention committee, with diplomatic groundwork and political manoeuvring done by Captain O'Connell and the bureau in Washington.[2] Cohalan believed that it was 'absurd' to use brass band methods to attempt to coerce delegates and party leaders.[3] 'For months the American leaders of the Irish cause had planned and worked to secure assistance from party conventions. The plans were working out smoothly and effectively.'

De Valera chose to work independently of the FOIF. The full Irish mission was summoned to the Windy City, taking O'Mara and Nunan away from the bond drive, as were the state chairmen who were asked to canvas delegates.[4] 'There was no chance of offending America that we did not take,' said McCartan of the brass band tactics adopted.[5] 'De Valera is not really a candidate at this convention,' ran a clever cartoon in the *Chicago Tribune*.

De Valera intended to appear before the resolutions sub-committee himself, but was persuaded of the impropriety of doing so. Instead, the delegation was led by Frank Walsh, a liberal labour lawyer at a Republican convention, and Congressman Mason. Their resolution asked the convention to favour full recognition of the elected government of the Republic of Ireland.[6] The resolution had no possibility of getting through the sub-committee. Just ten days earlier, the Mason Resolution had been diluted to an expression of sympathy, after which de Valera had written to the cabinet, 'It simply means that the Republicans are rather afraid of their constituents to declare strongly for Ireland'.[7]

Cohalan arrived in Chicago the day after de Valera. The FOIF leaders, including Mayor Grace of Charleston, finalised a resolution that they believed would get through the sub-committee, and ultimately the full committee.[8] The resolution called on the Republican party to place on record its sympathy with all oppressed peoples *and* to recognise the principle that the people of Ireland have the right to determine 'their own governmental institutions and their international relations with other States and peoples.'[9] The wording was a clear advance on an expression of sympathy.

A meeting was held on 8 June between de Valera and a committee of the FOIF delegation to find a compromise resolution, at which de Valera insisted on the Irish Republic wording.[10] One of those who attended the meeting, John Archdeacon Murphy of Buffalo, reported back to the full FOIF delegation of twenty-five prominent Irish–Americans from across the United States.

Finally, I asked him, 'Do I understand your position? Would you prefer to have defeated your Resolution, rather than victory upon Mayor Grace's Resolution?' He answered he would.[11]

Frank Walsh and Congressman Mason appeared before the resolutions sub-committee at 2pm on the following day. With only Senator Borah voting in favour, their resolution was rejected by a comprehensive vote of twelve to one. Two hours later, it was the turn of the FOIF delegation. Although a lifelong Democrat, Cohalan had nurtured close ties with many Republican senators and, as an American citizen, he could appear in front of the sub-committee, but he ceded to a FOIF delegation of Republican party members. The resolution was recommended by a vote of seven to six on the casting vote of the chairman. It was another victory for Cohalan and a further step towards recognition.

De Valera immediately came out in opposition; he planned to get his own resolution back on the agenda by attacking the FOIF one from the floor of the convention.[12] He told reporters the resolution left 'the Irish question exactly where it was so far as America is concerned'.[13] But the plan backfired catastrophically. There was no Irish plank in the final platform.[14] The *Chicago Tribune* described what happened while de Valera was busy 'denouncing' the Cohalan plank. 'While they were fighting, the full Republican resolution committee of fifty-five *killed* the Cohalan plank by a viva voce vote.'[15] The sub-committee chairman had also withdrawn his casting vote and the resolution was reported to the full committee as a tie.[16] The *New York Times* explained the rationale of the committee's decision: 'If the Irish were divided among themselves there would be less danger in ignoring them altogether.'[17]

The absence of an Irish plank on the Republican party platform was both an embarrassment and a huge setback to the recognition campaign. McCartan and others attributed the intensification of British military activity in Ireland to the failure in Chicago, though the British had already been regrouping for some months after their loss in the first battle of the intelligence war.[18]

A clearly satisfied Sir Auckland Geddes, the British ambassador to the United States, summed up the tactical failure.

> The incident illustrates in an interesting manner the immense influence Irishmen can exert on American politicians if they proceed wisely; and how ready American politicians are to withdraw themselves from that influence if they can find some colourable pretext for doing so.[19]

De Valera was forced to request a second letter of confidence from the cabinet. The message received by cable was necessarily much stronger in tone. Dáil Éireann in full session in Dublin 'unanimously re-affirms the allegiance of the citizens of Ireland to your policy, expresses complete satisfaction with the work you have performed.'[20]

But it was clear that de Valera had implemented the wrong strategy in Chicago, one that went against the advice of astute political operators, including McGuire who believed a straight recognition resolution could not be successful at a convention during the closing days of Congress in a presidential election year. As he explained to Cohalan, Ireland was 'far from their thoughts.' The Republican leadership had several months previously advised House leaders to 'soft-pedal or stop all Irish resolutions.' Since then the question had been one of 'battledore and shuttlecock' between both parties. 'This I had tried to point out to the President but with no success.'[21] He informed Cohalan that the failure in Chicago left Democrats 'chortling with glee.'[22] There was now no pressure on them to pass a strong resolution to retain the Irish vote that had been drifting towards the Republican party. McGuire asked after Cohalan's health and advised him to get a good rest that summer.

Aftermath

The *Gaelic American* reported on the Chicago convention under the headline, 'De Valera Prevented Action on Ireland'.[23] For the first time, Devoy criticised de Valera's *actions* rather than his policy statements, after a year in America. Devoy was forced into the criticism in order to refute false allegations that the FOIF had made no preparation in advance of the convention and that Cohalan had sprung the FOIF resolution on de Valera at the last minute.

Devoy made a tactical mistake in accusing de Valera of spending $50,000 on the convention campaign out of bond proceeds intended for use in Ireland. De Valera denied the size of the expenditure and countered that he had authorisation from home, having requested approval for expenditure of up to $500,000 to influence the presidential campaign and up to $1 million to obtain recognition of the Irish Republic. A letter written on 8 June confirmed cabinet approval, though the Dáil did not give authorisation until 29 June.[24] On 19 April, however, Collins had authorised expenditure by de Valera of between $250,000 and $500,000 at his discretion. Collins did not know at the time if formal Dáil approval would be required.

De Valera proposed another straight recognition resolution at the Democratic convention in San Francisco at the end of June. It, too, was rejected. He had no choice; he could hardly row back to a more achievable target after criticising the Cohalan resolution in Chicago. The FOIF decided not to attend the convention; it had come out in support of Hiram Johnson in the presidential campaign.

The defeat in San Francisco caused de Valera to belatedly appreciate the benefit and necessity of the FOIF education campaign.

> A more systematic and thorough organisation of the friends of the cause in America is now shown necessary and will be made. *An intensive campaign of education will be carried into every State and will reach every citizen. The heart of America is with us. We must capture its intellect.*[25]

Boland, too, now understood what Cohalan meant when he said that America would only grant recognition when it was in her strategic interest. 'I fear ... that we will not achieve Recognition until it is expedient for America to so recognise us.'[26]

21

POST TRUTH

Round two

McCartan and Maloney saw another opportunity to take down Cohalan in the wake of de Valera's faux-pas in Chicago; it being plainly necessary to explain away the failure at the convention and to deflect from the *Gaelic American*'s attribution of fault on de Valera. The chosen strategy was to pin the blame on Cohalan in another orchestrated press campaign, in both the Irish weeklies and the daily papers across the country, and through messages to the leaders at home.

Cohalan knew what was coming. At the convention, after it became known that there was no Irish plank on the final platform, supporters of de Valera put it about that Cohalan had deliberately opposed a strong resolution for his own political ambitions. Reporters were told that he supported the candidacy of Democrat William McAdoo 'and that he wanted a weak plank adopted by the Republicans so that the Democrats could gain votes by adopting a strong plank.'[1] This was patent nonsense given Cohalan's known support for the candidacy of Hiram Johnson and the *Gaelic American*'s endorsement of the Californian senator. Another rumour was circulated that Cohalan had made a bargain with Johnson not to push an Irish Republic resolution at the convention. Although meant as a criticism of Cohalan, it would have been a sensible tactical manoeuvre. If Johnson became president, with Senator Borah as his secretary of state as speculated, the most proactive Irish supporters would occupy the White House and Foggy Bottom.

The irony of the renewed attack was that McCartan had lost confidence in de Valera. He wrote to McGarrity proposing a conference of friendly Americans to put an end to the feuding, but he did not want de Valera and Boland invited. 'My experience of him and Harry is that they come to a conference not knowing what they want; have an unconscious contempt or seem to have such for opinions of others. The Chief presides and does all the talking … thinks he has co-operation when he only gets silent acquiescence.'[2] Maloney was also critical of de Valera, complaining to McGarrity of his 'political bluff'.[3] But they were content to use de Valera as the means to topple Cohalan and, if necessary, Devoy.

First into battle was William Randolph Hearst fulfilling his pledge to support de Valera. On 18 June an editorial appeared in the *Chicago Herald–Examiner* under the headline, 'We Congratulate the Irish Upon the Tact and Wisdom Displayed by Their President in America'.[4] Bizarrely, the editorial included a retraction statement from Father McCabe, former president of De Paul University, whose comments appeared somewhat counterproductive.

I much regret the misstatements in the interview that appeared this morning in The Herald and Examiner, which would imply that I was at variance in any way whatsoever with President De Valera, or that I considered indelicate or unwise the recent steps that he has seen fit to take as a counsel in our country pleading for his nation.

The editorial added that 'the Hearst papers do not believe that Father McCabe or any other loyal Irish–American is at variance with President De Valera.' Accusations that he had 'butted into' American politics were denied; de Valera's campaign never once over-stepped the 'bounds of good sense and good taste'.

McCartan then 'fired a broadside' at Cohalan in a series of press interviews.[5] He told a reporter from the New York *World* that the judge, 'privately and on several occasions, had tartly hinted that there was no such thing as an Irish Republic.'[6] In an interview with the *New York Call*,

McCartan coined the phrase 'Cohalan Americans' who brought 'contempt upon the whole Irish Race in this country'.[7] The *New York Times* reported McCartan stating that Cohalan had been 'playing with Ireland since the armistice was signed, but selling it every time.'[8] Cohalan had been tolerated because 'the rank and file did not detect his slick work and those he put in power were all merely Cohalan Americans.'

'Treason Most Odious' was the headline in the *Irish World*.[9] Devoy and Cohalan were accused of being part of an underhand conspiracy; they were despots, malignant defamers and sub-cellar plotters. Lacking honesty and decency, they had twisted de Valera's statements in the *Westminster Gazette*, had changed the Mason Bill into a mere resolution of sympathy and were perniciously active at the Republican convention. 'Let us be plain-spoken,' declared the paper. 'Insensate vanity and unbounded ambition are at the bottom of the attacks upon President De Valera ... Their vision is bound by narrow, selfish, personal interests.'

The *Irish Press* declared that Irish–American politicians had defeated the Republic's cause in Chicago.[10] The failure to have an Irish plank included in the platform was 'in part if not entirely due to the fact' that Cohalan had 'refused to cooperate' with de Valera. His policy was to work for the nomination of Senator Johnson 'and nothing else'. He had attacked de Valera in an editorial for the *Gaelic American*. He did not recognise and makes 'no serious attempt to secure recognition for the Republic of Ireland.' The paper published the letter of confidence from the cabinet on its front page.[11]

De Valera then arranged for the Irish foreign affairs minister to put criticism of Cohalan and Devoy into the official Dáil record.

> This portion of my report would be incomplete if I did not refer to the attitude of Supreme Court Judge Daniel F. Cohalan and John Devoy toward President De Valera and his minion. The ministry learns that these two men have never given their whole-hearted support to the President in his mission.

At the very outset they used their utmost endeavour to prevent a launching of the Bond Drive, and they attempted to force the President into the position of accepting their dictation in all matter of policy connected with his mission.

The President has definitely refused to allow his judgment or his action to be dictated by these men and the success of his tour and of the Bond Drive are proof of his wisdom in the matter.[12]

The leaders in Ireland might have been convinced of the success of the struggling bond drive, but people in America knew different. So McCartan and Maloney deflected fault from the Irish mission on to Cohalan. In his New York *World* interview, McCartan declared that Cohalan had been against the bond from the moment of de Valera's arrival.[13] He had said to a prominent Irish–American, 'This fellow won't do; We'll have to pack him home again without selling any bonds.' And Cohalan had told Frank Walsh, 'We cannot allow the sale of Irish bonds.' When the drive launched, Cohalan had pretended to support de Valera while hoping 'to wean him away from the idea of Bonds by masterful inactivity'. He attempted to get control of the money by having his friend Edward McSweeney appointed director of the drive, he wanted American trustees appointed by himself 'of course' to take charge of the money and, after failing to get his hands on the funds, he began to plot the president's destruction before he grew too strong.

Cohalan issued a measured response to the press attacks. 'There is no division in the ranks on any question of principle and I am confident there will be none. Most of those whose names have been mentioned have been working tirelessly and unselfishly for the recognition of the Irish Republic.' He hinted at de Valera's inability to negotiate the American political system. 'I am in this work as an American whose first and only loyalty is to my own country, and as one who for many years has made close study of our governmental machinery and our political methods and institutions.'[14]

The *Gaelic American* was less measured in its response to the 'false and vicious charges', declaring that McCartan had come under the 'evil influence' of Maloney, the 'cleverest and most insidious British agent of modern times'.[15] Devoy repeated his charge that the plot to destroy Cohalan had been planned at the British embassy. He addressed the bond drive accusations against Cohalan under the headline, 'Lies About The Bonds'.[16] Denying that Cohalan was opposed to the bond drive, he went on to say that 'all the Irish leaders in America were opposed to making the call for the Bonds *before* the Victory Fund ... was fully collected.' He explained that the delay in the start of the bond drive was caused by the selection of 'utter incompetent and improper agents', referring to the unnamed Callahan and Elder. McCartan had filled them up with 'falsehoods and calumnies' and they had gone round the country at big salaries attacking Cohalan and other leaders, while lauding President Wilson and the League of Nations. Further delays lasting several months were due to 'bad business methods.'

Messaging to Ireland from Boland and Nunan ensured that Cohalan and Devoy were perceived as the aggressors. When McCartan had gone home to explain away the *Gazette* interview, he had 'forgotten' to mention Cohalan's stand for recognition of the Republic, even at the price of war with Britain, at the Mason Bill hearing, and his statement at the Senate hearing that recognition of the Republic was only a matter of time.[17] Counter letters from Devoy proved futile, as Piaras Béaslaí explained:

> We in Ireland, engaged in a fierce and bloody struggle, were not in a position to study the niceties of American politics. We could only see in the whole controversy an attempt to undermine the influence of the man we had chosen as our representative. In any case it was obviously impossible for us, in the face of the enemy, to 'let down' the man we had elected as President.[18]

Tempest
William Barry, a fireman on a transatlantic passenger ship, was arrested in Southampton carrying pistols, ammunition and letters. Barry was

described by the magistrate as being part of 'a system regularly employed to convey communications between revolutionary leaders in Ireland and their agents and sympathizers in America.'[19]

On 13 July the *Philadelphia Public Ledger* and the *Brooklyn Eagle* published the letters found on Barry. Carl Ackerman, a correspondent for both papers, declared that the letters 'reveal for the first time, in the words of American Sinn Feiners, the tempest within the ranks of Irish leaders in the United States.'[20]

Boland's diary reaction to the publication of the seized letters was understated. 'Barry's capture gives the full report of Chicago and Sean Nunan's letter makes things awkward for us'.[21] Boland added cryptically, 'practice code messages, on the run from Chicago.'

In one of the letters Nunan advised Collins that it was time for action against Clan-na-Gael and that the fight was 'now on' against the Cohalan group. He was also sending '400 rounds, 900 automatic revolvers, forty-eight of filling for same, two spare magazines, and a leather case.'[22] Nunan had enough 'hardware' on hand to keep the messenger well stocked for some time to come.

But it was a letter from Nunan to Griffith on the Republican convention which caused the most difficulty for the Irish mission, and de Valera in particular. The account of what happened in Chicago, which was scripted for private consumption by the leaders in Ireland, bared little relationship to what had actually happened before and during the convention. Nunan claimed that de Valera had met Irish leaders in Chicago at the office of Hugh O'Neill, a prominent FOIF leader, where inclusion of a recognition plank in the party platform was agreed at the suggestion of ex-Congressman Gorman, not de Valera. A committee which had been formed to arrange a date and time to present the resolution failed to report back to de Valera, and 'from that day onward they deserted the President altogether.'

Hugh O'Neill publicly denied a meeting took place in his office. The mayor of Chicago 'denied emphatically' that he attended any conferences in the office of Hugh O'Neill.[23] The mayor said that he called upon de

Valera when he came to Chicago, but any private conference mentioned in the letters 'is all fiction.' Mayor Thompson was later close to Al Capone which might explain Boland's 'on the run from Chicago' comment.

The letter continued with the arrival of Cohalan in Chicago, which 'doubtless' accounted for the desertion of the Irish leaders who 'boycotted' de Valera; he was not consulted about Cohalan's resolution, which was a 'great surprise' to him (no mention was made of the meeting on 8 June with the FOIF leaders, or the lengthy preparatory work done in Washington in advance of the convention, of which de Valera was aware). It was claimed that the chairman of the resolutions sub-committee had withdrawn his casting vote because the resolution 'would not be satisfactory to the representatives of the Irish people [so] it was useless to pass it.' The letter did not refer to de Valera's public opposition to the Cohalan resolution, which had resulted in its defeat.

In a bind, de Valera 'utterly repudiated' the account of events in the letter.[24] He explained how the letter '*might* have been written.'

> Whether Mr. Nunan in fact made this memorandum or not, I do not know, as I have not seen him since I gave him verbal instructions to make it before I left for San Francisco. It is not impossible that he sent such a memorandum in the form of a letter with his *own personal comments* to Ireland.

Press coverage of the fracture in the Irish movement reached fever pitch. Boland noted that the row was becoming 'very nasty' in New York with the *Gaelic American*, *Irish World* and *Irish Press* 'lashing the fires'.[25] Pro-English newspapers gleefully reported on the debacle in Chicago, the post-convention criticism of Cohalan and the exposures in the seized letters.[26] On the media frenzy, McCartan later concluded:

> We formed into camps of de Valeraites and Cohalanites each denouncing the other for the ruin of our hopes – to the scandal of America and our own degradation. And while our frenzy lasted we forgot Ireland.[27]

But Devoy had not forgotten Ireland. The *Gaelic American* described the letters as 'painful reading' designed to deceive the leaders in Ireland by misinformation.[28] The claim in the letter that de Valera did not know that the FOIF committee had a plan for the convention, and so had to act himself, was 'too ridiculous to waste any words upon'. Devoy concluded that approval of the warfare conducted in America, which had been going on for a full year, had been obtained from the leaders in Ireland through misrepresentation.

In the wake of the fallout from the Chicago debacle, McGuire informed Cohalan that 'politicians think the divisions in our circles have nullified the fears of the "Irish vote."'[29]

22

ENDGAME

Dishonour

Cohalan and Devoy found themselves in a knotty and ironic position; attacked by the official head of the Irish Republic to which they had given a lifetime of service in establishing. 'It is easy enough for an Irishman to defend himself against the English Government,' Devoy commented in the *Gaelic American*, '… but it is quite another matter when he is unjustly and viruntly attacked by an Irish leader who has the confidence of his countrymen.'[1]

They retained strong support within the FOIF and Clan-na-Gael leadership in New York. Cohalan's official report on the convention was adopted by a vote of sixty to fifteen at a National Council meeting. They had the backing of at least 70% of Clan-na-Gael leaders.[2] But they were losing the support of the rank and file members nationwide. Resolutions passed by many FOIF branches pledged loyalty to de Valera. The propaganda message against them was working. The FOIF branch in Lynchburg noted 'with much regret, and no little indignation' statements in the press showing some FOIF leaders making the fight for recognition of the Republic 'subservient to their own petty pride and political aspirations.'[3]

The constant battles and strife took a heavy toll on Devoy. After spending seven hours in his company, a concerned McGuire wrote to Cohalan. 'I could see the heart of the great veteran was breaking and I resolved to do my utmost in a final effort to compose the differences as far as they could & make every sacrifice possible.'⁴ Back in the role of peacemaker, he was determined to save the FOIF organisation, in whose mission he believed, and Clan-na-Gael, of which he was chairman. He was also determined to defend the reputations of Cohalan and Devoy, who were needed to keep the organisations growing. McGuire warned Cohalan that the 'vile talk now going on over the country beggars description and the morale is very seriously affected.'

His task became increasingly difficult when Boland, with whom he remained a good friend, threatened to sever the connection between Clan-na-Gael and the Irish Republican Brotherhood in Ireland. On 17 August, after agreeing a compromise with Boland to avert the move, McGuire wrote to Devoy to justify his reasons and show that the compromise was in his best interests. 'The action taken … was most necessary to either avert or prevent a split which would cut off the old organization from the revolution and soon destroy it, hasten the end of the *Gaelic American* and shorten your own life under the strain of a deadly and useless struggle, falsely condemned as a traitor in Ireland while misunderstood and abused in this country.'⁵ He tried explaining to Devoy that no defence of 'Americanism' would save the Clan from 'execration in the pages of Irish history'.

Two days later, McGuire appealed to Cohalan to accept the compromise. 'As the President is said to be leaving the country this fall the wisest plan will be to accept the proposals in good faith and your leadership in the F.O.I.F. will carry the ideas through in different form but effectively & no one but you can do this invaluable service.'⁶ He reminded Cohalan of the reputation risk he faced if a compromise was not reached. 'All Irish quarrels start over Issues or Principles or Methods but invariably wind up in Personalities where the vilest epithets & calumnies are uttered & the character of men aspersed or destroyed.' McGuire stressed upon Cohalan that he 'must' make sacrifices again to protect the Clan and the FOIF. 'De Valera is the only one whom revolutionary, cleric, nationalist, labor agrees on and regardless of temperament etc., etc., no effort should be spared to save the organizations here for useful work.'

McGuire then arranged a conference between Boland and Devoy on 24 August. After the meeting, Devoy reported to Cohalan that de Valera was intent on gaining control of the FOIF by forcing through constitutional changes, but he wanted Cohalan to be the leader. Boland had admitted to Devoy that Frank Walsh 'is a failure because he has no organizing ability and you have. So he wants you as leader but evidently to do what you are told.'[7] McGuire did not escape Devoy's criticism, either. 'He wants peace at any price and everything which interferes with that is wrong. He is even ready to deplete our treasury to carry out very doubtful schemes by them.'

Increasingly exasperated by personal criticism, and fuming at moves to take control of the American organisations, Devoy changed editorial policy in the *Gaelic American* to direct attacks on de Valera. This only served to give credence to the view propagated by McCartan and Maloney that it was Devoy who was fomenting division in the Irish movement. In attempting to show de Valera in a bad light, he also earned the wrath of Collins whom he greatly admired.

On 11 September Devoy reprinted an article from the *Philadelphia Public Ledger* reporting on a schism in Sinn Féin. The article was accompanied by a picture of Collins in full military uniform over the text 'Ireland's Fighting Chief'. Moderates, identified as de Valera and Griffith, were 'convinced that Ireland can get the substance of freedom within the Empire for the asking'. The extremists, of whom Collins was the 'strong man', were holding out for a republic. The subtext was that Collins had taken over leadership of the Irish people.

Devoy must have taken some pleasure in reprinting the story. He claimed privately it was not an attack on de Valera, but there was a hint of one, and it was at least mischievous. 'I expect to be told it is an attack on D.V. Well, it is not an attack, but it is a suggestion about Mick. He must have an idea of the ultimate leadership in his Corkonian head.'[8]

Three weeks later Collins wrote to Devoy that it was a 'matter of regret' that he had reproduced the 'ridiculous statements.' His tone was conciliatory, however; the introductory comments to the report were 'quite fair' and he acknowledged that the article was reprinted 'with reserve'.[9] A formal statement for publication formed part of the letter.

> Everyone here at home knows well there is no difference, and knows equally well it is this fact that has been the great strength of our position. Anything which I have said about 'no negotiations' has been said more forcibly and much more ably by both President de Valera and the Acting President, Mr. Griffith.

De Valera may not have been satisfied with Collins' mild rebuke of Devoy. On 14 October Collins issued a more robust criticism on the pretext that at the time of his first letter he had not fully realised the 'complete extent of the bad effects' from reproduction of the article.[10] Collins declared that every member of the cabinet supported de Valera 'against any and every *group* in America who have either not given him the cooperation which they should, or have set themselves definitely to thwart his actions.' He hoped for an apology from Devoy to the president 'for misrepresenting him and by way of apology to other men whose names you have used against their wishes and their inclinations, towards weakening the President's position.'

The *Gaelic American* published the correspondence from Collins next to an editorial reply.[11] Devoy made clear his admiration for Collins, 'there is no man in Ireland for whom the editor has greater respect'. But he rhetorically asked if he agreed with the theory which seemed to be implied in his letter that a 'censorship similar to the English' should be exercised over Irish papers in America, 'or that they should not freely discuss the utterances and actions of Irish leaders in a time of national crisis.' Citing the reference to 'groups' that had not given proper support to the president, he said it showed that Collins 'believes the official lies that have been sent to Ireland and that he has an utterly false notion of actual conditions in America.'

Devoy declared that he had nothing for which to apologise. In fact, he demanded an apology from de Valera and Boland for the 'dishonor' done to him and Cohalan by the statement which they had caused to be inserted in the records of Dáil Éireann. 'John Devoy will insist on an apology for that grievous wrong until his dying day'. And neither would he be deterred by threats of assassination made against him by young Irishmen 'led astray by the most hideous propaganda of falsehood'.

Time to go

'The loan here has not been satisfactory,' de Valera admitted to a gathering in the Waldorf Astoria on the morning of 18 September.[12] The meeting had been hastily arranged after a failed attempt to gain control of the FOIF at a tempestuous National Council meeting the evening before. Not getting what he wanted, de Valera had stormed out of the room, but was persuaded to return, after which he asked those who supported him to gather in the morning, when he informed them that he intended to set up a new organisation. Admitting to the underperformance of the bond drive was the pretext for his action.

> The misrepresentation with respect to the Cuban statement, the misrepresentation as to the happenings in Chicago, and the general campaign conducted to excuse these misrepresentations, coupled with the attacks and counter-attacks which they called forth in different sections of the press, have done us an incalculable harm in the loan as in other respects.
>
> Checks made out in February have been withheld till a few days ago; subscriptions originally made out for large sums, have been cut down; workers have been discouraged and the public disgusted, all through a situation which, one would imagine, was almost wilfully created.

De Valera did not mention the registration crisis at bond headquarters, which had continued to damage the bond drive, even leading to accusations of fraud. 'Owing to the slowness of the delivery of the bonds from New York, unjust suspicions have been manifest by some of the subscribers,' reported the chief organiser in Philadelphia in an update in the *Irish Press* a week earlier.[13] One contributor to the bond drive complained to Lynch:

Some time ago we subscribed to the Irish bond Issue ... After signing the pledge and making the initial payment, however, we have heard nothing further and can secure no information ... It does seem as though quite an amount of money has in this way been lost to the Cause. The condition seems to hold all over.[14]

Angry subscribers unjustly blamed the FOIF for the delay in receiving their certificates, with Lynch receiving hundreds of complaints at 250 Broadway, despite bond administration being in the hands of O'Mara and Nunan at the ACII headquarters.[15] Even Devoy had not received the certificate for his own subscription, which he had made months earlier. 'And there are thousands of others in the same position,' he reported in the *Gaelic American*.[16] He blamed those who were publicly attacking him; while they engaged 'in this harmful propaganda the legitimate work of sending the Bond Certificates to contributors is neglected.'

The bond administration system in Philadelphia was in chaos. 'Many of the subscription cards are still in the hands of the collectors,' reported the chief organiser.[17] 'The subscribers calling at this office to finish payments go away disappointed when their money cannot be accepted.' Many ward leaders had failed to return up-to-date records to headquarters; many had made no returns; some had done 'absolutely nothing.' He threatened to publish the names of the delinquents. There had also been a lack of interest among 'many of our well-to-do citizens.'[18]

On 27 September the ACII announced the closure of the first loan of the Republic of Ireland.[19] New subscriptions would cease to be accepted on 14 October. 'A final and supreme effort to increase the results should at once be made. Bond certificates are being issued to all subscribers *as rapidly as possible*.' The final sum raised in America for the first Dáil loan was $5.2 million, though not all of that had been received at the date of closure.[20] De Valera had missed his $10 million target by almost 50%.

After the failed takeover of the FOIF at the Waldorf and de Valera's announcement that he intended to set up a new organisation, McGuire made another effort at compromise with Devoy, who updated Cohalan on the outcome of their discussion. Devoy had told McGuire 'very plainly' that he was done making agreements that were never kept. He had enough of de Valera's 'absurd notions of his Presidential Prerogative and his attempts to treat us as a pack of schoolboys or servants.' The failed attempt to take control of the FOIF was the final straw, 'they did their best to make a split and failed.' Devoy summed up the outcome of the meeting for Cohalan.

> James [McGuire] got indignant at my "stubbornness" and said Harry and I were one as bad as the other and that I should accept his suggestion. I told him these "agreements" were shams and the only thing to do was to get D.V. to stop his warfare on us.[21]

On 18 October Boland severed the relationship between Clan-na-Gael and the Irish Republican Brotherhood. He then established a new organisation, 'Clan-na-Gael Re-organised'. Ironically, he had to send the severance letter to his friend McGuire, chairman of the Clan-na-Gael executive committee. Twelve days later Devoy carried a front-page headline in the *Gaelic American*, 'Clan-na-Gaels Work for the Bonds'. He contrasted the $627,916 raised in New York, a success 'backboned' by the Clan, with the campaign of falsehood accusing them of 'failing to support President De Valera and of opposing the Bond Drive.'[22]

One month later de Valera launched the American Association for the Recognition of the Irish Republic (AARIR).[23] The FOIF haemorrhaged members to the new organisation. The split in the Irish movement was complete.

The cabinet in Dublin requested de Valera to defer presentation of a formal demand for recognition of the Irish Republic to the United States government until the new president and Congress came into office, and asked him to remain until the demand for recognition was made.[24] Wanting to return to Ireland, de Valera ignored the cabinet. He asked Frank Walsh to lead a delegation, including McGuire and McGarrity, to present the official request.[25] Bainbridge Colby, the secretary of state, had made it known in advance that he would only meet American citizens. The recognition request was a futile act made five days before the presidential election, in which Wilson was not a candidate. No reply was received from the secretary of state.

De Valera left America on 10 December after an eighteen month stay. He returned to an Ireland of attacks, counter-attacks, arrests and brutal reprisals by the British throughout the country. Terence MacSwiney had died after refusing food for seventy-four days; eighteen-year-old Kevin Barry had been hanged; seventeen Auxiliaries had been killed in an ambush in Cork; fourteen civilians had been shot in Croke Park, on a day when thirty people were killed or fatally wounded, including twelve British intelligence agents.

EPILOGUE

Vindication

Four years later, on 3 September 1924, John Devoy celebrated his birth-day on Irish soil for the first time in more than half a century.[1] Six weeks earlier, the eighty-two year old had arrived in Cobh on the *President Harding*. An honour guard of fifty soldiers saluted the old warrior under a tricolour waving in the wind.

Ireland was recovering from the war of independence and the bitter civil war. The country had been dismembered by the partition of six counties under the Government of Ireland Act 1920. The honour guard comprised soldiers of the Irish Free State established by the later Anglo–Irish Treaty that ended the war of independence. The treaty included an oath of allegiance to the constitution of the Free State, and to be 'faithful to H.M. King George V'. Those opposed to the treaty considered it a betrayal of the Irish Republic. For others, including a majority of the elected representatives, it was another stepping stone towards a united Irish Republic.

Devoy had vacillated in his support for the treaty, stung by the de jure acceptance of partition, the oath and the retention of the 'treaty ports' by the British. His final backing of the Free State government of Michael Collins was consistent with his lifelong strategy of reaching for attainable goals. De Valera's rejection of the treaty influenced his decision. But not for personality reasons; he feared for an Ireland with de Valera at its head.

To mark his birthday Devoy was honoured with a state banquet. After the speeches, he expressed his thanks for the enthusiasm with which his health was drunk; 'I would not be human if I was not the jolliest good fellow in my own old town of Dublin tonight.'[2] He noted the progress made toward the realisation of the 'Fenian ideal', including his reception on arriving in Ireland by a detachment of an Irish army presenting arms, and a dinner he had at Collins Barracks, which he had previously visited in 1865 to recruit Irish men in the British Army to the Fenian movement.

But the returning hero was hurting inside. After six weeks of diplomacy, he could no longer hold back and the pain rushed out.

I tried to come over [for] Easter Week ... by getting the naturalisation papers of an old friend who had recently died, and who was very like me, but his nephew refused to give them to me. I have often since then regretted that I failed and was not shot with Tom Clarke and Sean MacDermott.

That would have spared me the worst agony of mind I have ever endured when from 1919 to last year, I was called a traitor for standing by the Irish Republic by the man who first lowered its flag and who sent men bribed with money which I had helped to collect to repeat the lie all over the United States and to make the worst split in all Irish history, which he later brought to Ireland to bring ruin and disaster upon her...

God knows Ireland ought to have learned the lesson that Splits have proved her ruin in the past, but the man *you* sent to America made the most disastrous one in history. We have recovered from it in America and you are recovering from it here, and the Republican ideal, to which he gave a bad setback, will eventually triumph.[3]

De Valera had been released from prison three days before Devoy had set sail from America.

Devoy had watched from afar as Ireland had been ripped apart by a civil war that he blamed on the *Westminster Gazette* interview, which for him made compromise inevitable.

Loss

Devoy had reconciled with Collins after the signing of the treaty. In early 1922 Collins wrote to him that his 'good opinion is of concern to us here'.[4] Devoy was not shy, however, in reminding Collins how the situation had come to pass that compromise had to be accepted in the treaty.

> I am utterly opposed to De Valera's attempt to upset the 'Free State Agreement'. The first blow to the Republic was dealt by him in the Cuban interview. These infamous actions by de Valera were approved or condoned *by all of you.*[5]

Collins apologised to Devoy for the severance of Clan-na-Gael from the home organisation, explaining that the IRB envisaged setting up 'a world-wide Irish federation, each separate part working through the government, and in accordance with the laws of the country where it had its being.' He explained rather weakly, 'Unfortunately, some of those we sent to America did not understand the vital principle of that idea.'[6]

Most of the Clan-na-Gael leadership had remained loyal to Devoy. The 'Re-organised' Clan established by Boland had failed to become a material force, for whom McGuire's decision to withdraw entirely from the Irish movement had been a serious setback. Resigning as chairman of Clan-na-Gael and refusing to join the new organisation, McGuire explained to Boland that he would not join any other Irish society because 'they all go bad in the end'.

> The rivalries of individuals for leadership or control of our organizations are the curse and the bane of the movement … In every case there has been a boss or a clique dominating and the struggle against the caucus and dictatorship has resulted in paralysis of the hopes and aims of pacific but earnest men.[7]

McGuire had warned Boland that his new organisation had attracted 'several ambitious disturbers who are invariably factional, quarrelsome and unworkable'. Any new organisation made up of "old timers" would be bound to be 'barren of good results'. But he offered him his personal support, and was able to assure him after visiting the State Department that there would be no interference with his work.

The American Association for the Recognition of the Irish Republic collapsed little more than a year after its founding. The first bloom of enthusiasm had faded by August 1921 fuelled by internal disputes.[8] Membership crumbled when de Valera opposed the treaty, though the FOIF never recovered from the trauma of the establishment of the rival organisation.

McGuire was in poor health, while neglect of his business interests, already suffering due to a sharp decline in the shipping industry, were factors in his decision to withdraw from Irish affairs. But he gave another more revealing reason to Boland: the view he had formed of de Valera from inquiries and after meeting various friends. He began by saying that de Valera had done 'the greatest work of any Irishman of his time in dealing with the great issues and with people in the mass.'[9] But he could never work with de Valera again.

> I am sorry to observe that he is a lamentable failure in meeting delegations or committees or groups in conference. ... In details and methods he appears to most of his visitors as lacking in decision, changeable, unsteady and many men go away feeling they cannot work with him or under him *safely*.[10]

Harry Boland was still in the States when he celebrated his thirty-fourth birthday in April 1921. Frances McGuire, wife of James, made him a tie as a gift, 'for one whom we all like and admire so much.'[11] This high regard for Boland was also waiting at home for him where, as soon as he returned, he did everything in his power to broker an accord between de Valera and Collins on the treaty. A letter McGuire wrote him the following April recommended that the dispute should be settled by a plebiscite; 'the feeling here among your friends is in effect that whatever the majority of people of Ireland should determine, is the best settlement to accept.'[12] But Boland sided with de Valera in opposition to the treaty. Three months after receiving the letter from McGuire, Boland was dead – a passionate, heart-on-sleeve young man taken in his prime.

In a fond farewell in the *Gaelic American*, both affection and hurt can be found in Devoy's words. Boland had 'a splendid record until he fell under the evil influence of de Valera … [who] … made him the instrument for the doing of things which Boland, left to himself, would never of thought of.'[13] Boland's father had died when Harry was just eight years old, and he had always enjoyed the company of his father's generation, in particular the old Fenians, who provided a link to the father he barely knew and filled an emotional gap. Devoy, who had known Boland's father well, and without children of his own, might have become a natural mentor to him. He might have moulded the pugilistic revolutionary, whom he described as lacking 'intellect or fine feeling … [and] … wholly devoid of political judgement', into a more rounded person and a more accomplished political operator.

Across America, Boland's shooting was greeted with dismay. Six days after his death, McGuire sent a warning to Collins that Irish–Americans opposed to the treaty planned to assassinate him as well as Richard Mulcahy, the defence minister, in revenge for the deaths of Boland and Cathal Brugha. But Collins was in no mood for threats. Still only thirty-one, he was head of the embattled government and commander of the national army; he had barely time to mourn the loss of his good friend. He replied to McGuire 'for whom I have a very great respect' through an intermediary.

> I would ask you as a personal favour to tell him that he need not waste his time nor his energy in inducing any of the American-Irish *not* to come here to slay Dick Mulcahy and myself.
>
> I have not the slightest doubt that we should be able to stand up to such gentlemen … It is a pity that they did not show the same desire to come to help us when we were all fighting for our lives against the British … Please tell this to Mr J.K. McGuire, just as I put it, and tell him my message to his friends is – *'Let them all come'*.[14]

Three days later, Collins was shot dead.

Ten months after the passing of Boland and Collins, McGuire, the former 'boy mayor', died of a heart attack aged fifty-four. Devoy wrote a warm farewell to his friend.

> Personally James K. McGuire was a most amiable, genial and likeable man. He was very proud of his descent from the fighting Fermanagh McGuires and spent much time during trips to Ireland in visiting that county. Even those who differed most strongly from him in opinion freely acknowledged his downright sincerity and honesty of purpose, and the news of his death will be received with sorrow throughout the country.[15]

Devoy commented that McGuire was with Boland 'night and day during the purchase of the only large consignment of arms and ammunition sent to Ireland during the Black and Tan warfare.' He could not fully forgive McGuire, however, for the concessions he was willing to make to conciliate de Valera.

Honour

Diarmuid Lynch had continued as national secretary of the FOIF after de Valera left America. Four months before Devoy's feted return to Ireland, Lynch addressed the IRB veterans' banquet at the Hotel Astor in New York. 'Looking back now on the history of Ireland since December 1921, many are tempted to speculate on what might have been'.[16] He could well have speculated on his own fate; if he had not sided with Cohalan and Devoy, if he had not resigned his seat in Dáil Éireann, if he had not lived up to his own principles. He might have been in Ireland where his leadership skills, organisation flair and American experience would have been invaluable to the emerging Irish state. Instead, he was fighting bitter legal battles for control of the bond drive proceeds.

Lynch had resigned from the Dáil in 1920 following the publication of the letters seized on William Barry, one of which was written by Nunan, a former comrade of Lynch in the GPO, to Collins.

> Now, Michael, something should be done about Diarmuid. It is absolutely outrageous that he, a member of Dáil Éireann, should be supporting those who are opposing in every way the endeavours of the President. I think that it should be put up to him to resign either his seat in the Dáil Éireann or the Secretaryship of the F.O.I.F.[17]

Nunan disingenuously added, 'I can't make out what has come over him.' In another letter to Griffith, Nunan wrote that Lynch had become 'unworthy to represent any Irish constituency and a grave *menace to our cause.*'[18] He was accused of being part of a plot against de Valera. Few at home questioned the apparent remarkable transformation of the man who had arranged for his secret prison wedding to match the date and exact time of the beginning of the Easter Rising. Nunan raised the spectre of a man called Thomas Fogarty, who had been sent to Ireland by the FOIF with letters of introduction from Lynch. On hearing the Fogarty tale, Lynch immediately cabled his good friend Terence MacSwiney. 'Fogarty got no commission whatever from and was not authorised to act or speak for myself or Friends. Advise Dublin.'

Lynch knew that his position was untenable before the publication of the seized letters. He had wanted to resign, but was concerned that his 'actions would have been misconstrued by the enemies of the Irish Republic.'[19] In his resignation letter to the Dáil, Lynch explained his decision. 'I now feel more free to continue my efforts here for the recognition of the Irish Republic on lines which long and practical experience in America have shown me to be for the best interests of the Irish Cause.'

Boland expressed regret at the resignation in his diary. 'Diarmuid proved himself a good man when the call came. I am really sorry for him and Mrs. Lynch.'[20] But a heartbroken Kit, the prison bride, writing to her family in Ireland had little time for Boland, or de Valera.

> The President and other men from home, acting on the advice of a number of men ... are allowing men such as John Devoy, Judge Cohalan, Diarmuid and others who have served the cause just as faithfully to be

hounded through the country *by certain Irish–American Newspapers* ... Dev could put a stop to this disgraceful work by just a raise of his hand but instead he and H. Boland, etc. encourage it by their silence.[21]

When Terence MacSwiney had been imprisoned and commenced his hunger strike, Lynch sent a formal protest to the US secretary of state. Muriel MacSwiney wrote to Lynch while at her husband's bedside.

I have been thinking of you often since the time we were all in Dundalk together. There is little I can say about Terry. I see him every afternoon. He is in great pain at times. I showed him your cable; he was pleased to get it.[22]

Lynch paid a long price for opposing de Valera and acting in what he saw as the best interests of the Irish Republic. The principled 1916 veteran, and former occupant of seven English prisons, knew what it meant to live according to MacSwiney's prophetic words, 'it is not those who can inflict the most but those that can suffer the most who will conquer'.

Love

'John', she said in a voice loud enough for the deaf old man's ears, 'why didn't you write? I waited for you for twelve years'. Devoy said nothing for a moment. Then, at last, he replied, 'And I've been waiting for you all my life'.[23]

Devoy had reunited with his long lost fiancé, Eliza Kenny Kilmurray, when in Ireland. There was even speculation of marriage. Their relationship continued by letter when he returned to America, where he fell into a familiar routine; fierily editing the *Gaelic American*, helping those in need and battling the ravages of time. He quietly raised a subscription for Kathleen Clarke, Tom Clarke's widow, who was on the edge of poverty. Mrs. Clarke sent her gracious thanks, 'I can sleep at night when I go to bed instead of laying awake with the strain and worry of how to keep going. People tell me I am looking years younger and ask what am I doing with myself. I smile but don't let them into the secret'.[24]

Devoy sent Eliza a picture taken shortly after he had arrived in New York for the first time. On the back of the photo he wrote: 'To Mrs. E. Kilmurry (nee Eliza Kenny), in loving memory of our engagement when she was a fine girl of 20 and with deep regret at the misfortunes which separated us.'[25] Eliza replied with a photo of herself and her niece. Reminded of the hurt that he had caused her, Devoy inscribed on the back: 'Mrs. E. Kulmurry of Naas, ne Eliza Kenny of Tipper, County Kildare, engaged to John Devoy at the time of his arrest ... waiting for him for 12 years after his release in 1871'.[26] The thoughts of a different life both pleased and haunted Devoy.

Their fondness grew over the following two years. Eliza's letters became more tender and she signed 'with best love'.[27] But letter writing for John became more difficult as his eyesight deteriorated. 'It must be a great trial on you when you can't read or write,' Eliza wrote sympathetically.[28] He promised to visit in 1927, but Eliza had been suffering from health problems too. Before the promised visit could take place, he received word from his nephew that she had died. Unable to travel for the funeral, he was again 3,000 miles from the only true love he had known in a long lonely life. He lived his final years in a room in West 107th Street in the care of two sisters; his rent and other expenses being paid by a secret fund set up by Cohalan and Lynch. On 29 September 1928, around one in the morning, the French legionnaire, Irish revolutionary and 'greatest of the Fenians' died in his own bed.

Devoy's body was carried to Ireland aboard the *President Harding* for a full state funeral. In Dublin, his coffin was borne through the streets atop a gun carriage with full military honours, before burial in Glasnevin near his old friends. The *Times of London* saluted Devoy as 'the most bitter and persistent, as well as the most dangerous, enemy of this country which Ireland has produced since Wolfe Tone'. If he was bitter, it was the fault of those that had ruled his country and exiled him from it, and if persistent it was because he was prepared to fight for Irish freedom for however long it took, and if he was the most dangerous it was because of his intelligence, innovativeness and rationality in pursuit of the Fenian ideal of an independent Irish Republic.

Devoy advocated not only for freedom for the people of Ireland, but for the freedom of all peoples under the yoke of imperialism. He warned against the tendency of people to follow men instead of principles and sound policies.[29] It was maybe fortunate that he died before the peaceful transfer of power to de Valera in 1932, and the launch of the *Irish Press* newspaper, which had been partly funded from the proceeds of the bond drive, and named after the Philadelphia newspaper that had vilified him. Devoy's Fenian ideal had not been achieved at his death but he was confident that it would happen.

> The final settlement has yet to come – and it will come, not through an English Act of Parliament, but from the united action of the Irish people themselves.[30]

CONCLUSIONS

Overview

De Valera had the intellectual and physical stature to fill out the figure-head role of 'President of the Irish Republic' in America. First impressions were of a courteous, frugal and earnest man. He carried an air of integrity and sincerity. Taking up arms in 1916, sentenced to be shot and saved only by 'his American citizenship', his story-book escape from Lincoln Jail, the ease at which he eluded the British and his mysterious arrival in America, all added to his appeal.[1] He drew the working-class Irish to him; he was not a politician (to them) and not of the establishment; he had a genuine Catholic faith.

But de Valera's time in America between June 1919 and December 1920 was marked by strategic mistakes and tactical errors in the conduct of the bond and recognition campaigns, as well as an unnecessary divisiveness. He lacked the interpersonal and management skills to deliver his objectives. His lack of interest and understanding of 'elaborate organisation' – planning, communication, delegation and commercial awareness – resulted in what Edward McSweeney perceived in the bond drive as 'no adequate systematization of the work, and no clear or definite idea of the handling of the mass of detail necessary for such a campaign.'[2] He had attention to detail, a valuable skill, but it was often directed in the wrong direction, and he continually procrastinated, a weakness he recognised in himself. 'If I could only acquire [the] habit of doing things on the spot. I trust I am not too old to improve.'[3]

A remarkable self-belief and self-admitted stubbornness, combined with an almost contradictory insecurity and a jealous streak, was not compatible with inspiring motivation and trust. There was only one voice; compromise and teamwork were not possible. A toxic 'corporate culture' is revealed in the later letters of his earliest supporters in America.

I am sorry to observe that he is a lamentable failure in meeting delegations or committees or groups in conference. ... In details and methods he appears to most of his visitors as lacking in decision, changeable, unsteady and *many men go away feeling they cannot work with him or under him safely.*[4] – James K. McGuire.

My experience of him and Harry is that they come to a conference not knowing what they want; have an unconscious contempt or seem to have such for opinions of others. The Chief presides and does all the talking ... *thinks he has co-operation when he only gets silent acquiescence.*[5] – Patrick McCartan.

I would advise you [de Valera] to promptly send someone to this country who has your confidence, if such a person exists, and having done so *don't constantly interfere with his work.*[6] – James O'Mara.

De Valera survived self-inflicted wounds – the *Gazette* interview, the Republican convention and the bond campaign – through the (sometimes reluctant) support of those using him to leverage their own agendas, or because professed loyalty to the 'Irish President' was the only option without damaging the Irish cause. McCartan and Maloney leveraged de Valera's presence in America in their failed liberal takeover of the leadership of the Irish movement, and the fallout from the dispute enabled Boland to justify his failed attempt to take control of Clan-na-

Gael. Disgruntled factions challenging the New York 'clique', and the ambitious quarrelsome 'disturbers' identified by McGuire to Boland, gladly sided with him in his dispute with Cohalan and Devoy. The Hearst newspaper organisation pursued its own anti-imperialist agenda through support of de Valera. The cabinet in Dublin, with no choice in the matter, had to issue two letters of confidence.

Raising $5.2 million, equivalent to over $75 million today, cannot be dismissed as a failure, but it was a colossal lost opportunity, missing the $10 million target by almost 50 per cent, an opportunity cost of over $70 million today! The launch delays and poor organisation resulted in reputational damage to the Irish movement. Moreover, de Valera's rejection of Edward McSweeney's plan, which had envisaged raising $20 million, had been a mistake. The $10 million target had been achievable as late as February 1920 if, as McGuire noted, they could 'perfect the organisation'. Charles Wheeler had told McGarrity that if unity could be maintained, 'you would get not $10,000,000, but nearer $50,000,000'; while an exaggerated estimate, it is an indication of the opportunity left behind.

Official recognition of the Irish Republic by the United States government was not a realistic objective in the timeframe envisaged by de Valera. Pro-English sentiment in the White House and Congress was too strong to support straight recognition. De Valera's unexpected arrival in America and desire for almost instant success through an appeal to public opinion interfered with the FOIF's stepping stone recognition strategy in Washington, nationwide campaign of education and focus on elevating the status of the Irish Race (often by challenging an increasing anglicisation of America). The rash decision to establish the AARIR one month before he left America, after failing to take control of the FOIF through constitutional means, unnecessarily split the Irish movement.

John Devoy perceived de Valera as another in the long line of revolutionaries coming from Ireland that misunderstood America and who believed they knew the country better than those that had been born there or made it their home. Devoy had shown himself capable of working with leaders from Ireland in the past, but he formed a low opinion of de Valera considering him egotistical, insincere and being of poor judgement. Devoy's question to McCartan written on the train from New York could equally have been asked of de Valera. 'Does it ever occur to you that your assumption of infallible judgment is absurd?'[7] He believed de Valera setback the Republican ideal through mixed messaging and the divisions he created in America, and replicated in Ireland.

Devoy merited greater respect for his achievements; not to be harassed to the point of regretting that he had not gone over for Easter Week to be shot with his friends.[8] He found vindication and some solace on his return to Ireland in 1924, but never forgave the man who caused him to be accused of being a traitor to the Irish Republic.

Cohalan was character assassinated in public by McCartan and Maloney and in private by de Valera; accused of capitalising Irish support for personal, social, political and financial gain, and selling his 'priceless birth right for a mess of mephitic pottage'.[9] He became a despot and a malignant defamer, one accused of treason, of plotting, of being part of an underhand conspiracy, of being a dead weight. All this within months of de Valera stating at a National Council meeting that he had received 'every assistance' and always found him 'ready with advice and help.'[10]

Unlike F. Scott Fitzgerald, Cohalan's vocation was the elevation of the Irish Race to equality in American society. The establishment of an Irish state with its people free from English colonial rule was crucial to achieving that goal. He fought for Irish independence as an American. De Valera's insecurity prevented him from leveraging Cohalan's record of political achievement and bipartisan access in Washington for the Irish cause. As Devoy asked of McCartan when he first attempted to challenge Cohalan's leadership, *And who would you put in his place?*[11]

One can only speculate on what could have been achieved in America if the Friends of Irish Freedom had continued its growth trajectory and if de Valera, instead of being the catalyst for its destruction, had used his speaking tours to attract new members. McGuire saw the potential for 5,000 branches across the country. There would have been factional fights, but likely not to the point of being an existential threat to the organisation. The sharp decline in interest in Irish affairs among the Irish in America in the wake of the treaty debate and the civil war might have been averted. There would have been disagreements, but probably not the collapse in membership that the AARIR experienced.

Was the cost of de Valera's time in America the absence of a powerful united organised diaspora providing political, financial and humanitarian support to the new Irish state in the decades that followed?

Bond: A lost opportunity

The $10 million bond drive target was airbrushed from history. In his book *With De Valera in America*, published in 1932, McCartan did so with a simple, appealing and effective line: 'McGarrity had advised President de Valera to ask for ten million dollars, and he would get five'.[12] McCartan did not mention the *Irish Press* regretting that de Valera did not go for $25 million, or de Valera's rejection in St. Louis of McSweeney's $20 million plan, or that McGarrity believed 'several times' $5 million could be subscribed within one week.

As it became clear that the target would not be achieved, de Valera wrote to Griffith lowering expectations to 'at least three or four times the sum we set out here to obtain.' He was referring to the initial arbitrary target of $1.25 million set in Dublin in early 1919. The lowered expectation equated to a total of between $3.7 and $5 million. 'It would be a great triumph,' he informed Griffith, 'if we secured the full Ten Million Dollars.' There was to be no triumph, however. Instead, achieving four times the target set in Ireland became part of the bond drive narrative.

Many factors played a part in the underperformance of the bond drive: handing management of the campaign to the nameplate ACII, and attempting to turn it into a rival to the FOIF; failing to listen to the legal and operations advice of the *millionaire group* and the FOIF leaders; believing a bank could be secured to act as a financial agent; delaying engaging a specialist bond certificate printer; recruiting and inadequately supervising Elder and Callahan; insufficient marketing support; proposing the radical Monroe Doctrine and Cuban policies during the campaign, and the public attacks on Cohalan and Devoy that alienated many potential subscribers, including wealthy Irish–Americans.

Issuing bond certificates to subscribers continued to be a problem until the end of 1921. In March of that year, Nunan replied to a request from McGarrity for certificates to be delivered to him for subscribers. 'I have gone carefully over all books and lists which reached us from Philadelphia and I cannot find any trace of any of these.'[13] Towards the year end Nunan wrote to McGarrity again. 'We have had many complaints from Chester, both from people who say they paid in full and from people who say they paid in part, and we have no reply to give them.'[14] In December Nunan published the names of hundreds of people in Philadelphia whose certificates had been returned undelivered due to inaccurate names and addresses.[15]

Other factors that played a part in the underperformance of the bond drive were outside the control of the organisers, including influenza, pneumonia, weather, pro-English propaganda and the opposition, albeit mild, of the United States government.

Division: Taking sides

In a letter to Collins on 18 January 1921, just over a month after leaving New York, de Valera explained his role in the conflict.

> You will not, of course, make the mistake of thinking that the division began with my advent in America. It existed in reality long before; my coming only gave it a new turn, and brought it to a head, so to speak.

My view, when I was over, was that the best attitude of the Irish representative would be to be friendly to both groups, *without making any
attempt to bring the groups more closely together*, except in so far as through
his influence he could *prevent them from wasting their energies fighting one
another.*[16]

De Valera's arrival in America certainly gave the division a new turn
by empowering a minority liberal faction within the Irish movement,
mainly controlled by people born outside America, which had allied
itself with powerful progressive, socialist and pacifist leaders in New
York. The incumbent leaders of the Irish movement, an older generation that had built the Irish organisations from the ground up, were
lifelong Democrats who pragmatically worked both sides of the aisle in a
combined fight for American sovereignty, the status of the Irish Race in
America and Irish freedom.

De Valera did not make any attempt to bring the groups closer
together, even for the expected short duration of his stay and to ensure
the success of the bond drive. His attitude towards both groups was not
a friendly one, and he made no attempt to prevent them from fighting
one another.

De Valera's invented 'ulterior motives' of Cohalan are revealing
– jealousy, envy, resentment or some 'devilish cause', and to compel
de Valera to be a mere rubber stamp. Cohalan had no cause for such
motives; he was a judge of the New York Supreme Court, confident in
his Americanism and proud of his 100% Irish heritage. He would not
have expected de Valera to be a rubber stamp. By contrast, de Valera
was a political figurehead in a foreign country, an Irish leader born to
a Hispanic father who had been given up as a child by his mother. He
wanted the Irish leaders in America to rubber stamp the decisions made
in Ireland. While Cohalan was confident in his opinions, seldom made
mistakes and rarely had to explain himself, de Valera constantly had to
justify his actions, either to the press or to cabinet, as he did with his
well-used refrain, 'I never in public or private say or do anything here

which is not thoroughly consistent with my attitude at home as you have known it.'

Recognition: Mixed messaging

In the same letter to Collins, de Valera revealed that while working for recognition, his 'main political objective' was the obtaining of America's influence, if she was to join the League of Nations, in securing Ireland a place within the League.[17] In a letter to Griffith, after the Gerry reservation had been passed in the Senate (which stated that when the Irish people attained a government of their own choice 'it should promptly be admitted as a member of the League of Nations'), de Valera wrote that the reservation 'was what I had been *always* wishing for, and it came finally even beyond expectations.'[18]

He admitted to Collins that recognition would only be got 'in case of a war with England though, of course, we should never cease our demand for it.' He informed Boland that official recognition by the United States government could not be secured *'except in a crisis in which America's own interests are involved* and when it might be convenient to hit England through us.'[19] De Valera was espousing the view of Cohalan and the FOIF; either he had been converted over time, or he did not believe that recognition was possible while he was in America. If the latter, it begs the question as to why he kept referring to the bond drive as being 'secondary' to recognition.

Devoy believed the attempt to remove Cohalan and himself was 'deliberate preparation' for the implementation of the Cuban and Monroe Doctrine policies, 'which he knew we would not stand'.[20] He accused de Valera of lowering the flag in the *Westminster Gazette* interview, making compromise inevitable in the treaty, which de Valera refused to accept. McCartan believed the Cuban interview intimated that de Valera was prepared to accept 'much less than complete sovereignty.'[21]

De Valera also delivered mixed messaging on the League of Nations. In Fenway Park, he had called for a new League covenant to be framed in Washington, a political non-starter. Two weeks later, at the Chicago

Cubs baseball park, he acknowledged the 'American grounds' for opposing the League. He had learned his lesson (temporarily) not to meddle in domestic politics. He stopped publicly calling for a new League of Nations and he restricted his opposition to Article 10, a legitimate complaint for a representative of the Irish government in America.[22]

But if his main political objective was to secure a place for Ireland within the League, it meant that he was working privately to secure passage of the Treaty of Versailles, despite the negative consequences of the territorial integrity provisions of Article 10 of the League of Nations. It would explain his letter to Griffith that he was 'trying to give Wilson to know that if he goes for his 14 points as they were and a true League of Nations men and women of I.[rish] blood will be behind him.[23] It might also explain his meeting with Shane Leslie at the Long Island estate of Bourke Cockran, and his sending of McCartan to criticise and threaten with repudiation Captain O'Connell for opposing Senator Walsh's resolution.

Westminster Gazette: The real story

In *Assignment: America, De Valera's mission to the United States*, which was approved by de Valera prior to publication in 1957, Katherine O'Doherty provided an inaccurate timeline on the events surrounding the *Westminster Gazette* interview in support of the narrative that Cohalan and Devoy had misrepresented and distorted the interview *before* it appeared in Ireland.

The *Gaelic American* commented on the interview on 14 February, eight days after the report appeared in the New York *Globe*, seven days after the *Westminster Gazette* and *five days* after the first press comments in Ireland. Devoy was reasoned and restrained in his editorial comment, making a plea for debate on the proposals in a 'frank, and friendly spirit … without heat or passion … and with all respect to President De Valera'. There was no attempt at misrepresentation or distortion, though O'Doherty's description of the interview built an almost believable case.

He [de Valera] was prepared to do this because he knew that the Westminster Gazette reached Dublin on the evening of the day on which it was published and that the first comment would be from Ireland, where he felt sure his arguments and his purpose would be understood.

He was not aware that there was an arrangement between the New York Globe and the Westminster Gazette by which special articles in the one might be used in the other, and that Hernan represented both publications.

The interview appeared in the Globe a day before it appeared in the Westminster Gazette, on 7th February, 1920, with the result that the first comment came from Cohalan and Devoy quarters, who took advantage of it to misrepresent it completely, so that the interview when it appeared in Ireland was accompanied by this distortion.[24]

The *Irish Independent* and *Freeman's Journal* reported on the interview on 9 February, five days before the *Gaelic American* was published. A 'prominent Dublin Sinn Feiner' told a reporter from the *Irish Independent* that 'the utmost caution should be observed with regard to messages purporting to represent declarations of Irish leaders abroad'.[25] The *Freeman's Journal* reprinted the *Gazette* report under the headline, 'Mr. De Valera's reported offer to Britain'.[26] A special section entitled 'The Status Of Cuba' noted the leasing of Guantanamo harbour to the United States and the prior military intervention in the country. The *Morning Post's* Dublin correspondent reported back to London that 'Many of the old Nationalists appear to think that it is something of a climb down on the part of the President'.[27]

O'Doherty described the meeting between the reporter and de Valera.

It *so happened* that a newspaper representative, W. J. Hernan, who frequently visited the Irish Legation in pursuit of 'copy' or, perhaps, hoping for a 'scoop', asked on February 5th for a special interview with the Irish President on the plea that he would like it for the Westminster Gazette.

> Mr. de Valera handed to Mr. Hernan the draft of the proposed speech
> on which he was actually working at the time. Hernan, having read it
> through, thought that the part dealing with Britain's security would serve
> his purpose and Mr. de Valera agreed that he might use it.

On the morning of the interview, de Valera was preparing to leave on a
tour of New England to re-launch his new security proposals. It is too
much of a coincidence that Hernan 'so happened' to be in the office
looking for 'copy' or a 'scoop' that morning, or that he, not de Valera,
selected the piece on Britain's security for publication. In fact, the interview was most likely arranged *in advance* by McCartan and Maloney
through Alfred McCann, an Irish-American friend of theirs on the editorial staff of the *Globe*.[28]

McCann was a pioneering though controversial natural foods cam-
paigner who exposed negative industry practices in pseudoscientific
articles. He had facilitated the publication of copy for McCartan and
Maloney previously, and spoke at an Irish Progressive League meeting.[29]
McCann lived in Yonkers where de Valera had trialled his new policy
proposals for the first time on 1 February; he was one of the speakers
that evening.[30] Devoy commented to a friend that the 'appearance of
the interview in the Globe suggests McCann, a member of its staff, as
the intermediary, and he is a worshipper of Maloney – which brings
Maloney in with a finger in the pie'.[31] The New York *Globe* was the *only*
American newspaper to report and comment editorially on the interview
on the day after it was given by de Valera.[32]

In his book, McCartan denied that he or Maloney knew Hernan at
the time of the *Globe* interview. He wrote that Maloney enlisted Hernan
'*whom none of us knew*' in *1921* to publish propaganda material in Europe
and he praised the splendid work done by 'this *unknown*' Hernan.[33]
But is it possible that Maloney, with his strong connections to the liberal New York press, and McCartan, editor of an Irish paper (albeit in
Philadelphia), did not know the American correspondent of the liberal
Westminster Gazette, whose articles appeared in the *New York Globe*, and

who 'frequently' visited the Irish mission in pursuit of copy. McCartan's denial of knowing Hernan in 1921 is even less credible considering it was a year after the most controversial interview ever given by an Irish politician to an American reporter! Boland noted in his diary on 9 May 1920, 'Chief, Hernan and I walk back to Waldorf.'

De Valera distanced himself from Maloney in later years, who is mentioned once in O'Doherty's book, compared to 190 mentions in McCartan's account of the same period. The approved biography by Longford and O'Neill noted that de Valera was 'very careful' in dealing with Maloney and that he met him 'no more than twice during the whole of his time in America.'[34] There is evidence that Maloney accompanied de Valera on tour; in November 1919 Devoy wrote in a letter, 'I forgot to mention about Maloney, who was brought West to speak with D.V., I asked Harry last night how he came to be selected and he said he was sent to them. "Who sent him"?" "Walsh, I think.""[35]

O'Doherty's sole reference to Maloney was to his humanitarian initiative in setting up the 'large and very powerful' American Committee for Relief in Ireland. According to Kelly Anne Reynolds, an authority on Maloney, de Valera had been reluctant to support the endeavour, which raised $5,069,194 in three months.[36]

De Valera and Collins: Show me the money

On 9 February 1920, three weeks after the launch of the bond drive, the entrepreneurial Collins wrote to de Valera.

> The necessity for the money is now beginning to press. The Bank can absorb an enormous amount [the National Land Bank set up using a dummy corporation to disguise its ownership], as quite apart from its Land activities other enterprises are making applications which might with great advantage and success be granted.[37]

Three months later, on 12 May, Collins demanded of Boland that 'we could do with a great deal more money quickly.'[38] At that stage $3 million had been raised, of which $545,000 was on deposit in four banks (two in New York and two in Massachusetts).[39] On 8 June, the cabinet wrote to de Valera that 'large schemes in connection with Land, Fisheries, and other *urgent problems* are at present under consideration, and the amount of money required will be contingent upon the extent to which these schemes are adopted.'[40] The cabinet letter concluded that the 'Secretary for Finance is of opinion that arrangements might be made for the immediate transmission of £500,000 [$2.2 million].'[41]

Despite this, the first half of 1920 saw only $235,000 (£58,880) sent to Ireland, to the frustration of Collins and other members of the cabinet.[42] Two more bank drafts were sent in July totalling $105,000.[43] Another draft for $40,000 had been received in June, but this was related to money voted to Ireland by the Friends of Irish Freedom 'held since last year by Mr. O'Mara's instructions.'[44]

Increasingly frustrated at the lack of funds coming from America, Collins accused Boland on 14 August of having 'misled us very seriously in this connection'.[45] The money coming from America was 'nothing short of being disastrous.' Boland reluctantly informed Collins the reason for de Valera's refusal to send the money. 'The Chief ... is particularly anxious that you at home be satisfied that you can safeguard the money ... to allay his fears, will you, in your next despatch, assure him that you can safeguard the funds? I have a copy of your financial report, and it certainly is very creditable to you.'[46] Collins bluntly replied to Boland to tell de Valera 'our chief way of safeguarding it up to the present has been by spending it — that is to say, by investing it in land'.[47]

By the end of October, just $650,500 (£147,841) had been remitted home, when over $4.5 million had been raised and the cash balance available was $3.2 million.[48] Meanwhile, over double the amount sent from America had been raised by the loan fund in Ireland.

By the end of March 1921, three months before the truce, $851,500 (£193,523) had been remitted home.[49] The cash balance in America was $3,830,152.[50]

The total *official* receipts of the Dáil government in 1919 and 1920, including only funds received in Ireland, was £618,323, or $2.8 million, equivalent to $41 million today. Of this, 60% came from the loan in Ireland, 30% from the loan in America and 10% from the Self Determination Fund.

Dáil government receipts: 1919 and 1920				
Loan and SDF Subscriptions	To 31.10.19 6 months	To 30.04.20 6 months	To 30.12.20 8 months	Total 20 months
Internal	10,160	144,598	220,278	375,036
External	-	58,880	127,566	186,446
Loan: Ireland and America	10,160	203,478	347,844	561,482
SDF	42,054	2,945	11,842	56,841
	52,214	206,423	359,686	618,323

NA, DE 2/7, 015, 177, 182 (exludes refunds and interest)

The total outlay of the Dáil government in the same period was £374,026, or $1.7 million, equivalent to $25 million today. Spending on economic development activity, including funding the National Land Bank, accounted for a surprising 70% of total expenditure in that period. The loan was also used to fund the setting up of the legislative, executive and judicial arms of the fledgling state, but, again surprisingly, only 6% of Dáil expenditure in its first two years went on the Department of Defence, though other funds were used to purchase arms. Expenditure on military activity, however, ratcheted up substantially in 1921. In the six months before the truce in July of that year, the Department of Defence accounted for 35% of government spending and, despite the signing of the truce, for 48% of expenditure in the second half of the year.

Dáil government spending: 1919 and 1920				
Loan and SDF	**To 31.10.19** **6 months**	**To 30.04.20** **6 months**	**To 30.12.20** **8 months**	**Total** **20 months**
Loan	23,406	42,683	279,176	345,265
SDF	6,672	8,765	13,324	28,761
	30,078	51,448	292,500	374,026

NA, DE 2/7, 015, 177, 182.

The Friends of Irish Freedom gave $115,046 of critical funding to Ireland between July 1919 and February 1920, *before* the first bond drive funds were transmitted home. These funds were kept off balance sheet; on 19 August 1919 Collins verbally told the Dáil that a sum of $25,000 received from America was not shown separately in the financial statement, but it was included in his general report.[51] The amount contributed to Ireland by the FOIF increased to $215,046 including the $100,000 contribution to the bond drive, and to $254,046, including $9,000 sent to Ireland for St. Enda's School (February 1920) and $30,000 'For Irish Relief' (3 January 1921). The FOIF also gifted $26,748 to cover de Valera's tour expenses, bringing the total contribution to Irish affairs to $280,794, equal to one-third of the bond proceeds remitted home by March 1921.[52]

De Valera and Collins: Organisational lessons

De Valera raised just three times the amount raised by Collins in Ireland, where the enemy's 'chief objective' was the suppression of the loan and the demographic profile was much less attractive. Collins raised £371,849, or $1.7 million, beating his target by almost 50%. The success of the loan in Ireland was underpinned by strong leadership, smart recruitment, attention to detail, an appreciation of systems, processes and controls, and an innovative marketing programme.

Collins leveraged the existing Sinn Féin organisation structure in Ireland. De Valera chose to hand direction of the bond drive to the nameplate ACII, under the direction of the reluctant Frank Walsh. He chose not to use the established administration systems and branch network of the FOIF. 'Had our advice been heeded as to the manner in which the Branch units could have been utilized to best advantage,' wrote Diarmuid Lynch, 'we are confident that the results would have been more satisfactory.'[53]

De Valera had limited administration experience, while Collins added a layer of professionalism to a natural flair for organisation during his time in London. Unable to comprehend the scale of organisation required to deliver a national bond campaign in America, de Valera listened to McCartan who believed the bond drive was a 'relatively simple affair'.[54] In a backhanded compliment to Collins' administration system, the head of the British 'Raid Bureau' wrote that he was able to gather a substantial amount of information because 'the Irish had an irresistible habit of keeping documents'.[55] Not everyone appreciated the amount of paperwork this generated, especially some of the military leaders in the field.

Collins thrived on organisational challenge. De Valera avoided organisation. When faced with a struggling campaign, de Valera countenanced using a draft plan entitled, 'Scheme to sell bonds *without an organised machine*'.[56] When the Dáil was declared a prohibited body and newspapers were suppressed in Ireland, Collins expanded his nationwide organisation. Four provincial organisers and forty-three sub-organisers were transferred from the payroll of Sinn Féin to the funding campaign.[57] He increased the print run of the prospectus to 400,000, distributed 3,000,000 promotional leaflets and sent 50,000 customised letters to prominent Sinn Féin supporters.[58]

De Valera recruited people that were subservient to him. Collins surrounded himself with competence.

De Valera had limited interpersonal and meeting skills. Collins could be arrogant and impatient, and he was absolutely intolerant of laziness and inefficiency. He grumbled to Cathal Brugha, 'If you saw the bloody pack down there, & their casual, indefinite, meaningless purposeless way of carrying on'.[59] At a low point in the funding campaign in Ireland, he spilled out his frustration in a letter to Boland. 'This enterprise will certainly break my heart if anything ever will.'[60] But disagreements were aired openly; people knew where they stood with him. He was not the easiest person to work for and, as is often the case, was liked by those who worked most closely with him and disliked by those with whom he had only infrequent contact.

Neither leader could access a bank to act as a financial agent for their campaigns. De Valera failed to put an administration structure in place to compensate. Collins, who had some investment banking exposure in London, understood that distribution was crucial to successful fundraising. In the absence of an established distribution network, he built his own – A financial 'Ho Chi Minh trail' between Dublin and the four corners of the country. Couriers had to distribute the prospectus, promotional material and receipts for the loan, and carry subscriptions (cheques, notes, coin, gold) back to Dublin for processing.

Collins believed in the power of marketing. De Valera accepted McCartan's advice that publicity was 'not a thing to worry about.'[61] He also rejected McSweeney's funding plan, which included a substantial marketing budget. Collins implemented a broad publicity campaign, including full-page newspaper advertisements (until the newspapers were suppressed) and a seven-minute promotional film. 'Of course, it is an awful disadvantage to be excluded from the Press,' he wrote to de Valera.[62] De Valera did not promote the bond drive when speaking in front of his great audiences. In contrast, his fellow TDs in Ireland were imprisoned for promoting the loan to even small gatherings.

De Valera saw the bond campaign as secondary to his political objectives. It was almost a nuisance to him. In contrast, the Sinn Féin leaders in Ireland recognised that 'Upon the loans, the future of Dáil Éireann and the republican movement depended.'[63] Collins loved Ireland 'not in theory but in practice', wrote Mary Frances McHugh in the immediate aftermath of his death.

Financial Civil War

On 7 January 1922, Dáil Éireann approved by a narrow majority the Treaty between Great Britain and Ireland. The new Provisional Government was in desperate need of finance. An important meeting took place on 23 February between members of the Provisional Government and the three trustees of the Dáil funds – de Valera, Stephen O'Mara (who had replaced his brother James) and Bishop Fogarty. The latter was the only one of the three trustees on the pro-Treaty side. Without the agreement of de Valera and O'Mara, both Treaty opponents, the new Provisional Government could not access funds held in the names of the trustees, although neither could de Valera and O'Mara without the support of Bishop Fogarty.

The American funds presented a particular headache for Collins. The balance of cash in America on 31 January 1922 was \$2,461,590.[64] The money was held in the name of Stephen O'Mara only. It was unanimously agreed at the meeting that title should be transferred to the trustees and that the funds should remain in America. There was no guarantee, however, that O'Mara would act on the decision, especially if the split over the Treaty widened, which it did.

Negotiations to settle differences between the opposing sides proved futile. Pro-Treaty Sinn Féin and Anti-Treaty Sinn Féin candidates campaigned against each other in the general election in June 1922. Treaty supporters won by a significant majority and a bloody civil war erupted.

Bitter, complex and protracted legal disputes erupted between the opposing sides for control of the funds in Ireland and America.[65] In December 1925, the Irish Supreme Court upheld an earlier ruling in the High Court in favour of the Free State. De Valera 'refused or neglected' to cooperate with the decision, despite copies of the High Court decision and the Supreme Court order being personally served on him. In February 1927, the court made an order appointing an alternative trustee to de Valera facilitating the discharge of the funds.

In June 1927, Judge Curtis A. Peters ordered that the American money be returned to the bond-certificate purchasers. He appointed receivers to organise the disbursement of the funds.[66] De Valera made a direct appeal to bondholders to transfer bond certificates to him to fund his political activities, in particular to part-finance the foundation of the *Irish Press* newspaper.

Distribution of the funds by the receivers was delayed by legal challenges and administration problems. According to Francis Carroll, 'it was not until 1930 that the receivers had completed sufficient paperwork to make a repayment of the money to the bondholders, and then to only 131,249, just over one-third of the 303,578 original purchasers.'[67] Judge Peters approved the receivers' report authorising the repayment of $2,539,783, or $.58 for every dollar. The final receiver payments were not made until 24 February 1933.

The Free State had passed legislation for the full repayment of the Loans raised in Ireland and America in 1924, before the final court judgements. The government publicly committed to repaying the American bonds *in full*, but had delayed the process due to the benefit that would accrue to de Valera from the bond certificates that had been assigned to him. In December 1932, after de Valera acceded to power, the cabinet approved the repayment of $1.25 for each dollar subscribed, less the amount paid by the receiver ($.58), providing a 25% return. In a heated debate in the Dáil, Desmond Fitzgerald, the former Minister for External Affairs, said the bill would 'mulct the people of the country in about £1,000,000 in order that £100,000 may go into the pockets of the President [de Valera].'[68] The last payments were made in 1936. According to Carroll, a total of $2,487,651 was paid out to some 112,119 claimants.[69]

Repayment of the Loan in Ireland was made using Post Office Savings Certificates, beginning 1 June 1927. Subscribers to the Irish Loan received a 40% return on their investment, in line with the terms of the original prospectus which, unlike the American bond, paid interest. The 40% return consisted of the 5% interest rate paid for seven years and the repayment of the principal at 105%. The final date for receipt of applications was 30 April 1931.

Funds raised

The total funds raised in the First Dáil Loan in America was $5,235,167.[70] The cost of funding was $736,825 – a rather high 14.1% of the funds raised.[71] The number of subscribers was between 257,988 and 303,578.[72]

A second Bond drive launched on 15 November 1921 raised $619,640.[73] It was cancelled within weeks of the launch following the signing of the treaty in London. The total amount raised in America from the two Bond drives was $5,854,806.

The total official receipts by the Irish government from all sources in America was $6,484,915 to 31 January 1922 (Collins added an extra month to take account of receipts from the second Bond drive). This included the Self-Determination Fund (set up primarily to capture money being returned by the anti-conscription movement in Ireland), 'Refunds', interest and the 'Refugee Fund'.

Total outgoings came to $4,023,325, of which $2,160,363 or 33% of receipts, was remitted to Ireland; £863,858 (13%) was spent on the Bond campaigns; and $844,111 (13%) on the costs of the Irish mission, including the Waldorf.

The balance of funds held in America at 31 January 1922 was $2,461,590.

Receipts and Expenditure in USA to 31 January 1922 ($)		
Receipts		
First Bond Drive	5,235,167	81%
Second Bond Drive	619,640	10%
Self Determination Fund	184,173	3%
Refunds	125,830	2%
Interest	201,330	3%
Refugee Fund	118,775	2%
	6,484,915	
Outgoings		**Receipts (%)**
Costs - First Bond Drive	736,826	11%
Costs - Second Bond Drive	127,032	2%
Remittances - Home	2,160,363	33%
Remittances - Local	844,111	13%
Recoverable Expenditure	144,992	2%
Paris 6/11/19.	10,000	0.2%
	4,023,325	62%
Balance	**2,461,590**	

Source: 'U.S.A ACCOUNT', NA, DE 2/9, 021.

The official total collected by Clan-na-Gael for the Bond drive in New York City, as prepared by John Devoy, was $627,916.[74]

New York CnG Contribution to the Irish Republic Bond Issue ($)		
Brooklyn Clubs	369,780	59%
Manhattan and Bronx Clubs	200,765	32%
Collected byBunker Hill Club, Bronx, Members	50,000	8%
Cumann-na-mBan, Inc.	7371	1%
Total	**627,916**	

Source: Gaelic American, 30 October 1920.

AUTHOR'S NOTE

I commenced this book as a companion to *Crowdfunding the Revolution: The First Dáil Loan and the Battle for Irish Independence.*

It soon became apparent that much of the traditional narrative of de Valera's time in America – around the recognition campaign, the bond drive and his tours - did not stand up to the scrutiny of contemporary evidence, and when viewed from the perspective of the leaders of the Irish Race in America, and framed within post-war domestic American politics and geopolitical turmoil. This necessitated the broadening of the scope of the book.

As a result a number of important topics have not been addressed, or not been addressed in the detail they merit. These include the American Women Pickets Movement, the visit of Archbishop Mannix to America, the longshoremen strike, the suffrage movement, Marcus Garvey's support of Irish independence, and the American Commission on Conditions in Ireland and the American Committee for Relief in Ireland.

I would have liked to elaborate on the economic development activities of Dáil Éireann, including the work of the trade envoys and efforts to open direct shipping routes between America and Ireland. The purchase of arms and ammunition is only briefly touched upon. The cooperation of individual members of the New York Police Department and the New York City Fire Department would have been interesting to explore in more detail.

NOTES

Prologue

1 (Fitzgerald 1920), p. 290.

2 (Bruccoli 1981), p. 20.

3 (Bruccoli 1981), p. 12.

4 F. Scott Fitzgerald to John O'Hara, letter, 18 July 1933, Princeton University Library, *Life in letters*, pp. 233-34, (Bruccoli 1981), p. 23.

5 F. Scott Fitzgerald to John O'Hara, letter, 18 July 1933, Princeton University Library, *Life in letters*, pp. 233-34, (Bruccoli 1981), p. 23.

6 F. Scott Fitzgerald to John O'Hara, letter, 18 July 1933, Princeton University Library, *Life in letters*, pp. 233-34, (Bruccoli 1981), p. 23.

7 '"Such Friends": Maxwell Perkins and F. Scott Fitzgerald', blog post, 21 September 1917, American Writers Museum.

8 *The Evening World*, 13 July 1921, p. 5; *New York Times*, 14 July 1921, p. 10.

9 *New York American*, 30 January 1920, via *Irish Press*, 7 February 1920, p. 4.

10 Address to a Joint Session of Congress, 11 February 1918.

11 Lansing, Robert, *The Peace Negotiations: A Personal Narrative*, 1921, via (F. Carroll 2021), p. 36.

12 George Creel, *War, the World, and Wilson*, 163, via (F. Carroll 2021), p. 37.

13 President Wilson to Lansing, letter, 10 April 1917, via (Tansill 1957), p. 230.

14 Bruccoli, M.J., *Some Sort of Epic Grandeur: The Life of F. Scott Fitzgerald*, p. 38.

15 (Golway 2015), KL 3043.

16 (Golway 2015), p. 32.

17 'The elected Government of Ireland stood for social and economical deliverance, no less than for political deliverance', Collins to de Valera, 10 February 1920, Béaslaí 1922, pp. 414-16.

18 John Quinn, an American Home Rule advocate, said to Lord Balfour, 'I pointed out that the men who would go into the home rule parliament would be of a different breed and

kind than those who have gone into the Dublin municipal corporation'. Typescript of the interview with Balfour by John Quinn, John Quinn Papers, NLI, MS 1751, via (F. Carroll 2021), KL 4053.

19 (Creel 1919), p. 52.

20 (Tansill 1957), p. 322.

21 *Gaelic American*, 13 September 1919, p. 1.

22 (Lynch, History of the Friends of Irish Freedom 1930 - 1939).

23 (Doorley 2019), p. 20–23; 'Judge Daniel F. Cohalan & The Courtmacsherry Connection', Courtmacsherry & Barryroe History Group.

24 (Doorley 2019), p. 23.

25 The term 'Irish Race' was in regular use in 1919.

26 (Doorley 2019), p. 151.

27 McGuire to Cohalan, 20 September 1919, AIHS – American Irish Historical Society, via (Fahey 2014), KL 2214.

28 *NYT*, 6 October 1917, p. 11.

29 *NYT*, 2 October 1917, p. 1.

30 *NYTs*, 3 November 1917, p. 4.

31 *NYT*, 16 March 1918, p. 8.

32 Dr. Michael Doorley, Cohalan biographer, sourced the original document in the German diplomatic archives, along with several letters from Cohalan to Von Bernstorff. See (Doorley 2019), p. 85.

33 *The Southern Star*, 3 August 1912, via Courtmacsherry and Barryroe History Group; (Lynch, History of the Friends of Irish Freedom 1930 - 1939)

34 Leslie, S., November 1917, 'The Irish issue in its American aspect; a contribution to the settlement of Anglo-American relations during and after the great war', KL 1689.

35 (Fitzgerald 1920), p. 218.

36 Sproule, Michael J. (1997), *Propaganda and Democracy: The American Experience of Media and Mass Persuasion* (Cambridge, Cambridge University Press).

37 *Harper's Magazine*, March 1918, via (Lynch 1930 - 1939), Chapter XL.

38 Sproule, Michael J. (1997), *Propaganda and Democracy: The American Experience of Media and Mass Persuasion* (Cambridge, Cambridge University Press).

39 *NYT*, 22 December 1919, p. 3.

40 Lynch (1957), p. 198, via (McGough 2013), KL 1479.

41 (Lynch 1930 - 1939), Chapter XL

42 (McGough 2013), KL 1322.

43 (McGough 2013), KL 1159.

44 Pension files, Ref: 497, via (McGough 2013), KL 1270.

45 (McGough 2013), KL 160.

46 (McGough 2013), KL 1337; (Lynch 1930 - 1939).

47 (Lynch 1930 - 1939).

48 (Lynch 1930 - 1939).

49 (Lynch 1930 - 1939).

50 Devoy to McCartan, 21 April 1919, via (Lynch 1930 - 1939).

51 (Leslie 1917), p. 180.

52 *GA*, 27 March 1920, p. 1.

53 (Lynch, History of the Friends of Irish Freedom 1930 - 1939).

54 Devoy to McCartan, letter, 21 April 1919, via (Lynch 1930 - 1939).

55 Devoy to McCartan, letter, 21 April 1919, via (Lynch 1930 - 1939).

56 *IP*, 24 May 1919 p. 4.

57 *IP*, 28 June 1919, p. 4.

58 *NYT*, 15 October 1917, p. 4.

59 Devoy to McGarrity, (Golway), letter, McGarrity papers, NLI, MS 17,609, p. 201.

60 Devoy to McCartan, letter, 21 April 1919, via (Lynch 1930 - 1939).

61 Cohalan to Boland, letter, 6 September 1919, AIHS, Cohalan Papers, via (McGough 2013), KL 1576.

62 Maloney later claimed that the meeting in May 1917 with Lord Percy and Shane Leslie at the British embassy had not been pre-arranged. His was an 'inadvertent visit', which only happened through a series of coincidental events *(IP,* 9 July, 1921, p. 1). Maloney distanced himself from Leslie, whom he said he only 'knew slightly'. Diarmuid Lynch wrote that it was a 'small wonder, therefore, that Maloney in 1921 when defending his own actions should be meticulous in disclaiming any but a slight acquaintance with Leslie on his return to New York in 1917, and in minimising Leslie's standing at the Embassy in that year.' See

(Lynch, History of the Friends of Irish Freedom 1930 - 1939).

63 Biographical information on Maloney is mainly sourced from: Reynolds, K.A. (nd). 'Global Lives: Dr William J. Maloney', Century Ireland, www.rte.ie/centuryireland/index.php/articles/global-lives-dr-william-j-maloney; *IP*, 9 July 1921, p. 1; and (McCartan 1932), p. 77.

64 Oswald Garrison Villard to Maloney, letter, 1 May 1919, New York Public Library, Maloney CIHP, B.6, f.3, 2-3, via (Reynolds 2019), p. 43.

65 (McCartan 1932), p. 69.

66 (Golway), p. 117 and 140.

67 *GA*, editorial, 8 November 1919, p. 4.

68 Devoy to McCartan, letter, 21 April 1919, via (Lynch 1930 - 1939).

69 Devoy to McCartan, letter, 21 April 1919, via (Lynch 1930 - 1939).

70 Devoy to McCartan, letter, 21 April 1919, via (Lynch 1930 - 1939).

71 Devoy to McCartan, letter, 21 April 1919, via (Lynch 1930 - 1939).

72 Maloney to Villard, letter, 3 May 1919, Houghton Library, Villard Papers, via (Reynolds 2019), p. 43.

73 Report by Sir William Wiseman, Documents on British Foreign Policy 1919–1935, First Series, volume 5, pp. 980–83, via (Hopkinson 2002), KL 3865.

74 Senate Congressional Record, 6 June 1919, p. 729.

75 (Lynch 1930 - 1939)

76 Senate Congressional Record, 29 May 1919, p. 393.

77 Senate Congressional Record, 5 June 1919, p. 672.

78 John Quinn, an Irish–American Home Rule advocate, interview with Balfour, Quinn Papers, NLI, MS 1751, via (F. Carroll 2021), KL 4053.

79 *NYT*, 13 August 1919, p. 1.

80 *NYT*, 21 November 2019, 'The last time America turned away from the world'.

81 Sean T. O'Kelly to Dublin, 15 June 1919, No. 15, DFA ES Paris 1919, via DIFP.

Chapter 1

1 *NYT*, 24 June 1919, p. 1.

2 *NYT*, 25 June 1919, p. 4. On 4 April, the Dáil had approved a plan to raise a £250,000 bond in 'such amounts as to meet the needs of the small subscriber'. In June, the size of the bond was increased to £500,000, of which £250,000 was to be raised in Ireland and £250,000 in America. The plan was to issue a £1,000,000 loan with a *first tranche* of £500,000. See de Valera, É, 'Dáil Éireann debates', Vol. F No. 6. 10 April 1919.

3 *The Brooklyn Daily Eagle*, 25 June 1919, p. 2.

4 *NYT*, 22 June 1919, p. 12.

5 *NYT*, 22 June 1919, p. 12

6 *NYT*, 22 June 1919, p. 12

7 *IP*, 21 June 1919, p. 1.

8 *NYT*, 22 June 1919, p. 12.

9 *NYT*, 22 June 1919, p. 12.

10 *NYT*, 22 June 1919, p. 12.

11 *NYT*, 22 June 1919, p. 12.

12 *NYT*, 24 June 1919, p. 1.

13 *NYT*, 24 June 1919, p. 1.

14 *NYT*, 24 June 1919, p. 1.

15 *NYT*, 24 June 1919, p. 1.

16 *NYT*, 24 June 1919, p. 1.

17 *NYT*, 24 June 1919, p. 1.

18 (O'Doherty 1957), p. 43; Sean Nunan, Capuchin Annual, 1970, p. 238.

19 *NYT*, 25 June 1919, p. 4.

20 *NYT*, 24 June 1919, p. 4.

21 *NYT*, 25 June 1919, p. 4.

22 *NYT*, 25 June 1919, p. 4.

23 Collins to de Valera, letter, 14 October 1919, via (Béaslaí 1922), p. 356-57.

24 *NYT*, 25 June 1919, p. 4.

25 *NYT*, 26 June 1919, p. 20.

26 *NYT*, editorial, 25 June, p. 18.

27 The girls were Sheila O'Reilley and Mabel Clayton, living at 777 East 170th Street, *NYT*, 26 June 1919, p. 1.

28 40,000 (*NYT*, 30 June 1919, p. 4); 'at least 50,000' (*Boston Globe*), 70,000 (*IP*, 12 July 1919).

29 British Pathé silent newsreel with the intertitle, 'Boston Mass. Éamon De Valera, "President of the Irish Republic" is touring America raising funds for "Sinn Fein."', https://youtu.be/G8ljyohXLv0.

30 (O'Doherty 1957), p. 45–46.

31 *NYT*, 24 June 1919, p. 1.

32 (Lynch 1930 - 1939).

33 Devoy to Cohalan, letter, 24 June 1919, Cohalan papers, 4/4, via (Fitzpatrick 2003), p. 130.

34 Devoy to Cohalan, letter, 24 June 1919, Cohalan papers, 4/4, via (Fitzpatrick 2003), p. 130.

35 *GA*, 28 June 1919, p. 1.

36 *NYT*, editorial, 1 July 1919, p. 10.

37 *GA*, 12 July 1919, p. 1.

38 *Boston Post*, editorial, via *NYT*, 12 July 1919, p. 1.

39 *GA*, 12 July 1919, p. 1.

40 *NYT*, editorial, 1 July 1919, p. 15.

41 *NYT*, 4 July 1919, p. 7.

42 *GA*, 12 July 1919, p. 1.

43 *NYT*, 11 July 1919, p.1; *IP*, 19 July 1919, p. 1; *GA*, 19 July 1919, p. 1

44 *NYT*, 11 July 1919, p. 1; editorial, 14 July 1919.

45 *IP*, 19 July 1919, p.2.

46 *NYT*, 13 July 1919, p. 5; *IP*, 19 July 1919, p.2.

47 *NYT*, 14 July 1919, p. 13; *IP*, 19 July 1919, p. 1.

48 *NYT*, 14 July 1919, p. 13; (O'Doherty 1957), p. 52 – 55.

49 *IP*, 19 July 1919, p. 1; *NYT*, 14 July 1919, p. 13.

50 *IP*, 26 July 1919, p. 1,.

51 *New York Herald*, 4 August 1919, p. 5.

52 *New York Herald*, 4 August 1919, p. 5.

53 Itemised balance sheet for a lecture tour of the United States by Éamon De Valera, NLI, MGp, MS 17,651/6/8.

54 *St. Louis Globe-Democrat*, 4 August 1919, p. 9.

55 *NYT*, 9 July 1919, p. 3.

56 (Longford 1974), p. 99, citing Liam Mellows' diary, 8 July 1919.

57 *NYT*, 9 July 1919, p. 6.

58 (Creel, Rebel at large: recollections of fifty crowded years 1947), p. 48.

59 (Creel, Rebel at large: recollections of fifty crowded years 1947), p. 48.

60 Senate Foreign Relations Committee hearing, 30 August 1919, via *NYT*, 31 August 1919, p. 1.

61 *Gaelic American*, 20 September 1919, p. 6.

62 Henry White to Senator Cabot Lodge, via (Carroll, Thesis 1969), p. 40.

63 Sean T. O'Kelly to Dublin, 15 June 1919, via DIFP.

64 *NYT*, 31 August 1919, p. 1.

65 (Carroll, Thesis 1969), p. 49.

66 (Carroll, Thesis 1969), p. 40.

67 (Carroll, Thesis 1969), p. 40.

68 (Lynch 1930 - 1939). A further $10,000 was sent to Paris on 8 November

69 Sean T. O'Kelly to Daniel Cohalan, letter, 27 June 1919, Cohalan Papers, fl. 4, Box 13, AIHS, via (Doorley 2019), p. 130.

70 Sean T. O'Kelly to John Devoy, letter, O'Brien, W. and Ryan, D. (eds.), *Devoy's Post Bag*, Vol. 2, pp. 534-5, via (Doorley 2019), p. 130.

71 *NYT*, 5 July 1919, p. 5.

72 *NYT*, 2 July 1919, p. 5, 3 July 1919, p. 4.

73 *Chicago Tribune*, via *NYT*, 7 July 1919, p. 15. Kuno Meyer was held in high esteem in Ireland. Dáil Éireann used £300 ($20,000) out of the Loan proceeds in Ireland to pay for a portrait of Meyer for presentation to the Municipal Art Gallery. The cabinet also agreed to recoup £125 to the London office for the travel costs of Mrs Meyer and her daughter to America and the cost of their hotel stay in London. NAI, DE 2/7, 043, 055.

74 Other speakers included: Lincoln Colcord; Lindsay Crawford, the Protestant editor of *The Canadian Statesman*; Revd Norman Thomas; J. C. Walsh, special correspondent at the Paris Peace Conference for the *Catholic Weekly America*; Lajpat Rai, the Indian nationalist; Alfred W. McCann; and Brandon Tynan. See *New York Tribune*, 5 July 1919, p. 6.

75 *NYT*, 5 July 1919, p. 7.

Chapter 2

1 (Fitzpatrick 2003), p. 143.

2 Harry Boland to Michael Collins, letter 20 July 1921, via (Fitzpatrick 2003), p. 199.

3 *NYT*, obituary, 12 February 1933.

4 *NYT*, obituary, 28 March 1930.

5 (Tansill 1957), p. 348; (Doorley 2019), p. 132, William Cockran to Daniel Cohalan, 14 July 1919, fl. 3, Box 3, Cohalan Papers, AIHS.

6 *Gaelic American*, 12 August 1922, p. 2; (Lynch 1930 - 1939).

7 *Gaelic American*, 12 August 1922, p. 2; (Lynch 1930 - 1939).

8 *Gaelic American*, 12 August 1922, p. 2.

9 *Gaelic American*, 12 August 1922, p. 2.

10 *Gaelic American*, 12 August 1922, p. 2.

11 (McCartan 1932), p. 109.

12 (Lynch 1930 - 1939)

13 Lynch, D., Friends of Irish Freedom Circular, 19 November 1920, via *GA*, 18 December 1920, p. 1.

14 (Fitzpatrick 2003), p. 143.

15 Lynch, D., Friends of Irish Freedom Circular, 19 November 1920, via *Gaelic American*, 18 December 1920, p. 1.

16 (Lynch 1930 - 1939)

17 (Fitzpatrick 2003), p. 375, Note 34; (Lynch 1930 - 1939).

18 Lynch, D., Friends of Irish Freedom Circular, 19 November 1920, via *GAn*, p. 1, 18 December 1920.

19 (Lynch 1930 - 1939)

20 Harry Boland to Joe McGarrity, MGp, NLI, MS 17,578/1/3; *NYT*, 14 July 1919, p. 13.

21 Harry Boland to Joe McGarrity, MGp, National Library of Ireland, MS 17,578/1/3; *NYT*, 14 July 1919, p. 13.

22 Harry Boland to Joe McGarrity, MGp, NLI, MS 17,578/1/3.

23 Harry Boland to Joe McGarrity, MGp, NLI, MS 17,578/1/3.

24 *GA*, 16 July 1921, p. 5; 30 October 1920, p. 1.

25 *GA*, 16 July 1921, p. 5.

26 *GA*, 30 October 1920, p. 1.

27 Harry Boland to Joe McGarrity, MGp, NLI, MS 17,578/1/3.

28 Boland to McGarrity, MGp, NLI, MS 17,578/1/3.

29 *NYT*, 13 July 1919, p. 5.

30 Lynch, D., Friends of Irish Freedom Circular, 19 November 1920, via *GA*, 18 December 1920, p. 1.

31 Diarmuid Lynch to his sister Mary (Moll), letter, 20 July 1919, Lynch Family Archives, folder 5/16, via Ruairí Lynch, http://diarmuidlynch. weebly.com.

32 Diarmuid Lynch to an unknown recipient, probably Daniel Cohalan, letter, 19 July 1919, Friends of Irish Freedom Archives, AIHS, via Eileen McGough, and Ruairí Lynch, http:// diarmuidlynch.weebly.com.

33 *NYT*, 10 August 1919, p. 3; *IP*, 23 August 1919.

34 (Lynch 1930 - 1939)

35 *NYT*, 10 August 1919, p. 3; *IP*, 23 August 1919; (Lynch 1930 - 1939).

36 (Lynch 1930 - 1939). When Daniel O'Connell left the Bureau in March 1920, James K. McGuire was 'sorry to learn that Capt. O'Connell had gone. He has rendered good service and will be difficult to replace', (Fahey 2014), KL 2392; Boland wrote that 'O'Connell did good work', HBD, 13 February 1920.

37 *NYT*, 10 August 1919, p. 3; *IP*, 23 August 1919.

38 *Dictionary of Canadian Biography*, 'Pádraig Ó Siadhail', Vol. 15 (Toronto, University of Toronto).

39 Friends of Irish Freedom Archive, AIHS, via Eileen McGough, and Ruairí Lynch, http://diarmuidlynch. weebly.com.

40 (Lynch 1930 - 1939)

41 (Lynch 1930 - 1939).

42 (Lynch 1930 - 1939).

43 (Lynch 1930 - 1939).

44 Lynch urged the committees to make a 'whirlwind finish.' The total amount raised was $1,005,080. See *GA*, 16 August 1919; *IP*, 16 August 1919 and (Lynch 1930 - 1939).

45 *GA*, 18 December 1920, p. 1.

46 According to Lynch, Boland 'never consulted' with the special committee, and de Valera 'disregarded' it. The 'same week' (as a 16 August memo to Lynch), de Valera 'very emphatically stated that the committee appointed by the National Council had no further jurisdiction.' The Council dissolved the committee at its next meeting. According to Devoy, the committee was 'set aside' by de Valera without notifying its members. See *Gaelic American*, 30 October 1920, p. 1 and 18 December 1920, p. 1.

47 De Valera to Walsh, letter, 18 August 1919, NLI, MGp, MS 17,651/4/4.

48 Walsh to O'Kelly, 17 September 1919), via (Carroll, Thesis 1969), p. 330.

49 Walsh to Dunne, 12 August 1919, NAI, DE 2/245, 191; 18 August 1919, NAI, DE 2/245, 193.

50 De Valera to Boland, 11 June 1919, via (Fitzpatrick 2003), p. 124.

51 'We had already some idea that a difficulty existed in America, and Harry Boland was accordingly sent out to straighten matters.', Diarmuid O'Hegarty to Sean T O'Kelly, 25 June 1919, NAI, Gavan Duffy Papers 1125/21, via DIFP.

52 '[Boland] is meeting with good success', Diarmuid O'Hegarty to Sean T O'Kelly, 25 June 1919, NAI, Gavan Duffy Papers 1125/21, via DIFP

53 According to Devoy, '...when De Valera arrived later he ordered that no action whatever be taken in regard to McCartan. De Valera evidently wanted McCartan to continue his mischief making to prepare the way for the split which he afterwards launched, and which he evidently contemplated from the start.' GA, 12 August 1922, p. 2.

54 De Valera to Walsh, 18 August 1919, NLI, MGp, MS 17,651/4/4.

55 IP, editorial, 30 August 1919.

56 NYT, 24 August 1919, p. 12; IP, 30 August 1919.

57 McCartan papers, NLI, MS 17,681/3/1. Maloney came up with an impractical bond certificate numbering system designed to prevent 'exploitation of the poor people'; each certificate was to include the initial letter of the family name. See NLI, MS 17,681/3/8.

58 Walsh to Dunne, 12 August 1919, NAI, DE 2/245, 191.

59 Dunne to Walsh, 16 August 1919, NAI, DE 2/245, 189.

60 Walsh to Dunne, 18 August 1919, NAI, DE 2/245, 193.

61 De Valera to Griffith, 13 August 1919, DIFP, UCDA P150/96; 21 August 1919, DIFP, NAI, DE 2/245.

62 Michael Collins, Department of Finance Report, NAI DE 2/7, 159.

63 DE, debate, 20 August 1919, Vol. F No. 13.

64 'Upon this loan the whole constructive policy of Dáil Éireann depends', Report of the Honorary Secretaries of Sinn Féin on 21 August 1919 (Freeman's Journal, 22 August 1919, p. 5).

65 Walter Long, First Lord of the Admiralty, predicted that 'the Sinn Féin MPs would troop off to Westminster as soon as they discovered they could not draw their salaries' (Fanning 2013).

66 Michael Collins, Department of Finance Report, NAI DE 2/7, 159.

67 Chicago Tribune, 16 August 1919, p. 5; Chicago Herald and Examiner, 16 August 1919, via GA, 6 September 1919, p. 3.

68 Boland to Collins, 26 August 1919, O Murthuile, memoir, f. 91, via (Fitzpatrick 2003), p. 158.

69 Michael Collins' Own Story, Hayden Talbot, Hutchinson 1923, KL 299.

70 Collins to Boland, 10, 13 September and 6 October 1919, EdeVP P 150/1125, via (Fitzpatrick 2003), p. 159.

71 'According to O Murthuile, Memoir, f. 92, the pressure for Collins

departure came from Brugha and Stack.', via (Fitzpatrick 2003).

72 Collins to Boland, 10, 13 September and 6 October 1919, EdeVP P 150/1125, via (Fitzpatrick 2003), p. 159.

73 Nunan to Collins, 3 September 1919, DIFP, No. 25, NAI, DE 2/292.

74 Nunan to Collins, 17 September 1919, NAI, DE 2/292 (079).

75 Collins to Nunan, 6 October 1919, DE 02/292 (078).

76 Devoy ['Hudson'] to 'Dear Friend', 1 November 1919, MGp, MS 17,486/6/4.

77 GA, 16 August 1919.

78 NYT, 27 June 1919, p. 8.

79 (Béaslaí 1922), p. 337 – 338.

80 (Béaslaí 1922), p. 337 – 338.

81 (Béaslaí 1922), p. 337 – 338.

82 NYT, 27 June 1919, p. 8.

83 (Béaslaí 1922), p. 337 – 338.

84 De Valera to Collins, 6 September 1919, (Béaslaí 1922), p. 353.

85 Collins to de Valera, 6 October 1919, (Béaslaí 1922), p. 354.

86 De Valera to Collins, 16 September 1919 (Béaslaí 1922), p. 353.

87 Collins to de Valera, 14 October 1919, (Béaslaí 1922), p. 356.

Chapter 3

1 De Valera to Griffith, 13 August 1919, DIFP, UCDA P150/96.

2 Boland to McGarrity, MGp, NLI, 26 August 1919.

3 Boland to McGarrity, MGp, NLI, 26 August 1919.

4 Devoy to Boland, 6 September 1919, AIHS, Cohalan Papers, via (McGough 2013), KL 1576.

5 Devoy to Cohalan, 6 September 1919, via (Doorley 2005), p. 109.

6 Devoy to Cohalan, (Golway 2015), p. 223.

7 The Evening World, 15 September 1919, p. 12. One resolution referred to '10,000 American liberals' assembled together. See IP, 20 September 1919, p. 1.

8 IP, 20 September 1919, p. 1.

9 IP, 9 October 1919, p. 1.

10 NYT, 15 September 1919, p. 3; (McCartan 1932), p. 450; Other speakers included Martin Conboy, a lawyer and director of the draft in New York; Alfred J. Talley, Assistant D.A., and Rev. Grattan Mythen of the Protestant Friends of Ireland.

11 The Evening World, 15 September 1919, p. 12.

12 Colcord to Nuorteva, undated, McCartan papers, NLI, MS 17,682/8.

13 McGarrity to Friends of Irish Freedom National Council, 3 October 1919, FRIENDS OF IRISH FREEDOM archive, AIHS via Eileen McGough and Ruairí Lynch. www.diarmuidlynch.weebly.com.

14 (Golway 2015), p. 223 – 224.

15 GA, 20 September 1919, p. 1.

16 'Brooklyn to Give Great Welcome to De Valera', GA, 20 September 1919, p. 1.

17 (Golway 2015), p. 223 – 224.

18 *Newport Mercury*, 27 September 1919, p. 4.; (Hannigan 2008), KL 1088.

19 *NYT,* 25 September 1919, p. 1, 3.

20 *GA,* editorial, 11 October 1919, p. 4,.

21 De Valera to FRIENDS OF IRISH FREEDOM National Trustees, (Lynch 1930 - 1939); (Lavelle 2011), p. 144.

22 Itemised balance sheet for a lecture tour, NLI, MGp, MS 17,651/6/8.

23 De Valera to FRIENDS OF IRISH FREEDOM National Trustees, (Lynch 1930 - 1939); (Lavelle 2011), p. 144.

24 FRIENDS OF IRISH FREEDOM National Council, 3 October 1919, FRIENDS OF IRISH FREEDOM archive, AIHS, via Eileen McGough and Ruairí Lynch. www.diarmuidlynch.weebly.com.

25 Devoy ['Hudson'] to 'Dear Friend', 1 November 1919, MGp, MS 17,486/6/4.

26 Devoy to Cohalan, AIHS, Cohalan papers, via (Golway 2015), p. 224.

Chapter 4

1 Boland to McGuire, 10 September 1919, via (Fahey 2014), KL 2165.

2 (Schultz 2019), p. 8.

3 (Schultz 2019), p. 329.

4 (Schultz 2019), p. 329.

5 (Schultz 2019), KL 65.

6 Nunan to Collins, 19 August 1919, NAI, DE 2/292 082.

7 McGuire to Cohalan, 20 September 1919, via (Fahey 2014), KL 2195.

8 McGuire to Cohalan, 20 September 1919, via (Fahey 2014), KL 2195.

9 Boland to Cohalan, and reply, 4 and 6 September 1919, Cohalan Papers, 2/5, via (Fitzpatrick 2003), p. 131.

10 McGuire to Cohalan, 20 September 1919, via (Fahey 2014), KL 2195.

11 McGuire to Cohalan, 3 October 1919, AIHS, via (Fahey 2014), KL 2261; McGuire to Lawless, 30 September 1919, Lawless papers, Georgia Southern University; Shannon to McGuire, 30 September 1919, via (Fahey 2014), KL 2259; Lysaght to McGuire, 29 September 1919, via (Fahey 2014), KL 2259.

12 The Irish Republic, Charles N. Wheeler, Cahill-Igoe Company, Chicago, 1919.

13 Wheeler to McGarrity, 30 November 1919, MGp, NLI, MS 17,518/68.

14 Devoy to Luke Dillon, 28 November 1919, MGp, NLI, MS 17,610/2/1.

15 William E. Ellis, The Register of the Kentucky Historical Society, Vol. 92, No. 2 (Spring 1994), pp. 175-199.

16 William E. Ellis, The Register of the Kentucky Historical Society, Vol. 92, No. 2 (Spring 1994), pp. 175-199.

17 McGuire to Cohalan, 20 September 1919, via (Fahey 2014), KL 2195.

18 Devoy to a "Dear Friend", 1 November 1919, MGp, NLI, MS 17,486/6/4; Devoy to Luke Dillon, 28 November 1919, MGp, NLI, MS 17,610/2/1.

19 *IP*, 18 October 1919, p. 1,.

20 *NYT,* 28 February 1919, p. 17

21 McGuire to Cohalan, 20 September 1919, via (Fahey 2014), KL 2195.

22 Congressional Record – Appendix, 1960, Volume 106, Part 21.

23 McGuire to Cohalan, 3 October 1919, AIHS, via (Fahey 2014), KL 2261.

24 McGuire to Cohalan, 17 September 1919, AIHS, via (Fahey 2014), KL 2176.

25 McGuire to Cohalan, 3 October 1919, AIHS, via (Fahey 2014), KL 2261.

26 McGuire to Cohalan, 17 September 1919, AIHS, via (Fahey 2014), KL 2176.

27 McGuire to Cohalan, 17 September 1919, AIHS, via (Fahey 2014), KL 2176.

28 McGuire to Cohalan, 20 September 1919, via (Fahey 2014), KL 2195.

29 Sligo Champion, 18 October 1919, p. 5. The arrest date was given in the report.

30 The National Tribune (Washington), 28 October 1892, p. 7; *NYT,* Martin Conboy obituary, 6 March 1944, p. 19; *NYT,* 13 March 1934, p. 13; 8 August 1934, p. 15.

31 Boland to McGuire, 10 September 1919, via (Fahey 2014), KL 2165.

32 Boland to Cohalan, 11 September 1919, P150 1134, via (Lainer-Vos 2013), KL 1894.

33 Diarmuid Lynch, *GA,* 18 December 1920, p. 1. McCartan attributed the bond certificate solution to William Maloney, but much of McCartan's description of the Bond campaign does not match with contemporary evidence. See (McCartan 1932), p. 131. Katherine O'Doherty claimed that it was de Valera and McGarrity who proposed the solution and 'alone' consulted with Conboy. O'Doherty's description of the Bond campaign also does not match with the contemporary evidence, and paints the FRIENDS OF IRISH FREEDOM as obstructionist. See (O'Doherty 1957), p. 64.

34 Nunan to Collins, 17 September 1919, NAI, DE 2/292 (079).

35 Prospectus of the first issue of bond certificates, McCartan papers, NLI, MS 17,681/3/13.

36 (Lynch 1930 - 1939). In 1941, Robert Brennan and Frank Aiken called on Franklin D. Roosevelt. Brennan recorded that 'Mr. Roosevelt... recalled his first meeting with Mr. de Valera in 1919 or 1920, when he had been asked to advise on the matter of raising the Republican Loan without coming into conflict with U.S. laws. He recalled the raising of the loan that nobody expected to be repaid, and the magnificent gesture of the Irish Government in repaying the loan with interest.', Robert Brennan to Joseph P. Walshe, 10 April 1941, DIFP, NAI, DFA Secretary's Files, P35.

37 McGuire to Cohalan, 20 September 1919, via (Fahey 2014), KL 2206.

38 De Valera to Frank P. Walsh, 19 September 1919 [date is on another copy of letter], MGp, Villanova University.

39 Nunan to Collins, 17 September 1919, NAI, DE 2/292 (079).

40 De Valera to FRIENDS OF IRISH FREEDOM National Trustees, (Lynch 1930 - 1939); (Lavelle 2011), p. 144.

Chapter 5

1 Boland to Ned Boland, 23 September 1919, via (Fitzpatrick 2003), p. 131.

2 HBD, 1 October 1919.

3 *GA,* 11 October 1919, p. 2.

4 *GA,* 11 October 1919, p. 7; *IP,* 9 October 1919, p.1.

5 (Fitzpatrick 2003), p. 132.

6 *GA,* 11 October 1919, p. 2.

7 *IP*, 9 October 1919, p. 2.

8 HBD, 3 October 1919.

9 HBD, 4 October 1919.

10 Mellows to Boland, 29 September 1919, EdeVP, P150/1163, via (Fitzpatrick 2003), p. 141.

11 York Daily Record, 6 October 1919, p. 5.

12 HBD, 5 October 1919; Boland to McGarrity, 10 October 1919, MGp, NLI, MS 17,424/1/3.

13 HBD, 6 October 1919.

14 HBD, 6 October 1919.

15 HBD, 7 October 1919; Bucyrus Evening Telegraph, 7 October 1919, p. 5.

16 HBD, 8 October 1919.

17 HBD, 8 October 1919.

18 HBD, 9 October 1919.

19 HBD, 9 October 1919.

20 Boland to McGarrity, 10 October 1919, MGp, NLI, MS 17,424/1/3.

21 HBD, 10 October 1919.

22 The quotation is from the 1974 film directed by Jack Clayton, rather than the book itself, and portrays a key theme of *The Great Gatsby* and *This Side of Paradise,* and Fitzgerald's own early life.

23 Boland to McGarrity, 10 October 1919, MGp, NLI, MS 17,424/1/3.

24 HBD, 11 October 1919.

25 HBD, 12 October 1919.

26 The Huntington Herald, 10 October 1919, p. 14.

27 *NYT,* 11 October 1919, p. 8.

28 HBD, 13 October 1919.

29 Mellows to Boland, 6 Oct. 1919, via (Fitzpatrick 2003), p. 133.

30 HBD, 14 October 1919.

31 HBD, 16 October 1919.

32 HBD, 16 October 1919.

33 *Chicago Tribune*, 19 October 1919, p. 14; The Billings Gazette, 19 October 1919, p. 2.

Chapter 6

1 Boland to McGarrity, 10 October 1919, MGp, NLI, MS 17,424/1/3.

2 HBD, 9 October 1919.

3 *IP*, 9 October 1919, p. 3.

4 *GA,* 18 October 1919, p. 6.

5 Devoy to Cohalan, 9 October 1919, via (Doorley 2005), p. 115.

6 *GA,* editorial, 11 October 1919, p. 4.

7 Devoy to Luke Dillon, 28 November 1919, MGp, NLI, MS 17,610/2/1.

8 *GA,* 18 October 1919, p. 6,.

9 *GA,* 18 October 1919, p. 6,.

10 *GA,* 18 October 1919, p. 6,.

11 (Lynch 1930 - 1939).

12 Charles Wheeler to McGarrity, [incorrectly dated 18 June 1919], MGp, Villanova University.

Chapter 7

1 Walsh to de Valera, 2 October 1919, McCartan papers, NLI, MS 17,681/1/4.

2 Walsh to de Valera, 2 October 1919, McCartan papers, NLI, MS 17,681/1/4.

3 De Valera to McGarrity, MGp, NLI, MS 17,522/2.

4 (Fitzpatrick 2003), p. 151.

5 (Lynch 1930 - 1939).

6 (Lynch 1930 - 1939).

7 De Valera to McGarrity, MGp, NLI, MS 17,522/2. A memorandum with questions on the legality of the Bond issue and the banking issues was also prepared. See 'Memorandum regarding the Irish Republic bonds', McCartan Papers, NLI, MS 17,681/3/3.

8 Benjamin M. Kaye to Martin Conboy, 23 September 1919, MGp, Villanova University.

9 Michael Francis Doyle [incorrectly attributed to Frank P. Walsh] to the Land Title & Trust, MGp, NLI, MS 17,522/3.

10 Land Title & Trust to Michael Francis Doyle, 16 October 1919, MGp, NLI, MS 17,518/64.

11 Sean Nunan, Capuchin Annual, 1970, p. 236.

12 HBD, 22 October 1919; Sean Nunan, Capuchin Annual, 1970, p. 236.

13 HBD, 23 October 1919.

14 *IP*, 1 November 1919, p. 5,.

15 HBD, 24 October 1919.

16 Edward McSweeney, The Knights of Columbus, and the Irish-American Response to Anglo-Saxonism, 1900-1925, Christopher J. Kauffman, American Catholic Studies, Vol. 114, No. 4 (Winter 2003), p. 51-65, via JSTOR.

17 *GA,* 22 November 1919, p. 1.

18 (Lynch 1930 - 1939).

19 'Statement of Edward F. McSweeney' (undated typescript, responding to an attack by McCartan in the New York World, 22 June 1920), Cohalan Papers, 10/13, via (Fitzpatrick 2003), p. 144.

20 'Statement of Edward F. McSweeney' (undated typescript, responding to an attack by McCartan in the New York World, 22 June 1920), Cohalan Papers, 10/13, via (Fitzpatrick 2003), p. 144.

21 Devoy ('Hudson') to 'Dear Friend', 1 November 1919, NLI, MGp, MS 17,486/6/4.

22 'Statement of Edward F. McSweeney' (undated typescript, responding to an attack by McCartan in the New York World, 22 June 1920), Cohalan

Papers, 10/13, via (Fitzpatrick 2003), p. 144.

23 HBD, 24 October 1919.

24 HBD, 24 October 1919.

25 McCartan's papers, NLI, MS 17,681/3/9.

26 Collins to de Valera, 10 February 1920, via (Béaslaí 1922, 414–16); Finance Report to 30 April 1920, NAI DE 2/7, 090.

27 Collins to de Valera, 24 October 1919, via (Béaslaí 1922, 358); Freeman's Journal, 21 November 1919.

28 Dáil Éireann debate, 27 Oct 1919, Vol. F No. 14.

29 Clan-na-Gael circular letter, 27 October 1919, MGp, NLI, MS 17,657/12.

30 HBD, 28 October 1919.

31 HBD, 29 October 1919.

32 Devoy ['Hudson'] to 'Dear Friend', 1 November 1919, MGp, MS 17,486/6/4; GA, 30 October 1920, p. 1.

33 HBD, 29 October 1919.

34 William Elder: Ancestors and Descendants, Mary Louise Donnelly, University of Wisconsin, 1986.

35 HBD, 30 October 1919.

36 HBD, 31 October 1919.

37 Devoy ['Hudson'] to 'Dear Friend', 1 November 1919, MGp, MS 17,486/6/4.

38 HBD, 1 November 1919.

39 HBD, 1 November 1919.

40 HBD, 2 November 1919.

41 HBD, 3 November 1919.

42 HBD, 3 November 1919.

43 De Valera to Griffith, 21 August 1919, DIFP, NAI, DE 2/245.

44 (Lavelle 2011), p. 109.

45 (Fitzpatrick 2003), p.128.

46 De Valera to O'Mara, undated, via (Lavelle 2011), p. 138.

47 Griffith to O'Mara, via (Lavelle 2011), p. 139.

48 HBD, 3 November 1919.

49 HBD, 3 November 1919.

50 GA, 30 October 1920, p. 1.

51 HBD, 6 November 1919.

Chapter 8

1 HBD, 3 November 1919.

2 IP, editorial, 1 November 1919, p. 4,.

3 Devoy ('Hudson') to 'Dear Friend', 1 November 1919, MGp, NLI, MS 17,486/6/4.

4 GA, 8 November 1919, p. 4.

5 GA, 8 November 1919, p. 1.

6 GA, 8 November 1919, p. 1. Devoy published the Bond prospectus on the front page.

7 Devoy ('Hudson') to 'Dear Friend', 1 November 1919, MGp, NLI, MS 17,486/6/4.

8 IP, editorial, 1 November 1919, p. 4.

9 National Council Minutes, 7 November 1919, FRIENDS OF IRISH FREEDOM Archive, AIHS, via Eileen McGough, and Ruairí Lynch, www.diarmuidlynch.weebly. com.

10 On 9 July Boland had written to Griffith, 'we hope to leave behind us

here a concrete organization drawing its inspiration from home.', Boland to Griffith, 9 July 1919, DIFP, No. 19 UCDA P150/96.

11 HBD, 7 November 1919.

12 National Council Minutes, 7 November 1919, FRIENDS OF IRISH FREEDOM Archive, AIHS, via Eileen McGough, and Ruairí Lynch, www.diarmuidlynch.weebly.com.

13 National Council Minutes, 7 November 1919, FRIENDS OF IRISH FREEDOM Archive, AIHS, via Eileen McGough, and Ruairí Lynch, www.diarmuidlynch.weebly.com.

14 *GA*, 15 November 1919, p. 1.

15 *GA*, 15 November 1919, p. 1,.

16 (Lynch 1930 - 1939); *GA,* editorial, 22 November 1919, p. 4.

17 (Lynch 1930 - 1939).

18 HBD, 7 November 1919.

19 HBD, 8 November 1919.

20 HBD, 9 November 1919.

21 HBD, 10 November 1919.

22 HBD, 11 November 1919.

23 *IP*, 8 November 1919, p. 1; 15 November 1919, p. 4.

24 McGarrity to Harriman National Bank, 13 November 1919, MGp, NLI, MS 17,651/4/5.

25 Harriman National Bank to McGarrity, 19 November 1919, MGp, NLI, MS 17,652/5/13

26 New Netherland Bank to McGarrity, MGp, NLI, MS 17,651/4/6.

27 HBD, 21 November 1919.

28 HBD, 22 November 1919.

29 HBD, 23 November 1919.

30 Collins to Boland, 23 November 1919, de Valera papers, P150/1125, via (Fitzpatrick 2003), p. 145.

31 Collins to Boland, 23 November 1919, de Valera papers, P150/1125, via (Fitzpatrick 2003), p. 145.

32 *IP*, 8 November 1919, p. 2; Letter from the League to W.E.B. Du bois, 10 November 1919, W.E.B. Du bois papers, UMass Amherst.

33 *IP*, 8 November 1919, p. 2.

34 (O'Doherty 1957), p. 84.

35 *NYT,* 9 November 1919, p. 1.

36 *NYT,* 9 November 1919, p. 1.

37 *IP*, editorial, 6 December 1919, p. 4.

38 *NYT,* 9 November 1919, p. 1.

39 (Golway 2015), p. 176.

40 *NYT,* 11 November 1919, p. 1.

41 (Golway 2015), p. 221; *NYT,* 4 May 1920, p. 4; 19 April 1923, p. 1.

42 McGuire to Cohalan, 22 December 1919, via (Fahey 2014), KLs 2010.

43 *GA,* 6 December 1919, p. 7.

44 The lost Irish tribes in the South, Irvin Cobb,1919, McGarrity book collection, Villanova University.

45 *IP*, 29 November 1919, p. 1.

46 (O'Doherty 1957), p. 117.

Chapter 9

1 *GA,* 29 November 1919, p. 1.

2 *GA,* 29 November 1919, p. 1.

3 *GA,* 29 November 1919, p. 4.

4 *IP*, 22 November 1919, p. 4.

5   HBD, 19 November 1919.

6   *NYT,* 12 October 1919, section S, p. 95.

7   (Lynch 1930 - 1939).

8   *NYT,* 17 October 1919, p. 19.

9   *NYT,* 22 October 1919, p. 3. The historiographer was Michael J. O'Brien.

10 *NYT,* 18 October 1919, p. 1.

11 *NYT,* 18 October 1919, p. 1.

12 *NYT,* 19 October 1919, p. 20.

13 The *NYT,* 21 October 1919, p. 1.

14 Daniel T. O'Connell, memoir, via (Lynch 1930 - 1939).

Chapter 10

1   HBD, 24 November 1919.

2   HBD, 25 November 1919.

3   HBD, 26 November 1919.

4   (Lavelle 2011), p. 141.

5   HBD, 1 December 1919.

6   HBD, 30 November 1919.

7   HBD, 30 November 1919.

8   HBD, 30 November 1919.

9   HBD, 30 November 1919; Evening World, 2 December 1919, p. 14.

10 HBD, 4 December 1919.

11 HBD, 6 December 1919.

12 HBD, 6 December 1919.

13 *IP*, 13 December 1919, p. 1; *GA,* 20 December 1919, p. 1.

14 O'Mara to McGarrity, 6 December 1919, NLI, MS 17,651/4/2.

15 *IP*, 29 November 1919, p. 4.

16 Wikoff Smith to McGarrity, 12 December 1919, MGp, NLI, MS 17,522/4.

Chapter 11

1   *NYT,* 30 November 1919, p. 9.

2   *The Evening World*, 2 December 1919, p. 14; (Lavelle 2011), p. 148.

3   *The Evening World*, 2 December 1919, p. 14; (Lavelle 2011), p. 148.

4   (Lynch 1930 - 1939).

5   Devoy to Luke Dillon, 28 November 1919, NLI, MGp, MS 17,610/2/1.

6   Devoy to Luke Dillon, 28 November 1919, NLI, MGp, MS 17,610/2/1.

7   *NYT,* 13 July 1914, p. 1.

8   *NYT,* 13 July 1914, p. 1.

9   *GA,* 20 December 1919, p. 1.

10 Minutes, via (Lynch 1930 - 1939).

11 *GA,* 20 December 1919, p. 1.

12 *GA,* 20 December 1919, p. 1.

13 *GA,* 20 December 1919, p. 1; Minutes, via (Lynch 1930 - 1939).

14 Minutes, via (Lynch 1930 - 1939).

15 *GA,* 20 December 1919, p. 1.

16 Minutes, via (Lynch 1930 - 1939).

17 De Valera to Lynch, 10 December 1919, UCDA, de Valera papers, P150/1135.

18 'repeatedly exerted', (Lynch 1930 - 1939).

19 (Lynch 1930 - 1939).

20 Lynch Family Archives. Folder 5/19, via Ruairí Lynch. www.diarmuidlynch. weebly.com.

21 Costello 1995, 112.

22 Lynch to Joseph T. Lawless, 2 December 1919, Lawless papers, Georgia Southern University; FRIENDS OF IRISH FREEDOM archive, AIHS, via Eileen McGough, and Ruairí Lynch, www.diarmuidlynch.weebly.com.

23 FRIENDS OF IRISH FREEDOM archive, AIHS, via Eileen McGough, and Ruairí Lynch, www.diarmuidlynch.weebly.com.

Chapter 12

1 (Lynch 1930 - 1939).

2 *GA,* 29 November 1919, p. 4,.

3 FOIF archive, AIHS, via Eileen McGough, and Ruairí Lynch, www.diarmuidlynch.weebly.com.

4 HBD, 10 December 1919.

5 *NYT,* 12 December 1919, p. 19; *The Boston Globe,* 12 December 1919, p. 5.

6 *NYT,* 13 December 1919, p. 3.

7 *Washington Post,* 13 December 1919, p. 1; *Fall River Globe,* 12 December 1919, p. 17.

8 (McCartan 1932), p. 235 – 237.

9 *IP,* 20 December 1919, p. 2.

10 McGarry to Cohalan, 7 January 1920, FOIF Archive, AIHS, via Eileen McGough, and Ruairí Lynch. www.diarmuidlynch.weebly.com.

11 *GA,* 27 December 1919, p. 3.

12 *GA,* 27 December 1919, p. 3.

13 *NYT,* 13 December 1919, p. 3.

14 HBD, 13 December 1919.

15 HBD, 13 December 1919.

16 HBD, 14 December 1919.

Chapter 13

1 Nunan to Collins, 11 December 1919, NAI, DE 2/292 (076).

2 Liam O'Brian to Diarmuid Lynch, 10 December 1919, Lynch Family Archives, Folder 5/20, via Ruairí Lynch. www.diarmuidlynch.weebly.com.

3 *NYT,* 22 December 1919, p. 14.

4 Evening World, 19 December 1919, p. 2.

5 *IP,* 27 December 1919, p. 1.

6 *NYT,* 22 December 1919, p. 17.

7 *IP,* 27 December 1919, p. 1, 4.

8 *GA,* 27 December 1919, p. 8.

9 *NYT,* 12 January 1919,, p. 15.

10 HBD, 20 December 1919.

11 *NYT,* 21 November 1919, p. 17.

12 *NYT,* 21 November 1919, p. 17.

13 Prime Minister's Statement, 22 December 1919, Hansard Vol. 123.

14 *NYT,* 29 December 1919, p. 8.

Chapter 14

1 *GA,* 27 December 1919, p. 1; *IP,* 20 December 1919, p. 1.

2 NYPL, Bourke Cockran Papers, Box 13, Folder 2, via Letters of 1916 project, Maynooth University.

3 The absentee states were Colorado, Florida, Maine, Maryland, New Jersey, South Dakota, and in the Western sun belt Arizona, Nevada, New Mexico and Texas. *GA,* 27 December 1919,

p. 1; *IP*, 20 December 1919, p. 1.

4   Daniel C. O'Flaherty to Joseph T. Lawless, 17 November 1919 [incorrect date attribution as 27 November], Georgia Southern University, Lawless papers, Box No. 1, Folder No. 2.

5   O'Mara (using Frank P. Walsh's name) to Bourke Cockran, 19 December 1919, NYPL, Bourke Cockran Papers, Box 13, Folder 2, via Letters of 1916 project, Maynooth University.

6   O'Mara to Lynch, 17 December 1919, Cohalan Papers, 13/8, via (Fitzpatrick 2003).

7   The costs included hotels ($4,901), 'personal' expenses of de Valera ($749), and a large salary for Charles Sweeney ($2,037). The actual deficit was smaller as the cabinet in Ireland was settling the costs of Diarmuid Fawsitt ($5,000) and McCartan ($2,600). See Itemised balance sheet for a lecture tour of the United States by Éamon De Valera, NLI, MS 17,651/6/8.

8   McGarrity to O'Mara, 19 December 1919.

9   O'Mara to McGarrity, 22 December 1919, MS 17,518/48.

10   NAI, DE 02/292, 070.

11   HBD, 24 December 1919.

12   HBD, 26 December 1919.

Chapter 15

1   McGuire to Cohalan, 8 February 1920, AIHS, via (Fahey 2014), KL 2371.

2   McGuire to Cohalan, 10 February 1920, via Fahey 2014, KL 2386.

3   McGuire to Cohalan, 10 February 1920, via Fahey 2014, KL 2386.

4   McGuire to Cohalan, 8 February 1920, AIHS, via (Fahey 2014), KL 2371; *GA*, 14 February 1920, p. 1.

5   McGuire to Cohalan, 8 February 1920, AIHS, via (Fahey 2014), KL 2371.

6   McGuire to Cohalan, 19 August 1920, AIHS, via Fahey 2014, KL 2701.

7   HBD, 6 February 1920.

8   *NYT,* 7 February 1920, p. 9.

9   HBD, 6 February 1920.

10   HBD, 5 February 1920.

11   HBD, 5 February 1920; HBD, 7 February 1920.

12   HBD, 7 February 1920.

13   *NYT,* 6 January 1920.

14   *This Side of Paradise*, Fitzgerald, F. Scott, Amazon Classics, p. 208.

15   HBD, 17 January 1920.

16   Among those who escorted de Valera on the day were F. H. La Guardia, president of the Board of Aldermen; police Commissioner Richard Enright; Surrogate James A. Foley, son-in-law of Boss Charles F. Murphy; former State Senator Thomas McManus, better known as 'The McManus', who for 25 years had been political ruler of the midtown section of Manhattan west of Broadway; Chief Assistant District Attorney Alfred J. Talley; and William Harmon Black, former

Assistant District Attorney, and
Vice-Chairman of the National War
Labor Board when Frank Walsh was
Chairman. *GA,* 24 January 1920, p. 1;
IP, 24 January 1920, p. 1;
NYT, 18 January 1920, Section 2,
p. 35.

17 *NYT,* 18 January 1920, Section 2,
p. 35.

18 *GA,* 27 September 1919.

19 Yeates, P. 2012 *A city in turmoil—
Dublin 1919–1921: the War of
Independence.* Gill and Macmillan,
Dublin.

20 *NYT,* 17 January 1920, p. 1.

21 *NYT,* 19 January 1920, p. 9.

22 The Evening World, 13 April 1922.

23 HBD, 21 January 1920.

24 HBD, 22 January 1920.

25 *GA,* 31 January 1920, p. 5.

26 *GA,* 31 January 1920, p. 5.

27 (Lynch, History of the Friends of Irish
Freedom 1930 - 1939).

28 Nunan to Collins, 20 January 1920,
DIFP, No. 28, NAI, DE 2/292.

29 HBD, 31 January 1920.

30 HBD, 25 January 1920.

31 *NYT,* 1 February 1919, p. 18.

32 HBD, 20 February 1920.

Chapter 16

1 HBD, 28 January 1920; HBD, 29
January 1920.

2 Collins to de Valera, 9 February 1920,
NAI, DE 2/245 (178) and (180).

3 *GA,* 14 February 1920, p. 8.; *The
Yonkers Herald,* 2 February 1920,
p. 12.

4 *GA,* 14 February 1920, p. 8.; *The
Yonkers Herald,* 2 February 1920,
p. 12.

5 *NYT,* 2 February 1920, p. 16.;
'3,000', The News, 2 February 1920,
p. 7.

6 *The Daily News,* New York, 2 February
1920, p. 7.

7 *The Times,* London, 3 February 1920,
p. 12.

8 HBD, 1 February 1920.

9 HBD, 1 February 1920.

10 *Buffalo Evening News,* 3 February
1920, p. 9.

11 *IP,* 7 February 1920, p. 1; HBD, 2
February 1920.

12 HBD, 3 February 1920.

13 HBD, 3 February 1920.

14 HBD, 3 February 1920.

15 HBD, 4 February 1920.

16 *NYT,* 4 February 1920, p. 10.

17 HBD, 4 February 1920.

18 HBD, 5 February 1920.

19 *IP,* 14 February 1920, p.1; *GA,* 21
February 1920, p. 8.

20 *IP,* 14 February 1920, p.1; *GA,* 21
February 1920, p. 8.

21 Boston Globe 7 February 1920, p. 6;
IP, 21 February 1920, p. 6.

22 The Buffalo Times, 8 February 1920,
p. 27.

23 Westminster Gazette, 7 February
1920, p. 5.

24 *Westminster Gazette*, 7 February 1920, p. 5.

25 *Westminster Gazette*, 7 February 1920, p. 5.

26 *NYT,* 7 February 1920, p. 12.

27 *Chicago Daily Tribune*, 7 February 1920, p. 5.

28 *Westminster Gazette*, 7 February 1920, p. 5.

29 *Westminster Gazette*, 7 February 1920, p. 7.

30 *Westminster Gazette*, 7 February 1920, p. 5.

31 *Irish World* editorial, reprinted in the *IP*, 21 February 1920, p. 1.

32 *Irish Independent*, 9 February 1920, p. 8.

33 *Freeman's Journal*, 9 February 1919, p. 3.

34 *Irish Independen*t, 9 February 1920, p. 10.

35 *The Scranton Time*s, 20 February 1920, p. 1

36 *Irish Times* editorial, 9 February 1920, p. 4.

37 Patrick Moylett, BMH WS 767.

38 (McCartan 1932), p. 242 – 244.

39 Patrick Moylett, BMH WS 767.

40 Patrick Moylett, BMH WS 767.

41 The Sun (New York), 13 February 1920 via *IP*, 21 February 1920, p. 2.

42 The Sun (New York), 13 February 1920 via *IP*, 21 February 1920, p. 2.

43 (McCartan 1932), p. 239, p. 340.

44 (McCartan 1932), p. 239.

45 (McCartan 1932), p. 240 – 241.

46 *IP*, editorial, 14 February 1920, p. 4.

47 *IP*, 14 February 1920, p. 1 and 3.

48 (McCartan 1932), p. 242.

49 (McCartan 1932), p. 242.

50 De Valera Official Statement, via *GA,* 21 February 1920, p. 1. A different edit was made to de Valera's casual comment: 'Why Doesn't Britain do *Thus* in the Case of Ireland as the United States did in the Case Of Cuba?'

51 New York *Globe*, 14 February 1920, via *IP*, 21 February 1920, p. 1.

52 New York *Globe*, 14 February 1920, via (Lynch, History of the Friends of Irish Freedom 1930 - 1939).

53 New York *Globe*, 14 February 1920, via *IP*, 21 February 1920, p. 1.

54 New York *Globe*, 14 February 1920, via *IP*, 21 February 1920, p. 1.

55 New York *Globe*, 14 February 1920, via *IP*, 21 February 1920, p. 1.

56 *IP*, 21 February 1920, p. 1..

57 *IP*, 21 February 1920, p. 1..

58 HBD, 14 February 1920.

59 *GA,* editorial, 14 February 1920, p. 1

Chapter 17

1 (McCartan 1932), p. 240.

2 *Boston Post*, 9 February 1920, via *GA,* 21 February 1920, p.1; *Boston Globe*, 9 February 1920, p. 1.

3 *The Berkshire Eagl*e, 12 February 1920, p. 6.

4 *GA,* 21 February 1920, p.1; *Boston Globe*, 9 February 1920, p. 1.

5 Irish National Bureau newsletter, Issue 19, 20 February 1920, Lynch family

archives, via Ruairí Lynch. http://
diarmuidlynch.weebly.com.

6 *New York Sun*, 14 February 1920, via
IP, 21 February 1920, p. 2..

7 Mellows to Mrs Hearn, 9 March
1920, via (McNamara 2019),
p. 178.

8 Mellows to McCartan, 28 February
1920, via (McNamara 2019), p. 158.

9 Mellows to McCartan, 28 February
1920, via (McNamara 2019), p. 158.

10 Mellows to McCartan, 28 February
1920, via (McNamara 2019),
p. 158.

11 *IP*, editorial, 21 February 1920, p. 4.

12 *IP*, editorial, 21 February 1920, p. 4..

13 The News (New York), 23 February
1920, p. 2.

14 The News (New York), 24 February
1920, p. 6

15 The News (New York), 24 February
1920, p. 6

16 The News (New York), 24 February
1920, p. 6

17 (Tansill 1957), p. 365.

18 *GA*, England's Hidden Hand, 28
February 1920.

19 *GA*, WHO GIVES OUT THESE
LIES?, 28 February 1920.

20 *IP*, 28 February 1920, p. 7.

21 *GA*, 21 February 1920, p. 1.

22 HBD, 11 February 1920.

23 HBD, 12 February 1920.

24 HBD, 14 February 1920.

25 HBD, 15 February 1920.; *The Boston
Globe*, meeting advertisement, 15
February 1920, p. 1

26 HBD, 16 February 1920.

27 HBD, 16 and 17 February 1920.

28 HBD, 17 February 1920.

29 McGuire to Cohalan, 10 February
1920, AIHS, via (Fahey 2014), KL
2378 - 2387

30 McGuire to Cohalan, 10 February
1920, AIHS, via (Fahey 2014), KL
2378 - 2387

31 *NYT*, 21 February 1920, p. 10.

32 De Valera to the Cabinet, 17 February
1920, DIFP, NAI, DE 2/245, 159.

33 Boland to Collins, 30 January 1920,
De Valera Papers, P150/1125, via
(Fitzpatrick 2003), p. 153.

34 Boland [Woods] to Michael Collins
[Field], 26 February 1920, De Valera
papers, P150/1125, via (Fitzpatrick
2003), p. 153.

35 HBD, 18 February 1920.

36 Dictionary of Irish Biography, Anne
Dolan.

37 HBD, 18 February 1920.

38 HBD, 19 February 1920.

39 HBD, 19 February 1920.

40 HBD, 20 February 1920.

41 HBD, 20 February 1920.

42 HBD, 20 February 1920.

43 *NYT*, 22 February 1920, p. 10.

44 HBD, 21 February 1920; Cohalan to
De Valera, 23 February 1920, (Béaslaí
1922), Vol. 2, p. 9; and NAI, DE
2/245 (154).

45 Devoy to John McGarry (Schell), 26
February 1920 [filed as 20 February],
MGp, NLI, MS 17,486/6/7.

46 De Valera to Cohalan, 20 February 1920, (Béaslaí 1922), Vol. 2, p. 7; and NAI, DE 2/245 (157).

47 HBD, 21 February 1920.

48 HBD, 22 February 1920.

49 Devoy to John McGarry (Schell), 26 February 1920 [filed as 20 February], MGp, NLI, MS 17,486/6/7.

50 Cohalan to de Valera, 23 February 1920, (Béaslaí 1922), Vol. 2, p. 9; and NAI, DE 2/245 (154).

51 Cohalan to de Valera, 23 February 1920, (Béaslaí 1922), Vol. 2, p. 9; and NAI, DE 2/245 (154).

52 HBD, 24 February 1920.

53 (Schultz 2019), p. 121.

54 HBD, 24 February 1920.

55 HBD, 27 February 1920, UCDA, de Valera Papers, P150/1170; *NYT*, 3 November 1924, p. 17.

56 *GA,* 28 February 1920, p. 4.

57 The Executive Connection, Caroline Shaffer, 2010; *NYT,* 29 April 1910, p. 1.

58 The Nation, New York, 'Where Does England Stand?', 31 January 1920, via *IP*, 7 February 1920, p. 1.

59 *New York American*, 31 January 1920, via *IP*, 7 February 1920, p. 4.

60 *New York American*, 21 January 1920, via *GA,* 31 January 1920, p. 2.

61 HBD to Thomas J. Lynch, 25 February 1920, via (Maher 2020), KL 2071.

62 FOIF Archive, AIHS, via Eileen McGough, and Ruairí Lynch, http://diarmuidlynch.weebly.com; *NYT,* 26 August 1988, 31 October 1972.;

63 HBD, 26 February 1920. De Lue worked for the Boston Globe for sixty years as a reporter, travel writer, and as the newspaper's first night managing editor.

64 HBD, 13 February 1920.

65 HBD, 13 February 1920.

66 HBD, 27 February 1920.

67 *GA,* England's Hidden Hand, 28 February 1920.

68 *GA,* 28 February 1920, p. 4.

69 *GA,* 28 February 1920, p. 4.

70 Devoy to "Dear Friend", 26 February 1920 [filed as 20 February], MGp, NLI, MS 17,486/6/7.

71 Devoy to "Dear Friend", 26 February 1920 [filed as 20 February], MGp, NLI, MS 17,486/6/7.

72 Boston Globe, 1 March 1920, p. 1.

73 Fall River Globe, 1 March 1920, p. 3.

74 HBD, 29 February 1920.

75 HBD, 28 February 1920.

76 Devoy to "Dear Friend", 26 February 1920 [filed as 20 February], MGp, NLI, MS 17,486/6/7. The letter is a handwritten copy of Devoy's original typed letter. A handwritten note states, 'Copy of letter from H. to J. Schell'. 'H' is most likely Hudson (Devoy). 'J. Schell' is most likely John McGarry. The NLI states, 'Copy made by John T. Ryan'. The letter is in the McGarrity papers suggesting that Ryan sent the copy to McGarrity.

77 Devoy to "Dear Friend", 28 February 1920, NLI, MGp, MS 17,486/6/8. Both the 26 and 28 February letters are copied in the same handwriting,

begin 'Dear Friend' and are signed off 'Yours truly'. Although there is no mention of 'J. Schell', the recipient is on the FOIF National Council and is not based in New York suggesting McGarry. And the letter found its way into Ryan's possession. The letter is a handwritten copy of Devoy's original handwritten letter. A note states, 'Written in long hand by Hudson'. The NLI states, 'Copy made by John T. Ryan'. The letter is in the McGarrity papers suggesting that Ryan sent the copy to McGarrity.

78 Devoy to "Dear Friend", 26 February 1920 [filed as 20 February], MGp, NLI, MS 17,486/6/7.

79 McGuire to Cohalan, 10 February 1920, AIHS, via (Fahey 2014), KL 2378 - 2387

80 John T. Ryan to McGarrity, 13 March 1919, NLI, MGp, MS 17,486/6/10. It is most likely, but not confirmed, that McGuire is 'Dearborn' in the letter. 'Dearborn' is close to Cohalan and is well-known among the Irish leaders in America. McGuire, a fluent German speaker, had worked with German agents prior to America entering the war. The NLI identifies John T. Ryan as the main creator, and that the copy was written by him. The letter is in the McGarrity papers suggesting that Ryan sent the letter to McGarrity. The handwriting is the same as in later letters from Ryan to McGarrity, where both are clearly identified (see Ryan to McGarrity, 29 September 1928, NLI, MS 17,486/4/15). The letter is in the same handwriting as the copies made of the

Devoy letters on 26 and 28 February, and the letters to McGarrity on 28 February and 11 March.

81 *NYT,* 22 January 1919, p. 3.

82 *NYT,* 22 January 1919, p. 3.

83 *NYT,* 22 January 1919, p. 3; (Fitzpatrick 2003), p. 10.

84 John T. Ryan to McGarrity, 28 February 1919, NLI, MS 17,486/6/9. The NLI identifies John T. Ryan as the main creator, and that the copy was written by him. The letter is in the McGarrity papers suggesting that Ryan sent the letter to McGarrity. A note on verso reads 'McGarry letters from Devoy'. The handwriting is the same as in later letters from Ryan to McGarrity, where both are clearly identified (see Ryan to McGarrity, 29 September 1928, NLI, MS 17,486/4/15). The letter is in the same handwriting as the copies made of the Devoy letters on 26 and 28 February, and the letters to McGarrity on 28 February and 11 March.

85 John T. Ryan to McGarrity, 13 March 1919, NLI, MGp, MS 17,486/6/10.

86 Boland to Collins, 5 March 1920, NAI, DE 2/245 (135).

87 The note was appended to a letter from de Valera to Arthur Griffith, 6 March 1920, NAI, DE 2/245 (121).

88 John T. Ryan to McGarrity, 13 March 1919, NLI, MGp, MS 17,486/6/10.

Chapter 18

1 De Valera to Griffith, 6 March 1920, NAI, DE 2/245, 117.

2   Boland to Collins, 5 March 1920, NAI, DE 2/245, 135.

3   *GA,* 17 January 1920, p. 1; *IP,* 17 January, p. 7.

4   *IP,* 21 February 1920, p. 6.

5   *IP,* 21 February 1920, p. 6 and 8.

6   *GA,* 28 February 1920, p. 1.

7   *IP,* 21 February 1920, p. 6; *GA,* 28 February 1920, p. 1.

8   *IP,* 7 February 1920, p. 2.

9   James O'Mara (Frank P. Walsh letterhead) to McGarrity, 2 February 1920, MGp, NLI, MS 17,652/5/3.

10 E. A. Wright Company to McGarrity, 23 January 1920, MGp, NLI, MS 17,522/7; see also MS 17,681/7/4

11 E. A. Wright Company to McGarrity, 18 February 1920, MGp, NLI, MS 17,522/9.

12 HBD, 7 February 1920.

13 Letter from E. A. Wright to McGarrity, 6 March 1920, MGp, NLI, MS 17,522/11.

14 International Steel and Copper Plate Printers Union to McGarrity, 18 March 1920, MGp, NLI, MS 17,522/12.

15 International Steel and Copper Plate Printers Union to McGarrity, 18 March 1920, MGp, NLI, MS 17,522/13.

16 Letter from E. A. Wright to McGarrity, 26 March 1920, MGp, NLI, MS 17,522/14.

17 The *IP,* 1 May 1920, p. 3.

18 The *IP,* 1 May 1920, p. 3.

19 HBD, 29 April 1920.

20 On 6 March, the *IP* confirmed that the amount raised was 'in the neighbourhood of \$200,000', compared to the quota of \$1,000,000.

21 HBD, 8 February 1920.

22 *IP,* 14 February 1920, p. 2.

23 *IP,* 29 November 1919, p. 4.

24 *IP,* editorial, 29 November 1919, p. 4; *GA,* 17 January 1920, p. 1; *IP,* 17 January, p. 7.

25 *IP,* 7 February 1920, p. 1.

26 *IP,* 21 February 1920, p. 1.

27 *IP,* 14 February 1920, p. 1.

28 *IP,* 21 February 1920, p. 1.

29 *IP,* 21 February 1920, p. 1.

30 *IP,* 7 February 1920, p. 1.

31 *IP,* 28 February 1920, p. 1.

32 *IP,* 28 February 1920, p. 1.

33 *IP,* 28 February 1920, p. 1.

34 *IP,* 6 March 1920, p. 1.

35 *IP,* 7 and 14 February 1920, p. 1 and 2.

36 Michael Collins, Department of Finance Report, DE 2/7, 090, National Archives. See also Collins to Boland, 5 January 1920, EdeVP, P 150/1125, via (Fitzpatrick 2003), Note 75, p. 377. See https://ifiplayer.ie/historical-material-republican-loans/.

37 (Fitzpatrick 2003), p. 159.

38 (MacDonagh 1976).

39 *NYT,* 25 January 1919, p. 6.

40 *GA,* 7 February 1920, p. 1.

41 On 27 January the Health Commissioner of New York estimated the total number of influenza cases that day at over 3,600, and 420

pneumonia cases were reported. *NYT,* 28 January 1920, p. 1.

42 *NYT,* 28 January 1920, p. 1.

43 *GA,* 14 February 1920, p. 1.

44 Moore to Cockran, 8 February 1920, Box 17, Cockran Papers, NYPL, via (F. Carroll 2021), p. 72.

45 *NYT,* 25 January 1920, p. 27.

46 Mellows to Mrs. Ahern, 9 March 1920, (McNamara 2019), p. 178.

47 Mellows to McCartan, via (McNamara 2019), p. 158.

48 Mellows to 'Mrs. Ahern', 9 March 1920, (McNamara 2019), p. 177.

49 Mellows to 'Mrs. Ahern', 9 March 1920, (McNamara 2019), p. 175.

50 Mellows to 'Mrs. Ahern', 9 March 1920, (McNamara 2019), p. 178.

51 HBD, 28 October 1919.

52 HBD, 8, 9 and 28 October 1919; Boland to McGarrity, 10 October 1919, MGp, NLI, MS 17, 424/1/3.

53 McGarry to Cohalan, 7 January 1920, FOIF Archive, AIHS, via Eileen McGough, and Ruairí Lynch, http://diarmuidlynch.weebly.com.

54 *IP,* 21 February 1920, p. 1.

55 Peter Golden to Walsh, 5 February 1920, NLI, Golden Papers, MS 13,141, via Francis Carroll, 'American Opinion on the Irish Question', thesis, 1969, p. 318 - 319.

56 Helen Golden to Peter Golden, 16 February 1920, Golden Papers, NLI, via (F. Carroll 2021), p. 237.

57 James E. Deery to Peter Golden, 31 January 1920, NLI, Golden Papers, MS 13,141, via Francis Carroll, 'American Opinion on the Irish Question', thesis, 1969, p. 318 - 319.

58 Dr. W. Patrick Slattery to Frank P. Walsh, 3 January 1921, Walsh Papers, NYPL, via Francis Carroll, 'American Opinion on the Irish Question', thesis, 1969, p. 318. The comment echoed those of John J. Splain, campaign chairman in Connecticut, who complained to Bourke Cockran that it was 'hard to get our people enthused in this matter' and that he had received 'poor co-operation' from Irishmen and the Irish-Americans conducting the campaign. See James J. Splain to Cockran, 17 February 1920, NYPL, Cockran Papers, via Francis Carroll, 'American Opinion on the Irish Question', thesis, 1969, p. 318.

59 Dr. W. Patrick Slattery to Frank Walsh, 3 January 1921, Walsh Papers, NYPL, via Francis Carroll, 'American Opinion on the Irish Question', thesis, 1969, p. 337.

60 (Fitzpatrick 2003), p. 145.

61 Houston to Walsh, 7 February 1920, Box 125, Walsh Papers, NYPL, via (F. Carroll 2021), p. 73.

62 *NYT,* 8 February 1920, p. 87.

63 *NYT,* 11 January 1919, p. 9.

64 The Street, via *NYT,* 28 January 1920, p. 36.

65 *Wall Street Journal,* 4 February 1920, p. 1.

66 Collins to Boland, 19 April 1920, (Béaslaí 1922), Vol. 2, p. 14; and NAI, DE 2/245 (101).

67 Collins to Boland, 19 April 1920, (Béaslaí 1922), Vol. 2, p. 14; and NAI, DE 2/245 (101).

68 Collins to Nunan, 20 March 1920, (Fitzpatrick 2003), p. 165.

69 HBD, 7 March 1920.

70 HBD, 8 March 1920.

71 O'Mara to de Valera, 1 March 1920, via (Lavelle 2011), p. 154.

72 O'Mara to J.J. O'Kelly, 8 March 1920, via (Lavelle 2011), p. 156.

73 (Lavelle 2011), p. 151.

74 De Valera to O'Mara, 4 March 1920, via (Lavelle 2011), p. 155.

75 O'Mara to de Valera, 1 March 1920, via (Lavelle 2011), p. 154.

76 De Valera to Griffith, via (Béaslaí 1922), Vol. 2, p. 14; and NAI, DE 2/245 (103).

77 De Valera to Griffith, via (Béaslaí 1922), Vol. 2, p. 14.

78 De Valera to O'Mara, 4 March 1920, via (Lavelle 2011), p. 155.

79 De Valera to O'Mara, 4 March 1920, via (Lavelle 2011), p. 155.

80 De Valera to O'Mara, 4 April 1920, via (Lavelle 2011), p. 158.

81 (Lavelle 2011), p. 157. O'Mara offered his resignation from the Irish mission in April 1921 in disgust at de Valera's decision to drastically reduce the expenditure budget in America after he had returned to Ireland, and at his proposal to put an annual levy on AARIR members. 'I would advise you to promptly send someone to this country who has your confidence, if such a person exists, and having done so don't constantly interfere with his work.', O'Mara to de Valera, 25 April 1921,(Lavelle 2011), p. 245.

82 (Lynch, History of the Friends of Irish Freedom 1930 - 1939).

83 Report to the National Council, via (Lynch, History of the Friends of Irish Freedom 1930 - 1939).

84 ACII to Lynch, 9 January 1920, via (Lynch, History of the Friends of Irish Freedom 1930 - 1939).

85 (Lynch, History of the Friends of Irish Freedom 1930 - 1939).

86 (Lynch, History of the Friends of Irish Freedom 1930 - 1939).

87 (Lynch, History of the Friends of Irish Freedom 1930 - 1939).

88 On 9 January Boland informed Lynch that de Valera was anxious to fulfil his promise. (Lynch, History of the Friends of Irish Freedom 1930 - 1939).

89 Lynch to de Valera, 15 January 1920, NL/O'Mara papers, MS.21548/1; Lynch to de Valera, 27 December 1919, NL/O'Mara papers, MS.21547, via (Lainer-Vos 2013), KL 3231.

90 National Executive minutes, 9 February 1920, FOIF Archive, AIHS, via Eileen McGough, and Ruairí Lynch, www.diarmuidlynch.weebly.com.

91 (Lynch, History of the Friends of Irish Freedom 1930 - 1939).

92 (Lynch, History of the Friends of Irish Freedom 1930 - 1939).

93 (Lynch, History of the Friends of Irish Freedom 1930 - 1939).

94 (Lynch, History of the Friends of Irish Freedom 1930 - 1939).

95 HBD, 13 April 1920.

96 (Lynch, History of the Friends of Irish Freedom 1930 - 1939).

97 (Lynch, History of the Friends of Irish Freedom 1930 - 1939).

98 $2,995,643, Nunan to Collins, 17 May 1920, NAI, DE 2/292, 50. A £58,880, or $235,520 using an exchange rate of 4.0, bank draft payable to Dr. Fogarty. Statement of Receipts and Expenditures for the period ending 31st October 1919, and the half year ending 30 April 1920, and a note to 24 June 1920, DE 2/7 p. 087.

Chapter 19

1 De Valera to Griffith, 6 March 1920, NAI, DE 2/245 (117).

2 De Valera to Griffith, 6 March 1920, NAI, DE 2/245 (117).

3 De Valera to Griffith, 6 March 1920, NAI, DE 2/245 (117).

4 NAI, DE 2/245 (124).

5 De Valera to the Cabinet, 10 March 1920, NAI, DE 2/245 (147).

6 Minutes, via (Lynch 1930 - 1939).

7 De Valera to Griffith, 6 March 1920, NAI, DE 2/245 (117).

8 O'Hegarty to de Valera, 8 June 1920, NAI, DE 2/245, 081.

9 HBD, 13 April 1920.

10 HBD, 14 April 1920.

11 HBD, 15 April 1920.

12 Department of An Taoiseach, 'Information re. Russian Jewels given as security for loan made by Irish Government in 1920', BMH 372.

13 De Valera to Boland, 27 October 1920, DIFP, UCDA P150/108.

14 Department of An Taoiseach, 'Information re. Russian Jewels given as security for loan made by Irish Government in 1920', BMH 372.

15 *NYT,* 11 January 1920, p. 1.

16 *NYT,* 11 January 1920, p. 1.

17 Senator Borah to Senator Lodge, 24 January 1920, Borah MSS, via (Tansill 1957), p. 370.

18 Cong. Rec., 66th Cong., 2nd sess., vol. 59, 18 March 1920, 4502–22, via (F. Carroll 2021), p. 235. Note that the *NYT,* 19 March 1920, gives the text as '*self-government* is attained by Ireland'.

19 *NYT,* 18 March 1920, p. 1.

20 *The Boston Globe*, 20 March 1920, p. 1.

21 HBD, 22 March 1920.

22 New York Tribune, 22 March 1920, p. 1.

23 Senator Harding to Frank Walsh, 24 March 1920, NYPL, Walsh papers, box 124, via Carroll thesis, p. 307.

24 Cohalan to Borah, 2 February 1920, Borah MSS, (Tansill 1957), p. 371.

25 (Lynch, History of the Friends of Irish Freedom 1930 - 1939); *GA,* 21 February 1920, p. 1.

26 *GA,* 21 February 1920, p. 1.

27 Cohalan to Borah, 2 March
1920, Borah MSS, (Tansill 1957),
p. 372.

28 Cohalan to Hiram Johnson, 23 March
1920, Cohalan MSS, via (Tansill
1957), p. 372 – 373.

29 De Valera to Griffith, 6 March 1920,
DIFP, No. 31, NAI, DE 2/245.

30 Daniel T. O'Connell, *NYT*, 10
July 1920, p. 2. Lynch named the
congressmen as Mason, Kennedy
(Rhode Island) and Smith (New
York), (Lynch, History of the Friends
of Irish Freedom 1930 - 1939).

31 (McCartan 1932), p. 295. Lynch
gives the date of the National Council
meeting as 18 June and recounts a
similar outcome, (Lynch, History of
the Friends of Irish Freedom 1930 -
1939).

Chapter 20

1 (McCartan 1932), p. 331; (Lynch,
History of the Friends of Irish
Freedom 1930 - 1939).

2 Daniel T. O'Connell, quoted in
(Lynch, History of the Friends of Irish
Freedom 1930 - 1939).

3 Copy of draft minutes, MGp, MS
17652/3, NLI, via (Doorley 2019),
p. 150.

4 Nunan to Griffith, *GA,* 24 July 1920,
p. 2.

5 (McCartan 1932), p. 300.

6 *Chicago Tribune*, 11 June 1920, p. 1.

7 De Valera to Griffith, stamped as
received in Dublin on 10 June, NAI,
DE 2/245 (056).

8 (Doorley 2019), p. 148.

9 *Chicago Tribune*, 11 June 1920, p. 1;
(Doorley 2019), p. 148; (Lynch,
History of the Friends of Irish
Freedom 1930 - 1939).

10 (Doorley 2019), p. 150; Daniel T.
O'Connell, quoted in (Lynch, History
of the Friends of Irish Freedom 1930 -
1939).

11 Copy of draft minutes, MGp, MS
17652/3, NLI, via (Doorley 2019),
p. 150.

12 *NYT,* 11 June 1920, p. 1.

13 *Chicago Tribune*, 11 June 1920, p. 1.

14 *NYT,* 11 June 1920, p. 1.

15 *Chicago Tribune*, 11 June 1920, p. 1.

16 The Evening world, 11 June 1920,
p. 2; Boston Post, 11 June 1920,
p. 20.

17 *NYT,* 12 June 1920, p. 5.

18 (McCartan 1932), p. 337.

19 Geddes to Earl Curzon of Kedleston,
16 June 1920, via (Coogan 1993), KL
4313.

20 Diarmuid O'Hegarty to de Valera, 3
July 1920, NAI, DE 2/245 (054).

21 McGuire to Cohalan, 5 June 1920, via
(Fahey 2014), KL 2550.

22 McGuire to Cohalan, 14 June
1920(Fahey 2014), KL 2560.

23 *GA,* 19 June 1920, p. 1.

24 Diarmuid O'Hegarty to de Valera, 16
July 1920, NAI, DE 2/245 (035), and
8 June 1920, NAI, DE 2/245 (081)

25 *NYT,* 5 July 1920, p. 2.

26 Boland to Griffith, 11 August 1920,
NAI, DE 2/245, 023.

Chapter 21

1 *Chicago Tribune*, 11 June 1920, p.

2 McCartan to McGarrity, 12 July 1920, MGp, MS 17457/13, via (Fitzpatrick 2003), 189; and Cronin, Seán, The McGarrity Papers (1972), p. 83.

3 Maloney to McGarrity, 1 July 1920, MGp, MS 17621, via (Fitzpatrick 2003), 189.

4 Chicago Herald-Examiner, 18 June 1920, via *IP*, 26 June 1920, p. 1.

5 (McCartan 1932), p. 309 – 310.

6 New York *World*, via *IP*, 26 June 1920, p. 2.

7 New York Call, 22 June 1920, via *IP*, 26 June 1920, p. 2.

8 *NYT*, 22 June 1920, p. 29.

9 Irish World, date not available, via *IP*, 26 June 1920, p. 3.

10 *IP*, 19 June 1920, p. 1 and 4.

11 *IP*, 10 June 1920, p. 1.

12 Dáil Éireann Report on Foreign Affairs, June 1920, DIFP, No. 37 NAI DE 4/1/3. The report was seized in a raid by the British and widely published in America. See O'Hegarty to Boland, 29 September 1920, NAI, DE 2/245, 020.

13 New York *World*, via *IP*, 26 June 1920, p. 2.

14 *GA*, 3 July 1920, p. 5; *NYT*, 22 June 1920, p. 29.

15 *GA*, 3 July 1920, p. 1.

16 *GA*, 3 July 1920, p. 5.

17 (McCartan 1932), p. 246.

18 (Béaslaí 1922), p. 18.

19 *NYT*, 14 July 1920, p. 11.

20 *Brooklyn Eagle*, 13 July 1920, p. 1.

21 HBD, 14 July 1920.

22 Nunan to Collins, 21 June 1920, Philadelphia Public Ledger; *Brooklyn Eagle*, 13 July 1920.

23 *Brooklyn Eagle*, 15 July 1920, p. 16.

24 *Brooklyn Eagle*, 15 July 1920, p. 16.

25 HBD, 16 July 1920.

26 *NYT*, 22 June 1920, p. 29; 26 June 1920, p. 3; 10 July 1920, p. 2, 14 July 1920, p. 11.

27 (McCartan 1932), p. 309 – 310

28 *GA*, 24 July 1920, p. 1.

29 McGuire to Cohalan, 4 August 1920, AIHS, via (Fahey 2014), KL 2660.

Chapter 22

1 *GA*, 30 October 1920, p. 2.

2 Nunan to Collins, *Brooklyn Eagle*, 13 July 1920, p. 1.

3 *IP*, 24 July 1920, p. 5; For other examples see (McGough 2013), KL 1825.

4 McGuire to Cohalan, 19 August 1919, AIHS, via (Fahey 2014), KL 2697.

5 McGuire to Devoy, 17 August 1920, AIHS, (Fahey 2014), KL 2676.

6 McGuire to Cohalan, 19 August 1919, AIHS, via (Fahey 2014), KL 2702.

7 Devoy to Cohalan, 31 August 1920, AIHS, via (Fahey 2014), KLs 2769.

8 Devoy to Cohalan, 31 August 1920, AIHS, via (Fahey 2014), KLs 2769.

9 *GA*, 6 November 1920, p. 1.

10   *GA,* 6 November 1920, p. 1.

11   *GA,* 6 November 1920, p. 1.

12   *IP,* 9 October 1920, p. 1, 3.

13   *IP,* 11 September 1920, p. 7.

14   Charlotte Dunne to Lynch, 8 April 1920, NYPL/Maloney papers, folders 5– 9, via (Lainer-Vos 2013), KL 3248.

15   Diarmuid Lynch, *GA,* 18 December 1920, p. 1. See also (Lainer-Vos 2013).

16   *GA,* 31 July 1920, p. 2.

17   *IP,* 11 September 1920, p. 7.

18   *IP,* 11 September 1920, p. 7.

19   *IP,* 2 October 1920, p. 1. Second and deferred payments could be made up to 31 October, unless made direct to the ACII head office in New York when the date was extended to the end of November.

20   $5,235,166 to 31 January 1922, via 'U.S.A ACCOUNT, TOTAL TO 31 JANY. 1922', NAI, DE 2/9 (021).

21   Devoy to Cohalan, 20 September 1920, AIHS, via (Fahey 2014), KL 2801.

22   *GA,* 30 October 1920, p 1.

23   *IP,* 20 November 1920, p. 1.

24   O'Hegarty to Boland, 13 October 1920, NAI, DE 2/245,018.

25   *IP,* 6 November 1922, p. 2; *GA,* 6 November 1922, p. 4.

Epilogue

1   (Golway 2015), 259.

2   *Irish Times,* 4 September 1924, p. 6.

3   *GA,* 20 September 1924, p. 2.

4   Collins to Devoy, February 1922, via (Golway 2015), 251.

5   Devoy to Collins, February 1922, AIHS, FOIF papers, via (McGough 2013), KL 2059.

6   Collins to Devoy, February 1922, via (Golway 2015), 250.

7   McGuire to Boland, 16 November 1920, UCD-OFM, via (Fahey 2014), KL 2852.

8   Stephen O'Mara to de Valera, 12 August 1921, NAI.

9   McGuire to Boland, 16 November 1920, via (Fahey 2014), KL 2863.

10   McGuire to Boland, 16 November 1920, via (Fahey 2014), KL 2863.

11   (Fitzpatrick 2003), 220.

12   McGuire to Boland, 7 April 1922, UCD-OFM, via (Fahey 2014), KL 2984.

13   *GA,* 12 August 1922, p. 2.

14   Ronan McGreevy, 'Michael Collins dismissed death threat three days before he was shot', *Irish Times,* 4 December 2021.

15   *GA,* 7 July 1923, 1 and 5.

16   *GA,* 22 March 1924, p. 3. Originally sourced via (McGough 2013), KL 3003.

17   Nunan to Collins, 21 June 1920, *Brooklyn Eagle,* 13 July 1920, p. 1.

18   Nunan to Griffith, 21 June 1920, *Brooklyn Eagle,* 13 July 1920, p. 1

19   Lynch to Cohalan, 13 July 1920, AIHS, FOIF papers, via (McGough 2013), KL 1706.

20   HBD, 19 July 1920.

21 Kit Lynch to Lynch family members, 28 July 1920, via (McGough 2013), KL 1781.

22 Muriel MacSwiney to Diarmuid and Kit Lynch, October 1920, via (McGough 2013)KL 2002.

23 (Golway 2015), 257.

24 (Golway 2015), 262.

25 (Golway 2015), 261.

26 (Golway 2015), 261.

27 (Golway 2015), 262.

28 (Golway 2015), 262.

29 Irish Times, 5 September 1924, p. 6.

30 Irish Times, 5 September 1924, p. 6.

Conclusions

1 *NYT,* 22 June 1919, p. 12.

2 'Statement of Edward F. McSweeney' (undated typescript, responding to an attack by McCartan in the New York World, 22 June 1920), Cohalan Papers, 10/13, via (Fitzpatrick 2003), p. 144.

3 McCullagh, David, *De Valera Volume 1*, Gill Books, 2017, 30/3/20, EDV diary for 1920, P150/264.

4 McGuire to Boland, 16 November 1920, via (Fahey 2014), KL 2863.

5 McCartan to McGarrity, 12 July 1920, MGp, MS 17457/13, via (Fitzpatrick 2003), 189; and Cronin, Seán, The McGarrity Papers (1972), p. 83.

6 O'Mara to de Valera, 25 April 1921, via (Lavelle 2011), p. 245.

7 Devoy to McCartan, 21 April 1919, via (Lynch 1930 - 1939).

8 *GA,* 20 September 1924, p. 2.

9 *IP*, editorial, 1 November 1919, p. 4.

10 Minutes, via (Lynch 1930 - 1939).

11 Devoy to McCartan, 21 April 1919, via (Lynch 1930 - 1939).

12 (McCartan 1932), p. 231.

13 Nunan to McGarrity, 8 March 1921, McCartan Papers, NLI, MS 17,681/7/8.

14 Nunan to McGarrity, 1 November 1921, McCartan papers, NLI, MS 17,681/7/10.

15 *IP*, 17 December 1921, p. 2.

16 De Valera to Collins, 18 January 1920, (McCartan 1932), p. 362.

17 'Though I was working directly for recognition in America, I kept in my mind as our *main political objective*, the securing of America's influence, in case she was to join a League of Nations, to securing us also a place within the League. I am more than ever convinced that this should be the chief aim of our representatives after March 4th. Recognition we will only get in case of a war with England, though, of course, we should never cease our demand for it.' De Valera to Collins, 18 January 1920, (McCartan 1932), p. 362.

18 De Valera to Griffith, 25 March 1920, NAI, DE 2/245, 103.

19 De Valera to Boland, 30 May 1921, NAI, No. 86, DFA ES Box 27 File 158.

20 Devoy to "Dear Friend", 26 February 1920 [filed as 20 February], MGp, NLI, MS 17,486/6/7.

21 (McCartan 1932), p. 239, p. 340.

22 *IP*, 19 July 1919, p. 1; *NYT*, 14 July 1919, p. 13.

23 De Valera to Griffith, 13 August 1919, DIFP, UCDA P150/96.

24 (O'Doherty 1957), p. 131 – 132.

25 *Irish Independent*, 9 February 1920, p. 8.

26 *Freeman's Journal*, 9 February 1919, p. 3.

27 *Irish Independent*, 9 February 1920, p. 10.

28 McCann on the editorial staff of the *New York Globe*, see (McCartan 1932), p. 76; McCann a friend of Maloney, see (McCartan 1932), p. 139; McCann was also a creationist author, see 'The nuts among the berries', Deutsch, Ronald M. (1961).

29 (McCartan 1932), p. 75 – 77, p. 112; McCartan shared a platform at a meeting of the Irish Progressive League on 4 July at the Lexington Theatre. See New York Tribune, 5 July 1919, p. 6.

30 *The Yonkers Herald*, 2 Feb. 1920, p. 12; The Yonkers Herald, 20 Feb. 1920, p. 1

31 Devoy to McGarry (Schell), 26 February 1920 [filed as 20 February], MGp, NLI, MS 17,486/6/7

32 The *Evening World*, a Pulitzer owned New York paper, carried an abridged report of the interview.

33 (McCartan 1932), p. 369, p. 463.

34 Éamon de Valera, Frank Pakenham Longford, Thomas P. O'Neill, Arrow Books, 1970, p. 105.

35 Devoy ['Hudson'] to 'Dear Friend', 1 November 1919, MGp, MS 17,486/6/4.

36 Irish Nationalist, Progressive Activist, or British Spy?, A Portrait of William J. M. A. Maloney, MD, FRCS, MC, MBE, LL.D, Kelly Anne Reynolds, thesis for the Master of Arts Program in Irish and Irish-American Studies, May 2019, NYU. See also Global Lives: Dr William J. Maloney, Kelly Anne Reynolds, Century Ireland.

37 Collins to de Valera, 9 February 1920, NAI, DE 2/245, 180.

38 Collins to Boland, 12 May 1920, EdeVP, P. 150/1125, via (Fitzpatrick 2003), 145.

39 'total…is $2,995,643', Nunan to Collins, 17 May 1920, NAI, DE 2/292, 50.

40 O'Hegarty to de Valera, 8 June 1920, NAI, DE 2/245, 081.

41 O'Hegarty to de Valera, 8 June 1920, NAI, DE 2/245, 081.

42 The £58,880 was an international bank draft payable to Dr. Fogarty, issued by the National City Bank of New York on 27 February 1920, and to be drawn at the National Provincial & Union Bank of England (NA, DE 2/7, 003). The £58,880 translates to $235,520 using an exchange rate of 4.0 (used by Collins at that time), though Collins wrote that he included the sum of $200,000, 'being the actual amount received here'. Statement of Receipts and Expenditures for the period ending 31st October 1919, and the half year ending 30 April 1920, and a note to 24 June 1920, DE 2/7

p. 087. On 27 February, Nunan asked Collins to cable O'Mara at 411 Fifth Avenue 'on receipt of the draft that Mr. O'Mara is sending' with the word "Congratulations" and sign cable "Mrs McGarry". Nunan to Collins, 27 February 1920, DE 2/292, 062.

43 £10,471, £15,706. NA, DE 2/7, 001 – 014.

44 £10,390 '…exchange rate of $3.85 on $40,001.50', Nunan to Collins, 27 May 1920, NAI, DE 2/292, 49; On 12 June 1920, Collins to Nunan, acknowledging receipt of the draft, Collins to Nunan, 12 June 1920, NAI DE 2/292, 44.

45 Collins to Boland, 14 August 1920, EdeVP, P 150/1125, via (Fitzpatrick 2003), 183.

46 Boland to Collins, 22 September 1920, NAI, DE 2/245, 16.

47 Collins to Boland, 15 October 1920, EdeVP P 150/1125, via (Fitzpatrick 2003), 183.

48 'U.S.A. Accounts', NAI, DE 2/9, 132.

49 'U.S.A. Accounts', NAI, DE 2/9, 132.

50 'U.S.A. Accounts', NAI, DE 2/9, 132.

51 'Michael Collins, Department of Finance Report, NAI DE 2/7, 159.

52 Lynch produced a table showing a total of $295,795, giving a $15,000 difference. FOIF archive, 9 January 1920, AIHS via Eileen McGough and Ruairí Lynch. www.diarmuidlynch. weebly.com. The difference may be related to sums transmitted to Paris for the Irish delegation. See (Lynch 1930 - 1939).

53 *GA,* 18 December 1920, p. 1.

54 *IP*, 29 November 1919, p. 4.

55 Ormonde Winter, Winter's tale: an autobiography (London, 1955), 303–4.

56 McCartan's papers, NLI, MS 17,681/3/9.

57 Collins to de Valera, 10 February 1920, via (Béaslaí 1922, 414–16); Finance Report to 30 April 1920, NAI DE 2/7, 090.

58 Collins to de Valera, 10 February 1920, (Béaslaí 1922), 414 – 416; Department of Finance report to 30 April 1920, DE 2/7 p. 090.

59 Mackay 1996, 119.

60 Collins to Boland, 19 April 1920, (Béaslaí 1922), p. 358.

61 *IP*, 29 November 1919, p. 4.

62 Collins to De Valera, 6 October 1919, (Béaslaí 1922), 355;

63 *Freemans Journal*, 22 August 1919, p. 5.

64 Translated by Collins to £559,452 at an exchange rate of 4.40. American Accounts for six months to 31st December, 1921, NAI, DE 2/9, 020. This also agrees to 'Cash Summary as 31st December, 1921', DE 2/9, 023.

65 For the court cases in America and Ireland, see (F. Carroll 2002), and for the court cases in Ireland, see (O'Sullivan Greene, 1920), KL 3576.

66 (F. Carroll 2002), KL 856.

67 (F. Carroll 2002), KL 1131.

68 (F. Carroll 2002), KL 1252.

69 F. Carroll, 2021, p. 81.

70 $5,235,166.64 to 31 January 1922, 'U.S.A ACCOUNT, TOTAL TO

31 JANY. 1922', NAI, DE 2/9, 021.
Other amounts have been stated
officially; $5,236,955 according to
Ernest Blythe, Minister for Finance,
on 13 December 1923 in Dáil
Éireann. $5,123,640 ('which, at
the rate of exchange prevailing at
that time, was roughly equivalent
to £1,600,000 sterling') in a Seanad
Éireann debate on 20 Jul 1933.

71 'U.S.A ACCOUNT, TOTAL TO 31
JANY. 1922', NAI, DE 2/9, 021.

72 257,988, (O'Doherty 1957), 66;
303,578, (F. Carroll 2002), KL 364.

73 'U.S.A ACCOUNT, TOTAL TO
31 JANY. 1922', NAI, DE 2/9, 021.
An alternative total of $622,730 ('or
approximately £190,000 sterling')
from 32,842 subscribers was given in
a Seanad Éireann debate on 20 July
1933.

74 GA, 30 October 1920, p 1.

BIBLIOGRAPHY

Béaslaí, P. 1922. *Michael Collins and the making of a new Ireland*, The Phoenix Publishing Co. Ltd, Dublin.

Bruccoli, M. 2002. *Some Sort of Epic Grandeur: The Life of F. Scott Fitzgerald*, Second Edition, University of South Carolina Press, Columbia.

Carroll, F. 2002. *Money for Ireland: finance, diplomacy, politics, and the first Dáil Éireann loans, 1919–1936*, Praeger, London.

Carroll, F. 1969. Thesis, Trinity College, Dublin.

Christopher M. Andrew, David Dilks. 1984. *The Missing Dimension: Governments and Itelligence Communities in the Twentieth Century*, Macmillan, London.

Costello, Michael. 1997. *Michael Collins, In His Own Words*, Gill & Macmillan, Dublin.

Costello, F.J. 1995. *Enduring the most: the life and death of Terence MacSwiney*, Brandon, Dingle.

Creel, George. 1947. *Rebel at large: recollections of fifty crowded years*, G. P. Putnam's Sons, New York.

Doorley, Michael. 2005. *Irish-American Diaspora Nationalism, The Friends of Irish Freedom, 1916-1935*, Four Courts Press, Dublin.

Doorley, Michael. 2019. *Justice Daniel Cohalan 1865 – 1946, American patriot and Irish-American nationalist*, Cork University Press, Cork.

Fahey, Joseph. 2014. *James K. McGuire: Boy Mayor and Irish Nationalist*, Kindle Edition, Syracuse University Press, Syracuse.

Fanning, R. 2013. *Fatal path: British government and Irish revolution 1910– 1922*, Faber and Faber, London.

Fitzgerald, F. Scott. 1920. *This Side of Paradise*, Amazon Classics.

Fitzpatrick, David. 2003. *Harry Boland's Irish Revolution*, Cork University Press, Cork.

Golway, James. 2015. *John Devoy & America's Fight for Ireland's Freedom*,Merrion Press, Dublin.

Hannigan, Dave. 2008. *De Valera In America: The Rebel Presidents 1919 Campaign*, The O'Brien Press, Dublin.

Hopkinson, M. 2002. *The Irish War of Independence*, Gill and Macmillan, Dublin.

Lainer-Vos, Dan. 2013. *Sinews of the Nation: Constructing Irish and Zionist Bonds in the United States*, Polity Press, Cambridge.

Lavelle, P. 2011. *James O'Mara: the story of an original Sinn Féiner,* History Publisher, Dublin.

Leslie, Shane. 1917. *The Irish issue in its American aspects,* Charles Scribner's Sons, New York.

ABBREVIATIONS

ACII   American Commission on Irish Independence
AARIR   American Association for the Recognition of the Irish
            Republic
BMH   Bureau of Military History
DIFP   Documents on Irish Foreign Policy
DoIB   Dictionary of Irish Biography
FOIF   Friends of Irish Freedom
GA   *Gaelic American*, Digital Library@Villanova University
GPO   General Post Office
HBD   Harry Boland's Diary, UCDA, de Valera Papers, P150/1170
IP   Irish Press, Digital Library@Villanova University
IRB   Irish Republican Brotherhood
KL   Kindle location
MGp   McGarrity Papers
NA/NAI   National Archives of Ireland
NLI   National Library of Ireland
NYT   *New York Times*
TD   Teachta Dála
UCDA   University College Dublin Archives
WS   Witness Statement

INDEX

Note: Page numbers followed by "n" refer to notes.

Martens, L., 70

Martin, Miss, xxviii, 7

Mason, W., 83, 162, 165-166

Mason Bill, 83–85, 158, 162-163, 173

Massey, R. H., 36

McAdoo, M., 169

McCabe, A., 44–45, 170

McCann, A. W., 36, 205

McCartan, P., xxx–xxxii, xxxiv, xxxviii, 6, 17, 26, 35, 37, 54, 59-61, 65, 66, 74–75, 83, 84, 106–107, 111-114, 116, 117, 121, 134–135, 159, 166, 169-173, 198-199, 205–206, 227n33, 234n7

McConaghy, J. W., 36

McGarrity, J., xxx, xxxiv, 5, 21-22, 24, 26, 35–37, 38-39 42, 48, 49, 52, 55-58, 61, 66, 68-70, 77, 83, 92, 144–146, 155, 170, 197, 200, 239n80, 239n84

McGarry, J., 84, 136, 138 150

McGough, E., 249n52

McGuire, F., 188

McGuire, J. K., 35-36, 40-45, 70, 97–98, 122, 123, 128, 131, 138, 140, 167, 176-178, 182-183, 188, 196, 199, 223n36, 239n80, 239n84

McHugh, M. F., 211

McKim, M., xxxiii

McQuillan, P., xiv

McSweeney, E., 58–59, 172, 195, 197

Meintes, J., 41

Mellows, L., 6, 17, 20, 46, 149-150 [

Meyer, K., 17, 222n73

Mitchell, J. P., xxv, xxxii

Monroe Doctrine, xvi, xxxvi, 13, 104-105, 108–113, 121, 128, 133, 200, 202

Moore, J. de, 21, 144

Morgan, J. P., 79, 146

Morning Post, 110, 204

Moylett, P., 111

Mulcahy, R., 189

Murphy, C. F., xxi, 17

Murphy, J. A., 165

N

Nation, The, xxxiii, 37, 112

National City Bank of New York, 19, 248n42

National War Labour Board, 15

Neutrality Act, xxiv, 8

New Netherland Bank, 68–69

New York Call, 170–171

New York Evening Post, xxxiii

New York *Globe*, 106–109, 112–114, 117, 203, 205

New York *Nation*, 132

New York Stock Exchange, 43

New York Times, xxiii–xxv, 5, 9, 11, 23, 50, 84, 85, 87, 90, 99, 102, 105, 106, 109, 152, 166, 171, 220n2

New York Tribune, 161

New York *World*, 170

Notre Dame University, 50

Nunan, S., 30, 31, 45, 98, 101–102, 104, 137, 152, 165, 182, 191, 200

Nuorteva, S., 37, 159